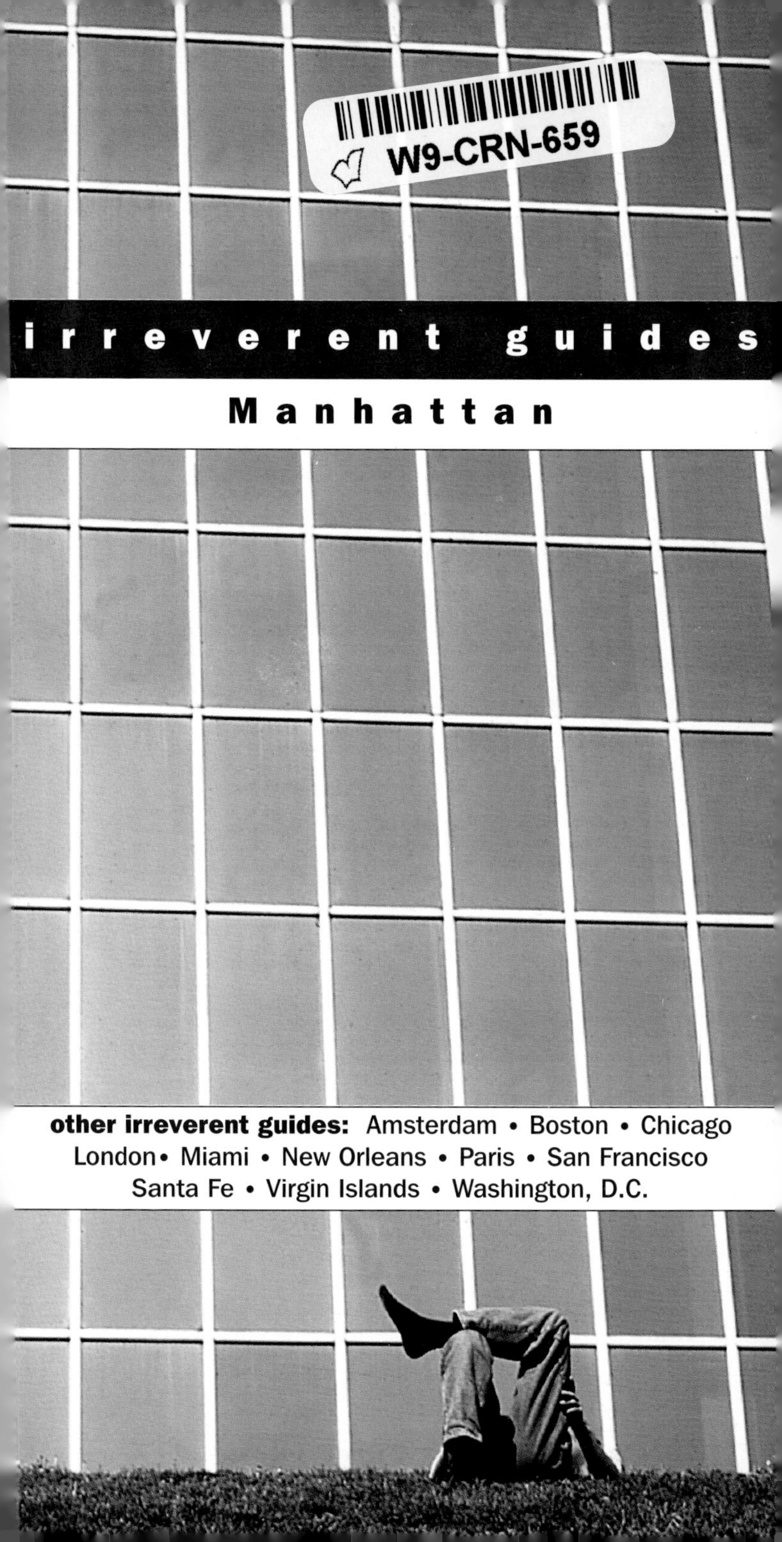

irreverent guides

Manhattan

other irreverent guides: Amsterdam • Boston • Chicago London• Miami • New Orleans • Paris • San Francisco Santa Fe • Virgin Islands • Washington, D.C.

irreverent

Man

guides

hattan

BY

SUSAN SPANO
MATTHEW DEBORD
AND
SHERILL TIPPINS

A BALLIETT & FITZGERALD BOOK

MACMILLAN • USA

Where to dig the oldest bones...

The American Museum of Natural History, see Diversions

Visit the crossroads of a million lives...

Grand Central Terminal, see Diversions

Eat very good seviche on very big plates...

Patria, see Dining

See museums that *are* art...

The Guggenheim Museum, see Diversions

Sleep off shopping binges...

Plaza, see Accommodations

And then start all over again...

Felissimo, see Shopping

Live it up with VIPs...

The Mark, see Accommodations

Work it off with everyone else...

Central Park Reservoir, see Getting Outside

Thai one on...

Kin Khao, see Dining

Measure books by the mile.

The Strand, see Shopping

what's so irreverent?

It's up to you.

You can buy a traditional guidebook with its fluff, its promotional hype, its let's-find-something-nice-to-say-about-everything point of view. Or you can buy an Irreverent guide.

What the Irreverents give you is the lowdown, the inside story. They have nothing to sell but the truth, which includes a balance of good and bad. They praise, they trash, they weigh, and leave the final decisions up to you. No tourist board, no chamber of commerce will ever recommend them.

Our writers are insiders, who feel passionate about the cities they live in, and have strong opinions they want to share with you. They take a special pleasure leading you where other guides fear to tread.

How irreverent are they? One of our authors insisted on writing under a pseudonym. "I couldn't show my face in town again if I used my own name," she told me. "My friends would never speak to me." Such is the price of honesty. She, like you, should know she'll always have a friend at Frommer's.

Warm regards,

Michael Spring

Michael Spring
Publisher

a disclaimer

Prices fluctuate in the course of time, and travel information changes under the impact of the varied and volatile factors that influence the travel industry. Neither the author nor the publisher can be held responsible for the experiences of readers while traveling. Readers are invited to write to the publisher with ideas, comments, and suggestions for future editions.

about the authors

Susan Spano writes the "Frugal Traveler" column for *The New York Times Travel Section*, won a Society of American Travel Writers Lowell Thomas Award in 1993, and has contributed articles and criticism to many newspapers and magazines. She lives in New York City.

Matthew DeBord is a writer and critic. He lives in New York City.

Sherill Tippins has worked as a freelance writer in New York for fifteen years.

photo credits

Page 1, Page 2, Page 4 (middle and bottom), Page 5, Page 6 (top and bottom), Page 7 (top and bottom), Page 8 (top and bottom): © Bo Zaunders; Page 4, top: © American Museum of Natural History.

Balliett & Fitzgerald, Inc.
Series editor: Holly Hughes / Executive editor: Tom Dyja / Managing editor: Duncan Bock / Production editor: Howard Slatkin / Photo editors: Rachel Florman, Sue Canavan / Assistant editor: Maria Fernandez / Editorial assistants: Sam Weinman, Jennifer Leben

Design by Tsang Seymour Design Studio
All maps © Simon & Schuster, Inc.

Air travel assistance courtesy of Continental Airlines

MACMILLAN TRAVEL
A Simon & Schuster Macmillan Company
1633 Broadway
New York, NY 10019

ISBN 0-02-860653-1
ISSN 1085-4770

special sales

Bulk purchase (10+ copies) of Frommer's Travel Guides are available to corporations at special discounts. The Special Sales Department can produce custom editions to be used as premiums and/or for sales promotions to suit individual needs. Existing editions can be produced with custom cover imprints such as corporate logos. For more information write to: Special Sales, Simon & Schuster, 1633 Broadway, New York, NY 10019.

Manufactured in the United States of America

contents

introduction

Almost every day I see tourists on the sidewalks of New York consulting guidebooks, being herded off sightseeing buses, sitting in sad cafes, and shopping in the wrong stores. All too often they look tired, or overloaded, or vaguely aware that they still haven't found the real New York, or simply too diligent in their pursuit of the city's incomparable sights—as if afterwards they're going to have to take a test. But a visit to the storied island of Manhattan shouldn't be a test. At best, it should unfold like the ridiculously lovable movie musical *On the Town*. Remember? With just 24 hours of shore leave, Gene Kelly wanted to track down the subway queen, gorgeous Miss Turnstiles—an enterprise that ultimately took him from the Bronx to the Battery, via the Museum of Natural History, where he and Ann Miller tap-danced so vigorously that they demolished the skeleton of a dinosaur.

A visit here should be like that—a serendipitous chain of events, sweeping one along from joy to disaster (New Yorkers particularly dote on disaster). Each day should have a motive (not a checklist). I can imagine a visit to New York focused on the search for a hip leather jacket, or Van Gogh's *Starry Night*, or the perfect bagel with lox.

But as you seek out your grail, whatever it may be, remain willing to get sidetracked. Let your purposeful self be subverted—that's when New York will yield up its distractions and its charms. For instance, not so long ago, I had drinks (a New York thing) with a friend on W. 57th Street; for complicated reasons, our conversation made me depressed, so I shucked all responsibilities and saw a big Hollywood flick in Chelsea, solely because it lay on a subway line nearby. I hated the film, walked out halfway through, yelled at a cabbie who almost ran me over, and then stomped down Eighth Avenue swearing under my breath at bums and baby carriages that crossed me. But on the way home, I passed the Cafe de Bruxelles on Greenwich Avenue—a little bit of Brussels in the Big Apple—where I started with a Manhattan (try them on the rocks with a twist rather than a cherry) and a coneful of peerless french fries, then finished with a bowl of mussels. The waiter was one of those ineffably handsome gay men heterosexual women want to change. And all of that, the hopelessly tangled layers of it, made me happy again. I got a tape of *Breakfast at Tiffany's* on the way home (another compelling cinematic myth of New York) and called it a day—good, depressing, and all.

Generally, though, New York has a way of intensifying whatever you're feeling, not turning it around. So if you embark, relatively happy, in the spring when the apricot trees are in bloom, you may have an epiphany. If you come to the city in the fall, *à deux* and in love, you could wind up getting married at City Hall. If you're on business and a little neurotic, you might come out of your meeting certifiably paranoid. And if you happen to be a little latently angry—well, don't come to me when your car gets towed or you get handcuffed by a cop.

The point is to give up programs and let New York do with you what it will. After all, the city's major attractions like the World Trade Towers, Rockefeller Center, Central Park, and the Brooklyn Bridge will never be exhausted—and (God willing) they'll all still be there the next time you come. What's more, they are never the same twice: transformed by sunset, quiet as the tomb after the bars close, or washed clean on a bright Sunday morning. You can visit them again and again. Nor are the the city's must-see sights the sole reason for a trip to New York. Indeed, it's the places in between that are really worth seeing, the no-name neighborhoods where New Yorkers buy their milk and eggs, where you begin to see the city undergoing relentless cultural change—Little Italy boxed in by sprawling Chinatown, the East Village parting ways with the West, the chic Upper East Side looking down its nose at Spanish Harlem, and suited Midtown stopped agog by the seedy razzletazz of Times Square. To reach them all you need is comfortable shoes and a willingness to roam.

A motorboat wouldn't hurt either, because New York is a city defined by water. It has 578 miles of ocean- and riverfront, mass transit ferries, a houseboat colony on Manhattan's Upper West Side, a yachting center on City Island, and bridges everywhere (in varying states of repair). "There now is your insular city of the Manhattoes," wrote Herman Melville in *Moby Dick,* "belted round by wharves as Indian isles by coral reefs. Right and left, the streets take you waterward." Two of the city's five boroughs are islands—Manhattan and Staten Island, of course. Queens and Brooklyn occupy the western end of Long Island, and the Bronx sits at the tip of a peninsula, hemmed in by the Hudson River and Long Island Sound.

Water is what first attracted European explorers to New York—like the Florentine, Giovanni da Verrazano, who called the Hudson "a very great river" when he spied it in 1524, pouring into a deep, protected port now known as New York Harbor. Eighty-five years later, Henry Hudson, a British navigator employed by the Dutch East India Company, sailed up the river (to which he gave his name), opening the way for colonization by the Dutch, who called their settlement at the southern tip of Manhattan island Nieuw Amsterdam. In the 1600s a Dutch governor general, Peter Minuit, swung one of the great real estate deals of all time by purchasing the island from Native Americans for bright trinkets worth about $27 today. And Peter Stuyvesant, who built himself a country plantation (in Dutch a *bouwerie*) in what is now the Lower East Side, never realized that in so doing he was naming a street—The Bowery—that would become the headquarters for New York's lighting wholesalers and for its bums.

Nothing stays the same in New York, but parts of the city do bespeak the past. Battery Park and Wall Street still whisper of the 17th-century Dutch; Washington Square recalls the golden days in the 19th century when monied citizens began moving north into Greenwich Village; the Lower East Side tells the tale of waves of immigrants who used the city as a way-station to a better life. Herald Square will always seem to me Batman's true Gotham, and whenever I walk along Fifth Avenue near Rockefeller Center, I imagine myself decked out in a Chanel suit in one of those great 1950s black-and-white Avedon fashion shots.

I arrived in New York in 1980, just in time to live through one of the city's more unlovely decades—Tom Wolfe's *Bonfire of the Vanities* and Jay McInerney's *Bright Lights, Big City* describe the greed and hypocrisy of those years well. But somehow, the air has cleared now. New York seems its bright old self again, and I keep falling in love with it every time I come home from a trip.

Not too long ago I found myself at Orso, a chic Italian restaurant west of Broadway on 46th Street favored by critics and producers (but too expensive for anyone who really works in the theater). I was stabbing at my ensalada bianca—believe me, this salad was blond, composed of celery, frisee lettuce, and fennel. My companions were all travel editors, who knew I moved about the globe often. Someone asked me which of all the cities in the world I preferred. With a leaf of endive poised near my mouth, I stopped. Venice and London came to mind. But then I put down my fork and said, "New York, of course."

Two out of three of them didn't believe me, I'm sure. They looked skeptical—which is understandable. We New Yorkers *do* have moments when all we can see is New York's crime, filth, uppity attitude, and wretched streetpeople; days when we have simply stopped taking pleasure in the city's perversity. During a bad evening rush hour, you may encounter temporary New York-haters pushing into over-crowded, subways, sourly telling their buddies that they're fed up and unwilling to take it anymore. If you happen to ask *them* for directions, watch out.

In Anchorage, Alaska, I read a newspaper article headlined "New York tries nice, doesn't wear it well," about the purported failure of a recent municipal friendliness campaign (which included the placement of air fresheners in taxicabs!). Surveys have been taken that rank New York (and Miami) tops for rudeness among American cities. And even the *New York Times* blazons the city's faults, like its residents' penchant for cursing. New Yorkers are all surly wise-crackers—or so the cliché goes.

I can't say how many times I've been told in some foreign land that I don't act like a New Yorker. "What is that?" I ask. The only thing that typifies New Yorkers is that they're atypical—and as worthy of study as any premier Manhattan sight. My hair stylist, who works out of his tiny apartment in the West Village, is a T'ai Chi master who always votes Republican; my kindly old Italian butcher packs a gun; the waiters in all my favorite restaurants are actors;

and one of my best friends, New York-born-and-bred, actually stops tourists on the street to give them helpful advice. New Yorkers brag a lot, but they also spend a lot of time on psychiatrists' couches. The accent everyone associates with New York is nowadays usually heard on the lips of the "bridge and tunnel" crowd—visitors from New Jersey or Long Island. The ratty looking guitar player in the subway may have once headlined at the Blue Note, and the Donna Karan-clad babes at the bar of the Cub Room in SoHo are actually in for the week from Denver or Cleveland.

However, it is wise to realize that New Yorkers *are* almost always in a hurry, which explains their terseness. *And* you should be careful—while incidents of murder and robbery have been falling (New York is no longer even in the top 125 most dangerous cities in America), crime does occur, with tourists as prime targets. A good scam is often greeted with admiration, because everyone in the city knows what it means to want to make a buck; you could get chiseled or cheated if you don't take care. Or you could find that New York is simply too loud and dirty for you. Like my very own parents, you could decide that one visit every five years is enough.

But I'm sure there are those among you who won't feel this way at all, who like Joan Didion in a wonderful essay called "Goodbye to All That" will speak of loving the city, "the way you love the first person who ever touches you." As a girl growing up in St. Louis, I remember seeking out a copy of the Sunday *New York Times* and poring over it, wondering who I would be if I lived there. As John Dos Passos wrote in his novel *Manhattan Transfer,* the city "is full of people wanting inconceivable things." Manhattan may be not so much a place as a formative power.

In some ways, perhaps it is a test, too. You get here and find yourself a little intimidated; someone yells at you for crossing against the light or charges you too much for a drink. But if you're one of the ones who's going to love New York, this is what happens: you get mad, decide not to take it anymore, and then start to walk around as if you owned the place. That's the New York attitude, and it travels.

Last spring I was on a bus crossing the Pampas of Argentina. Just outside Buenos Aires, Frank Sinatra started singing "New York, New York" over the loudspeaker—to signal, I suppose, that we were about to reach a big city. A city with the tango, beautiful broad boulevards, and fantastic steak. But not *the* city....

Manhattan Neighborhoods

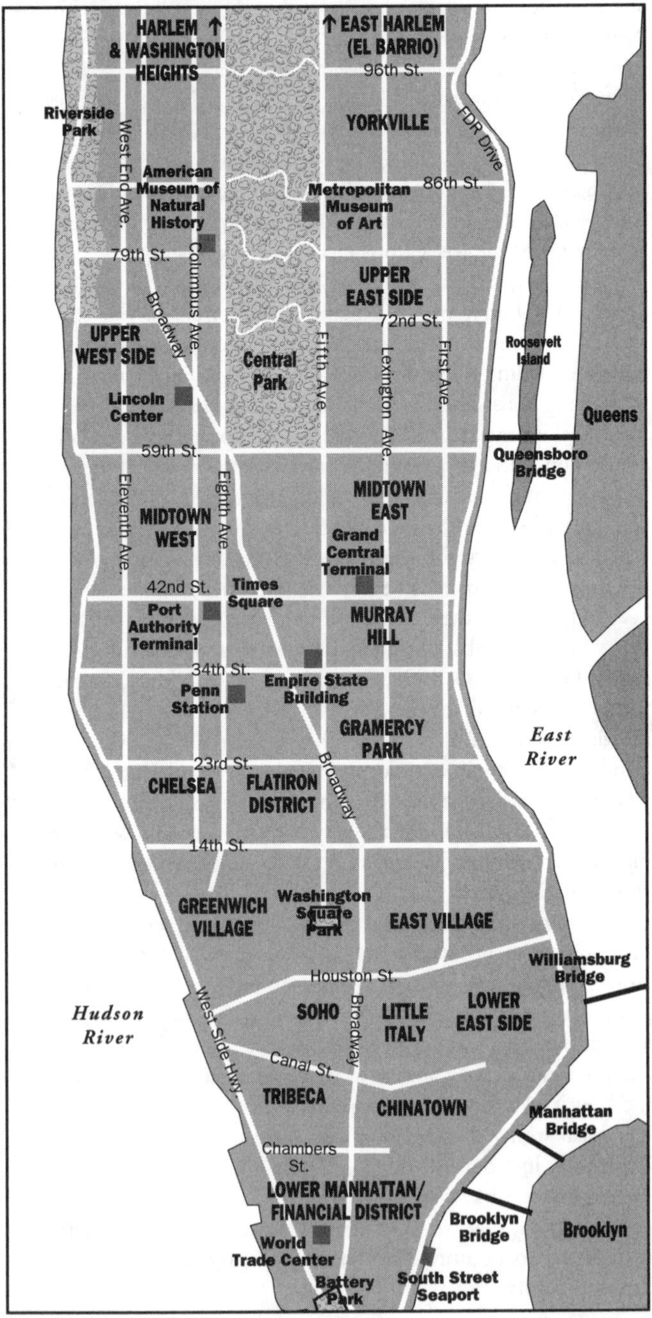

HARLEM & WASHINGTON HEIGHTS
EAST HARLEM (EL BARRIO)
96th St.
Riverside Park
YORKVILLE
FDR Drive
West End Ave.
American Museum of Natural History
Metropolitan Museum of Art
86th St.
79th St.
Columbus Ave.
UPPER EAST SIDE
Broadway
72nd St.
UPPER WEST SIDE
Central Park
Fifth Ave.
Lexington Ave.
First Ave.
Roosevelt Island
Lincoln Center
Queens
59th St.
Queensboro Bridge
Eleventh Ave.
Eighth Ave.
MIDTOWN WEST
MIDTOWN EAST
Grand Central Terminal
42nd St.
Times Square
Port Authority Terminal
MURRAY HILL
34th St.
Empire State Building
Penn Station
GRAMERCY PARK
East River
23rd St.
CHELSEA
FLATIRON DISTRICT
14th St.
GREENWICH VILLAGE
Washington Square Park
EAST VILLAGE
Williamsburg Bridge
Houston St.
Hudson River
West Side Hwy.
SOHO
LITTLE ITALY
LOWER EAST SIDE
Canal St.
TRIBECA
CHINATOWN
Manhattan Bridge
Chambers St.
LOWER MANHATTAN/ FINANCIAL DISTRICT
Brooklyn Bridge
Brooklyn
World Trade Center
Battery Park
South Street Seaport

you probably didn't know

Where to find the best New York panorama... The **Empire State Building** and **World Trade Center** are summits worth conquering, but they're on very beaten-track. Many feel that the best view of New York is from the harbor, aboard the **Staten Island, Statue of Liberty, or Ellis Island ferries, Seaport Liberty cruise boats** embarking from the South Street Seaport, or the **Circle Line**. From a watery vantage point, you get to see the great skyscraper cliffs of New York, and meeting in an awesome wedge at Battery Park, magnificently lit at sunset. But my favorite viewpoint is from the **Promenade** in Brooklyn Heights, cantilevered over the Brooklyn–Queens Expressway, providing nonpareil vistas of downtown and the Brooklyn Bridge. It's easy to get there; take the 2 or 3 train to Clark Street and walk toward the East River; then stroll back to Manhattan over the **Brooklyn Bridge**, with more magnificent views all the way.

How to see the lights... Just look up at the pinnacle of the **Empire State Building**, at 1,250 feet (1,472 if you count the TV tower at the top) the world's tallest skyscraper, at least until the World Trade Towers came along (which in turn were supplanted by the Sears Tower in Chicago...). After night falls, you'll see the lights, color-coordinated with the calendar. For instance, on Gay Pride Week in June they're lavender; on the Fourth of July, red, white, and blue, and so on.

How to see wildlife in the city (and not just cross-dressers and the extremely body-pierced)... Did you know that New York City is home to 70% of the state's breeding peregrine falcon population? They nest atop bridges and skyscrapers, in boxes placed there by officials hoping the falcons will keep down the local pigeon population; there's one pair that hunts pigeons and blue jays on the grounds of the New York Public Library on 42nd Street and Fifth Avenue. What's more, there have been reports of coyotes in the city, entering via the verges of highways leading south from Connecticut. And one day, I saw an opossum scrambling along Seventh Avenue in front of a jazz club—perhaps he'd just caught the show. Take that, Yellowstone.

How to stay out of trouble... Everybody's read about Midwestern tourists murdered in the subway, rapes in Central Park, and the old Times Square confidence scams. But in 1994, the murder rate in New York fell by 20%, robbery by 16%, and assault by 5%; in the first half of 1995, the murder rate hit a 25-year low. There are 34,028 law-enforcement officers in the five boroughs, 46 of whom patrol on horseback; there are even a few on 10-speed bikers, on the Upper West Side and in Brooklyn. Frankly, I've felt more nervous in Sofia and Marseilles, and found myself in riskier spots way out in the sticks. Most New Yorkers have cultivated a certain way of moving about the city that functions like a protective shield; they act as if they know where they're going, even when they don't, and rarely make eye contact with passers-by. (Remember that when you're tempted to brand all New Yorkers as rude.) The NYPD advises visitors not to flash their cash, credit cards, and expensive jewelry; men should keep their wallets in front pants pockets, and women shouldn't let their handbags dangle or hang from the backs of chairs; fasten all the locks on hotel room doors, and put your valuables in the safe. Other than that, use your common sense: Never, never walk down a street or enter a park if you see no one else around—whether it's light or dark outside. If you notice something out of line up ahead—like a gang of kids up to no good or a street person screaming obscenities—casually cross to the other sidewalk. Favorite spots for pickpockets include crowded buses, sardine-packed subway cars, and sidewalk crowds gathered around three-card monte games or street performers.

How to get about below... Paul Goldberger, architecture critic at the *New York Times*, once wrote, "There is no public environment in the United States as squalid as the New York City subway. It is dirty, cramped, smelly and altogether lacking in amenities as basic as a place to sit down." Lord knows, he's right; but, above all, what the New York subway system is, is old, some of it built almost a century ago. That it continues to get 3.4 million people around every day seems a miracle to me; and though it has frequently made me late and let me down, I stand behind it. Some 25 lines ply 238 miles of track under the city—for a map, ask at a token booth, or call the MTA at 718/330–1234, and also ask for the "Token Trips" brochure, describing how to visit 150 major attractions via the subway. Follow the color codes: red runs along Seventh Avenue and then Broadway, blue along Eighth Avenue and Central Park West, green along Lexington Avenue, orange on Central Park West and Sixth Avenue. (For more subway details, see Hotlines and Other Basics.) Once you're on the train, you'll notice many passengers burying their heads in books and newspapers (or surreptitiously reading their neighbors' books and newspapers over their shoulders). If you've forgotten to bring along reading material, look up at the ad posters above subway seats, like those that made a local celebrity out of a dermatologist named Dr. Jonathan Zizmor. Poetry Society of America posters raised the city's consciousnesses with often haunting lines of poetry by the likes of E.E. Cummings and Walt Whitman. Sleek car-long campaigns for high-profile advertisers like Fruitopia and Levi's have recently replaced the time-honored clutter of small ads, though—one more glossy improvement threatening New York's local color.

How to do lunch at an expensive restaurant and still have enough left over for dinner... Every year New York celebrates **Restaurant Week** (generally in June) with great bargains on lunches at some of the city's top restaurants. Amazing but true. In 1995, lunches at high-end eateries like Le Cirque, Lutèce, the Monkey Bar, Montrachet, and the River Cafe cost just $19.95 (with some restaurants extending the program through Labor

Day). Reservations made long in advance are generally required, because New Yorkers—who always know a good deal when they see one—don't mind snatching the goodies out of tourists' mouths. For information, contact the **New York Visitors and Convention Bureau** (tel 212/397–8222).

How to flag a taxi... The white lights on the roofs of yellow cabs indicate which ones are free; the yellow "Off Duty" light means the driver is on his way home—though he may still stop and ask whether your destination lies along his route. Look for people disembarking from a taxi, hold the door open for them, and then snag the cab. It is very bad form to plant yourself in front of someone else signaling for a taxi in order to get the next one first. That doesn't mean you won't see some New Yorkers doing it. Be aware that it can be hard to find cabs between 4 and 6pm, when drivers are changing shifts, and a good hard rainfall always make it doubly hard to catch a cab.

How to meet the dress code... Expensive finery isn't required here; though New York is a fashion industry center, your average New Yorker isn't as neurotic about clothes as your average person from Paris or Buenos Aires. New Yorkers do care about style, though, so what you wear doesn't matter as much as how you wear it; namely with confidence. If you're not sure you have the chutzpah to pull off a full-Cleveland (white shoes, white pants, white belt), there's always anything black, as close to a uniform as New York has.

Where to smoke... Can you smoke in New York? Sure, if you're outdoors. Otherwise, it's problematic. New smoking regulations have made it illegal to light up in restaurants seating more than 35 people. You can smoke at a bar, providing it's at least 6 feet away from tables where people are eating. Restaurateurs hate the new rules, which went into effect in 1995, but for now they're the law. Four cafes with streetside tables (in fair weather) at the Greenwich Village intersection of Bleecker and McDougal streets—**McDougal**, **Borghia**, **Carpo's**, and **Le Figaro**—have become a mecca for visiting smokers. In hotels, make sure to ask for a smoking room if you're a nicotine fiend.

Where to find the facilities... There's an excellent public restroom in **Bryant Park**, on 42nd Street between Fifth and Sixth avenues, which even has attendants, and a good one on the ground floor of the **New York Public Library** next door. But beyond this, stay out of toilets in public buildings—they're filthy and unsafe. Coffee shops and restaurants have bathrooms, though you should make a purchase before using them (even if it's only a cup of coffee to go); and of course, museums offer facilities, providing you buy an admission ticket first. I favor the restrooms in hotel lobbies, which are generally top-notch, though not always easy to find. The bathrooms at the rear of the second-floor lobby in the Grand Hyatt on 42nd Street between Park and Lexington avenues has never let me down. Or try the ladies and gents in the Plaza Hotel or the Waldorf-Astoria. If a concierge stops you, just say you're meeting a friend in the bar for a drink.

How to get a theater ticket... If you didn't call Ticketmaster, Tele-Charge, Teletron, Hit-Tix, or the theaters themselves months ago, you may be out of luck, at least for Broadway blockbusters—you can bet they won't be offered at the day-of-performance discount TKTS booth. **Ticket brokers** and the **concierges** at hotels can help out in a pinch, providing seats for hot shows at the last minute—though always at a substantial premium. But if you're intent on seeing a particular show, try the theater **box office** about an hour before show time, where you may meet someone desperate to unload tickets for the evening's performance. As curtain time approaches, many box offices free up house seats (which are routinely saved for the theatrical hoi polloi) and sell them off, first-come-first-served, at full price; and some theaters sell standing-room tickets at the last minute, generally at half price, which can provide better views than seats way up near the rafters. For more details, see the Entertainment chapter.

The best art museum nights... Insiders take advantage of "pay what you wish nights" at the **Whitney Museum of American Art** and **Solomon R. Guggenheim Museum** (Fridays), and the **Cooper-Hewitt National Museum of Design** (Tuesdays). These are three of the city's greatest museums; besides, the crowds often go off to dinner after about 5pm—leaving you free to wander in blissful solitude. On Friday and Saturday nights, the **Metropolitan Museum of Art** turns itself into a date venue, with drinks, music, and late closing.

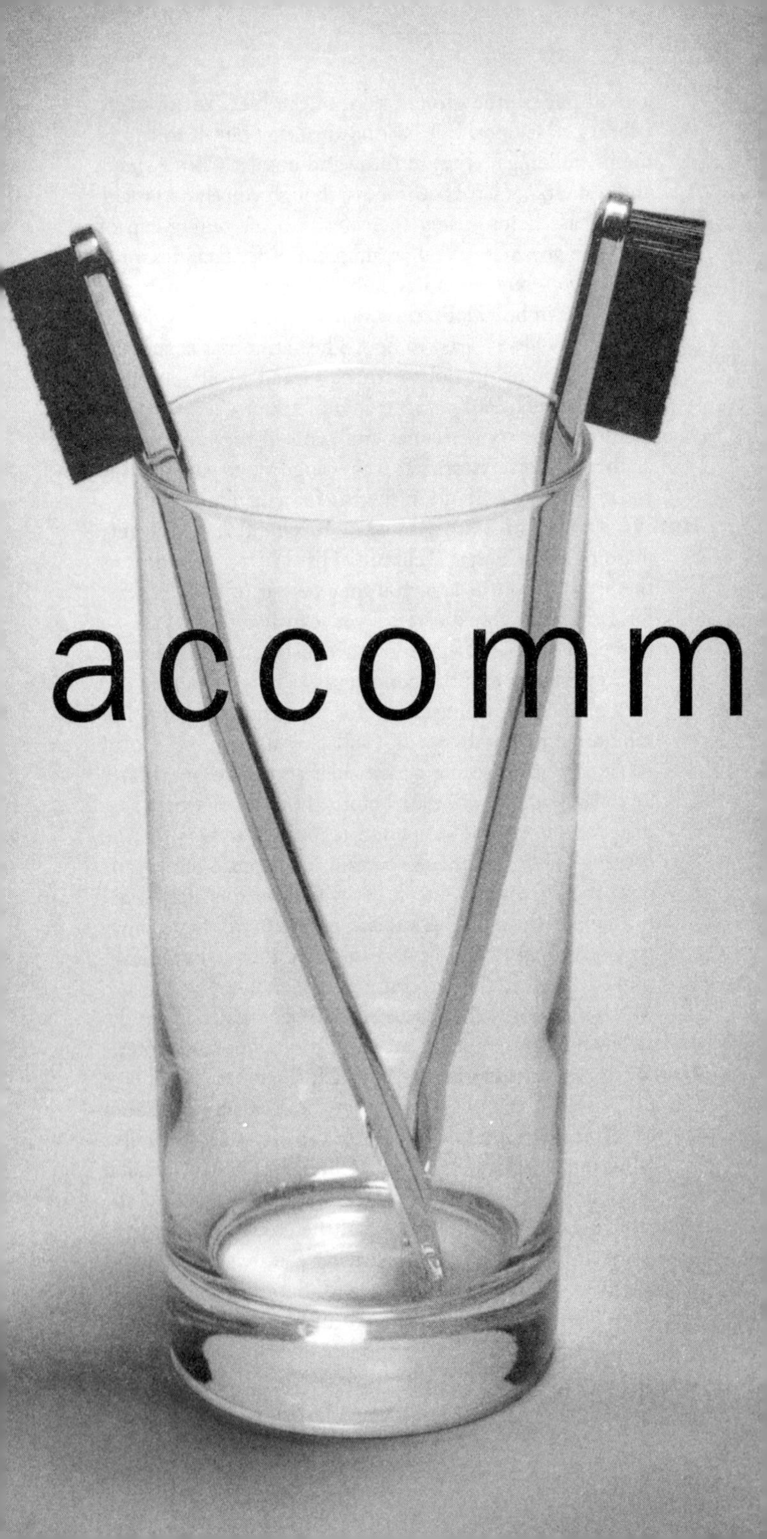
accomm

1

odations

You may enjoy roaming the streets of a new town, luggage in tow, letting fate dictate where you'll spend the night. Listen up: New York is not the place for that. Unless you want to spend your vacation in a motel off the turnpike in New Jersey, do your homework before you come: research the city, pick a neighborhood that suits your frame of mind, and then choose lodgings as close to it as possible—in your price range, if possible. Which isn't as impossible as it sounds. Behind the imposing facades of New York's luxury monoliths hover some perfectly charming and less expensive "boutique" hotels, where you're closer to the city's fascinating street life and yet often enjoy nicer furnishings and more attentive service. For an even more genuine taste of the real New York, consider going the bed-and-breakfast route, where accommodations range from penthouse apartments to walk-ups. We've listed one of the best B&B agencies below. Those who decide to stay in a mid-priced or luxury hotel should bear in mind that a hotel concierge can become more valuable in New York than your best friend. These miracle workers sit patiently behind their desks in the hotel lobby, ever-eager to locate last-minute theater tickets or recommend a little French restaurant that's perfect for popping the question (whatever that question may be).

Winning the Reservations Game

The standard recommendation in New York is to make reservations a month ahead—even longer if you plan to be here between Thanksgiving and Christmas. Don't accept the first room price offered, especially from the higher-priced hotels. There are nearly always discount packages to be had, from "summer holidays" to "Christmas getaways" to "romantic weekends." These packages are advertised in the free ***Big Apple Visitors Guide*** published by the New York Convention and Visitors Bureau (tel 800/NYC–VISIT, or pick it up in person at 2 Columbus Circle). Keep in mind that at some hotels, children under 12 stay free with their parents. And be sure to ask for corporate rates, even if you aren't part of a corporation. Desk clerks rarely check your credentials—they just want to fill the room. Sadly, what the hotel industry giveth with one hand, the city taketh away with the other. Hotel tax in Manhattan is a stiff 13.25 %, plus $2 per room per night. Taxes are not included in the price listings below.

Is There a Right Address?

There is a New York neighborhood for *every* personal philosophy and lifestyle, but traditionally the "right" residential address has been the East Sixties, Seventies, and Eighties—

the white-glove **Upper East Side**. Here one finds the city's most elegant and expensive shops, townhouses, hotels, and nearly all the members of New York's upper crust. Come summer, the East Side's a ghost town as the wealthy flee the heat for the Hamptons. Head across Central Park for the **Upper West Side**, a funkier, more family-oriented scene of gracious 100-year-old townhouses and grand old apartment buildings. Bounded on the north by Columbia University, by Lincoln Center on the south, and bracketed by Central Park and Hudson-hugging Riverside Park, this area's museums, theaters, affordable restaurants and hotels, and boutique shopping make it a pleasant place to hang. **Midtown**, running from Central Park South to the Thirties, is Manhattan's central business district and the chief hotel zone, convenient for tony Fifth Avenue shopping, the theater district, and not-for-the-timid Times Square. The best and costliest hotels are on Central Park South; room rates generally descend as you work your way south. Head south on Fifth Avenue and you'll bump into the triangular Flatiron Building at 23rd Street, which has lent its name to the very hot **Flatiron District**, where models and trendoids haunt a score of high-profile bars and restaurants. There are few hotels around the Flatiron, but you can enjoy the pulse of this happening area by staying in quietly genteel **Gramercy Park**, a few blocks to the east, or soon-to-be-hot **Chelsea** to the west, currently being gentrified by an ambitious gay community. Downtown starts at 14th Street, the northern border of **Greenwich Village**. The home of New York University and

New York's celluloid alter-ego

If you want to prepare yourself for a visit to the Big Apple, rent a flick. The classics are: Miracle on 34th Street *(1947) for sweetness and light at Christmastime;* Breakfast at Tiffany's *(1961) for bitter-sweetness à la Truman Capote, and Audrey Hepburn in Givenchy gowns;* The Sweet Smell of Success *(1957) with Tony Curtis and Burt Lancaster as two rats chasing celebrity and power; and Woody Allen's* Annie Hall *(1977), all about Upper East Side chic in the days before Woody and Mia's split revealed its seamy side. For a gritty taste of the city, try* Serpico *(1974) with Al Pacino, Greenwich Village, and corrupt factions in the NYPD;* The Godfather *(1971) and* The Godfather Part II *(1974) for the other side of the badge. If you want a love story, grab Cher's* Moonstruck *(1987) about a nice Brooklyn–Italian girl who wants something more from life than pasta.* Midnight Cowboy *(1969), perfectly perverse, sad, yet lovable, features Dustin Hoffman and Jon Voight as two New York losers.*

lively Washington Square Park, this neighborhood of quaint 19th-century brownstones is where generations of bohemians have made their mark. Jazz clubs, coffee shops, romantic restaurants, and proximity to Little Italy, Soho, the East Village (home of cutting-edge clubs and punky new bohemians), and the West Village (capital of gay America) should make this area ripe for hotels. Oddly enough, though, good hotels are hard to find here—unless you're willing to put up with tiny rooms, tenement housing, or a bed-and-breakfast room, you may have to commute to this playground. The southern tip of Manhattan—occupied by the **South Street Seaport** area to the east, the loft spaces of trendy **TriBeCa** to the northwest, **Battery Park City** to the west, and **Wall Street** at the very bottom—has only a few very luxurious hotels, drawn by proximity to the financial district. Compellingly urgent during the work week, strangely empty on weekends, this neighborhood is an especially memorable place to stay; squeezed between financial-industry towers you'll find soot-blackened churches whose cemeteries contain crooked, worn tombstones. The streets can be deserted and sometimes dangerous late at night, especially near the water. Stick to your hotel at those times, or take a ride uptown.

The Lowdown

Old faithfuls... Always the first to come to mind is the venerable **Plaza**, a French-Renaissance pile docked at the southeast corner of Central Park. Frank Lloyd Wright once claimed this was one of the few buildings he liked that he hadn't designed himself. In the early 1900s, New York's high rollers kept suites there, and the Plaza's blinding gold-and-crimson lobby (courtesy of former doyenne Ivana Trump, though Fairmont Hotels now manages the pile) continues to celebrate the joys of extravagant consumerism. Around the corner, the staid and elegant **Sherry-Netherland**, built in 1927 with a lobby fashioned after the Vatican Library, offers a better class of rooms with equally stunning park views, for substantially less than the Plaza. The recently refurbished **Waldorf-Astoria**, originally built in 1893, presides over Park Avenue, its Art Deco lobbies returned to their past splendor, though its guest roster is no longer as grand. Happily, the **Algonquin** functions much as it did in the days of Dorothy Parker and the Round Table—in the wood-paneled lobby, at least, where graying authors of both sexes, ensconced in armchairs, ogle young women in leopardskin coats.

For travelers with old money... In the old days, the luckiest visitors hung onto their trust-fund money by staying at the **Sherry-Netherland** as guests of relatives who occupied the apartments upstairs. Sherry residents invite guests less frequently now, it seems, so wealthy travelers have moved a few steps north to the **Pierre**, where the romantically frescoed downstairs rooms teem with European film directors, as well as American heiresses; even Hollywood types turn up frequently, now that Barney's has set up shop next door. Miraculously, the staff is alert and deferential, no matter who you are—unlike the help at the **Plaza-Athénée**, where you get the feeling you should show proof of a high income before walking through the door. The **Carlyle** on Madison Avenue has long been a bastion of good taste, though its reputation lately has slipped a notch. If you dislike feeling forced to dress for dinner, you may prefer the gracious **Stanhope**, where the high tea is perfectly English, and you can people-watch like a Parisian on the Terrace, sipping an aperitif and overlooking the tourist frenzy at the Metropolitan Museum of Art across the street. On Central Park South, the **Ritz-Carlton** feels like an exclusive club, given the small, opulently furnished lobby and the staff's legendary devotedness.

For travelers with new money... If your reason for being in New York is to spend cash, then the **Plaza**, at the top of the Fifth Avenue shopping district, in view of Bergdorf Goodman and FAO Schwartz, is the place to stay. Big hair, Dallas accents, and slack-jawed kids crowd the lobby, where plainsclothes security guards warily eye all but the wealthiest. Visitors bored with the Plaza might move up the ladder to the **New York Palace**, a modern black tower jammed behind the 100-year-old Villard Houses. Formerly owned by the infamous Leona Helmsley, The Palace lies in the shadow of St. Patrick's Cathedral, and its ornate public rooms put both the Plaza and St. Patrick's to shame—too bad the guest rooms don't live up to them. Visitors who've made their money in Hollywood would feel most at home at the **Mark**, a sleek East Sider where producers strike deals just crossing the lobby to the bar.

Places to misbehave... Just off Times Square, the **Paramount**, with its Whiskey Bar, whimsical acid-colored Philipe Starck furniture, and weirdly furnished (also very, very tiny) rooms, is the place to meet kindred souls if you work in advertising and are under 35. Media and show biz types prefer the **Royalton**'s Club 44, where you might catch a glimpse of Claudia Schiffer or Tina Brown before retreating to your higher-budget Starck bed upstairs. If this is too sophisticated-Disneyland for you, never fear: **Hotel 17**, a pensione for club-hoppers, just north of the East Village, may let you party in the dingy rooms where Madonna did her *Details* photo shoot, if you have modeling/MTV/acting credentials or they like the look of your fax.

Broadway bound... The **Millenium Broadway**'s 33 soundproof executive boardrooms and its sleek, black tower may be a corporate wet-dream to some, but at 44th Street off Broadway it's a sexy place for a theater-and-dinner weekend as well. The lobby's leather lounge chairs and black marble floors give way to cream-colored upstairs rooms whose glass walls offer killer city views. The more relaxed, Italian-owned **Michelangelo**, 5 blocks up Broadway, offers a choice of room design: Empire, Art Deco, or French Provincial. **Ameritania**, a former SRO hotel nicely renovated by gentrification genius Hank "Location, Location, Location" Freid, sits next door to the Ed Sullivan Theater (home of *Late Night with David Letterman*): it offers decent rooms with marble bathrooms and the very same views for $100 per night less than the Macklowe, and $200 less than the Michelangelo. Bottom-rung among the Broadway hotels is the 1,300-room **Milford Plaza**, which has much the same ambience as an airport terminal. Lines to the front desk form behind a velvet rope, and it's often necessary to wait 20 minutes just to pick up your room key. A prime destination for flight attendants and talk show guests, but at least there's *always* a room.

Picturesque views of the park... The **Ritz-Carlton**, from about the eighth floor up, offers the Central Park views people want on their honeymoons. Even the small fitness center lets you look at the trees while aerobicizing. Avoid the rear rooms—their windows face a wall. It's no surprise that the **Plaza**'s parkside vistas are as nice as the Ritz's—it's just a block down the road. Over on Central Park West, the **Mayflower** offers less opulent rooms-with-a-view for substantially less. Then there's the **Stanhope**, whose best quarters reveal the park and the Metropolitan Museum of Art as you've never seen them before.

Heartstopping views of the city... Check in after dark at the **U.N. Plaza-Park Hyatt**, and you'll open your curtains to a heart-stopping east-Midtown view of the city lights—guaranteed, since all rooms are on the 28th floor or above. The **Millenium**, across from the World Trade Center downtown, provides a New York Harbor panorama or skyline views from the higher rooms; take a dip in the pool overlooking St. Paul's Church. Any Midtown skyscraper-hotel is also likely to open up vistas worth writing home about: just ask for an upper floor.

Location, location, location... Best Western Seaport Inn, a fully restored, 19th-century, pink-brick building between the Brooklyn Bridge and South Street Seaport, provides an excellent departure point for walks around Old New York—and even delivers a bit of colonial sea-captain's ambience at a decent price, though the rooms are motel-like. The rooms at the **Washington Square Hotel** are disappointingly motel modern, too, but their mid-Greenwich Village location makes possible walks around NYU, Little Italy, Soho, and the East and West Villages. The comfy dowager **Mayflower** is a good, mid-priced starting point for walks around Central Park and the Upper West Side.

For culture vultures... For a long time, the dingy Empire Hotel, directly across from Lincoln Center, was a prime piece of New York real estate going to waste. Then the Radisson chain took over, changed the hotel's name to the **Radisson Empire**, and transformed the joint. From designers' models of opera sets in the tony brass-and-mahogany lobby to the CD players in every (sometimes quite small) room, this hotel should make arts aficionados very happy. Way uptown and to the east, **Hotel Wales**, a renovated Victorian with banners flying, offers a sweet, intimate alternative to the larger (and more expensive) hotels near Museum Mile. Downtown devotees might try the dreary-but-cheap **Washington Square Hotel** for its dinner-and-jazz package; or for easy access to SoHo galleries and clubs, try the **Incentra Village House**, a small, antique-filled inn full of turn-of-the-century Village bohemian aura. **Off Soho Suites**, a clean, bright, and inexpensive all-suite hotel in an unlikely Lower East Side neighborhood, is close to downtown plays, poetry readings, and galleries; many European and Australian travelers stay here, along with downtown musicians and those who write about them. Appropriately, a free *Village Voice* comes with your suite.

Endearingly eccentric... New York breeds rugged individualists of all types; among those who get off on sharing their life view with the world is James Knowles, the artist-owner of the **Roger Smith**, a lighthearted Midtown hotel decorated on the outside with a delightful, cartoon-like mural (inside it's jam-packed with an assortment of high-quality paintings and sculptures). Augustin Paege takes art one step farther at his wonderful little **Box Tree** hotel, where the walls, ceilings, and even the guest-room doors are playfully adorned. **The Inn at Irving Place**, just south of Gramercy Park, is so uncommercial it doesn't even have a sign; this luxuriously restored Victorian brownstone specializes in fashion models and celebrities who value their privacy.

Twilight zones... Even in New York there's eccentric, and then there's going too far. Lifetime Achievement Award goes to the **Chelsea Hotel**, where William Burroughs wrote *Naked Lunch* and Sid killed Nancy. The street is seedy, but the spacious renovated rooms with fireplaces can be a fun place to spend a night. The **Carlton Arms**, to the east, takes up where the Chelsea leaves off, letting young artists stay for free if they'll decorate their rooms—every surface, from the steps leading to the tiny second-floor lobby to hallways decked with "conceptual" clotheslines hung with lingerie and long johns, is an expression of what appears to be howling New-York-visitor angst (or plain psychosis). Less visually riveting, but still way out there, is **Hotel 17**, former stomping grounds for J.P. Morgan and, somewhat later, a bunch of winos, and the Weather Underground. Young manager Billy Candis advertises the place as offering "four times the fun, five times the glamour, ten times the cool, yet half the price" of other trendy hotels, in his bid for the media/fashion trade. The East

Gramercy location is off the track, though; bleached-blonde staffers man the entrance, while kaleidoscope-eyed guests mingle with unevicted tenants from the hotel's past as an SRO—characters with nicknames like "Soldier of Fortune," "Poltergeist Doctor," and "Norman Bates."

Luscious love nests... The **Michelangelo**'s spacious rooms, king-sized beds, and marble-clad Italian charm lend themselves to a perfect getaway weekend that might include a Broadway play. The **Lowell**, although prim-looking on the outside, coyly reveals fireplace-and-terrace suites designed to rekindle the coldest flame. A big hit with lovers is the **Sherry-Netherland**, for its park views, its expert service, and for Harry Cipriani's heavenly restaurant downstairs (or just order up room service from there if things get really hot and heavy). If you and your lover share the same gender, try the gay-friendly **Incentra Village Inn**, a double-townhouse in the West Village, filled with antiques, or the gay-frequented **Chelsea Pines Inn**, a bed-and-breakfast where each room is dedicated to a faded movie star, and breakfast in the rear garden makes for a romantic morning-after.

For stargazing... Celebrity hounds must absolutely stop by the **Royalton**, not only to scope out the talent, but to try to find the stalls in the overdesigned restrooms downstairs. If you consider checking out fashion models "stargazing," dine al fresco across from Gramercy Park's **The Inn at Irving Place**, or book a room at the East Side's **Franklin** and spend a few hours lurking in the post-modern breakfast room off the lobby. **Morgans** is where celebrities go when they don't want to be seen, but keep your eyes open as you pass through the small black-and-white lobby with the checkerboard trim, and you might catch one slipping out the anonymous East Side entrance. The bars at the **Mark** and the **Ritz-Carlton** are other good fishing spots. For literal stargazing, head for the **Days Hotel Midtown** with its rooftop terrace and pool.

Frumpy but lovable... So "Sin City" has lured you into naughty acts you regret the next morning? Come home to the **Mayflower**, a comfortable, somewhat frumpy establishment with paintings of clipper ships adorning a long lobby. Have a good dinner in the Conservatory Cafe, then go for a healthy jog across the street in Central Park, or to a chamber music recital at nearby Juilliard. Broadway performers and, for some reason, middle-aged British tourists seem to feel secure at the **Wyndham** on 58th Street, another matronly hotel, with its apartment-like rooms and small upholstered lobby.

Have I got a deal for you... Breaks on Manhattan hotel prices are urgently needed; fortunately, they're increasingly available. The clean, reasonably comfortable, no-frills **Malibu Arms** on the Upper West Side—farther up Broadway than some may want to go, in a cruddy though safe-enough neighborhood—caters to young Europeans and students with very limited budgets. The faded but surprisingly comfortable **Excelsior** offers reasonable rooms near Central Park for older fans of the Upper West Side. The **Ameritania** provides theater-district rooms with marble baths, a fitness room, and a waterfall in the lobby for less than $150 per night. The smart, pretty **Mansfield** on 44th Street is even cheaper, and you can hang out in the lobbies of the **Royalton** and the **Algonquin** down the block. **Off Soho Suites**, run by an attentive and very professional Egyptian family, answers downtowners' needs for low prices and sane desk clerks. And **Urban Ventures** can provide you with a bed-and-breakfast room in someone's apartment for well under $100 per night.

Suite deals... Especially popular with relocating corporate execs and families, suites are also taking hold among short-term visitors. Among the best suite hotels is the **Surrey** on the Upper East Side, with kitchenettes or full kitchens, spacious rooms, and somewhat lavish decor for this sort of hotel. Farther south, the **Shelburne Murray Hill** offers a more ornate lobby, with French antiques, but more anonymous-looking rooms; it also has a large basement gym that actually gets used. **Off Soho Suites**, in its funky Lower East Side location, is the best priced of the lot; the executive-class **RIHGA Royal**'s 600-square-foot suites with French doors and elaborate marble bathrooms should have most visitors feeling like kings, or at least like CEOs.

Taking care of business... The **Millenium Broadway**'s four-story Conference Center, state-of-the-art audiovisual facilities, and its own personal Broadway theater available for corporate presentations, make this an ideal venue for any kind of business activity. The staff are accustomed to serving business needs, and rooms feature dual-line telephones, interactive communication systems, and so on. **New York Hilton and Towers** serves mid-level business guests as efficiently here as the chain does elsewhere, though you shouldn't have to put up with the mass-market feel of the lobby and reproduction furniture in the rooms. The **Drake**, owned and operated by Swissotel, caters to no-nonsense types who want their suits back from the cleaners when promised; the best thing this place has going for it is a prime Midtown location at a reasonable price. Go up the price scale, and the clean-lined, Japanese-owned **RIHGA Royal** brings the corporate climber's ultimate fantasy to life, with its hierarchical room structure—"royal suites" have minimal luxury appointments, "imperial suites" are higher up, with city views, and "pinnacle suites" at the top offer chauffeured rides to and from the airport, personalized business cards, and private phone and fax numbers. Test your corporation—which room will it give you?

For the body beautiful... The **Peninsula** wins hands-down, with its 35,000-square-foot health club, glass-enclosed rooftop gym, 42-foot pool with a view of all Midtown, beauty salon, body and skin care, massage and facial service, sauna, and, finally, a sundeck. The **U.N. Plaza-Park Hyatt** isn't bad, with its 27th-floor health club, indoor pool, tennis courts, sauna, and exercise room. The **Lowell** can provide you with a sumptuous "Gym Suite," which consists of your own private windowed-and-mirrored gym, in addition to the usual large fireplace, full kitchen, and outdoor terrace for dining. (The gym is rumored to have been installed at Madonna's request, and is priced accordingly.) More economical bodily treats are available at the **West Side** and **Vanderbilt YMCAs**: one near Lincoln Center, the other close to Grand Central, both offering cheap if spartan rooms, most without private baths, with full use of the gym, pool, and other Y facilities.

For shopoholics... The **Plaza** is best, within sight of Bergdorf Goodman, FAO Schwarz, and most other places visitors like to shop. If you prefer Bloomingdale's, try the **Barbizon**: Rates are low (that's because rooms can be tiny), but tower suites have terraces and city views. The Italian-operated **Jolly Madison Towers** is popular among shoppers for its East Side location, efficient service, predictable if standard-issue furnishings, and reasonable price. If the boutiques along Madison Avenue will be your destination, try the **Carlyle**, set amid Lauren, Versace, Armani, et al.

So very literary... The **Algonquin** is still the obvious choice, and it can be amusing to watch Matilda the Algonquin cat lick her privates while you trade bon mots in the cozy, antique-filled lobby, where the Round Table actually held court. Meanwhile, editors of *Vanity Fair* and *Vogue* settle into the sleek postmodern bar of the **Royalton** across the street, where they can gossip all night while *New Yorker* editors try to listen in. The **Lowell** actually equips its suites' bookshelves with intersting volumes, and claims a number of authors among its loyal clientele—though you'd have to be a Clancy or Collins to afford this joint. And the **Chelsea Hotel** has a raffish literary past, numbering writers such as Dylan Thomas, William Burroughs, and Tennessee Williams among its former guests.

Money's too tight to mention... The **New York International American Youth Hostel** is the largest AYH in the U.S.; its freshly appointed Upper West Side landmark building takes up half a city block. Even if it didn't, you could easily spot it due to the crowds of Nordic backpackers converging on it from all directions. Rooms are dormitory-style and cost a pittance. The communal atmosphere in the roomy cafeteria, sunny library, pool hall, and large rear garden encourages interaction among the guests. Don't confuse the AYH with the privately owned **Chelsea International Hostel**—cramped quarters make this place a little too interactive. The **West Side** and **Vanderbilt YMCAs** do better, with private rooms, though there's still communal life in the bathrooms.

Decor to die for... The **Four Seasons**, for its sycamore-paneled dressing rooms and a columned Grand Foyer with a 33-foot onyx ceiling, conceived by architect I.M. Pei; the **Lowell** for its perfect mix of French antiques and modern accents; the **Box Tree** for best impersonation of a private home, complete with 17th-century oil paintings, Tiffany panels, and roaring fireplaces, all in a slender East Side double-brownstone; the **Pierre** for its frescoed Rotunda and mahogany-furnished rooms; and the **Peninsula**, for the art nouveau staircase rising to the salmon-pink Adrienne restaurant.

Family values... The **Excelsior**, situated across the street from the Museum of Natural History (and the New York Planetarium) and half a block from the playgrounds of Central Park, is perfect for little ones who love dinosaurs. In the morning, take the kids to the coffeeshop off the lobby for eggs and a visit to the serve-yourself candy stand. The suites at the **Surrey** on the Upper East Side provide enough space for kids and enough comfort for parents, as well as kitchens for making peanut-butter-and-jelly sandwiches when the kids can't face another restaurant. Worn furnishings at the **Gramercy Park Hotel** can take your kids' abuse, and many rooms have handy kitchenettes and sofabeds; pets are allowed, too. But best of all, the hotel will hand over a key to private Gramercy Park, where you can stroll with your baby from spring through fall. **Urban Ventures, Inc** (tel 212/594–5650). provides entire empty apartments, which can be a blessing if your children loathe hotels.

Elbow room... The **Drake**'s are spacious but disappointingly bland; the **Four Seasons**' are enormous but heartstoppingly priced; the **Michelangelo**'s are just right—especially on Valentine's Day and New Year's Eve weekends, when they're on sale.

Silent nights... Silence in New York sounds like an oxymoron, but there really are peaceful enclaves to settle into. Think of the faded Grand Hotel in the last small midwestern town you visited, put it in a turn-of-the-century New York neighborhood, and that's what the **Gramercy Park Hotel** is like. The antique-filled eight-room **Inn at Irving Place**, just a couple of blocks away, provides silence and privacy as well, but at a high price. **Morgans**, a cousin of the Royalton, insulates its reticent celebrity guests with blessed quiet, but the tradeoff is a room with no view, whose walls are the mottled gray-brown of the inside of a cardboard box.

Grand Hotel... The **Algonquin** again, for its very well-preserved downstairs. The **Best Western Seaport Inn** sits in the perfect spot for those curious about New York's early seafaring days, when Wall Street was a street with a wall and nothing more. The **Chelsea Hotel** will make you relive the Sixties, whether you want to or not—wall-to-wall paintings, piles of revolutionary tracts, tacky furniture, and a collection of dazed-looking residents and animals hanging out in the lobby help keep the Andy Warhol era going (you can't help wondering if these people are paid to hang out here). You can dine and dance in the grand ballroom at the **Waldorf-Astoria** as if World War II never happened; if there's no event in the ballroom, just while away some time in the glorious main lobby, near the famed bronze and mahogany clock. The **Plaza**'s more spacious rooms and the restaurants downstairs will have you feeling like you're on an ocean liner; fans of the "Eloise" books can imagine the little urchin goofing around here. The virginal **Barbizon**, once a women's residence for such transients as Grace Kelly, Ali McGraw, and Candice Bergen, retains a cloisterlike quality with narrow corridors and tiny, spare studio rooms. (You can loosen up a little in the Star Bar, with its zodiac-studded ceiling.) Both genders are allowed to stay here these days.

It's a small world... The **Holiday Inn Downtown** is not what you think it is—at least, not quite. Smack in the middle of Chinatown, the hotel hosts many Chinese guests, and its Pacifica Bar and Restaurant can cook up some excellent Cantonese cuisine. The **Fitzpatrick**, on Lexington Avenue in the East Thirties, is owned by an Irish company, which is obvious because *everything* in it is green. Irish lilts pour forth from the desk clerks' mouths, and Fitzer's, the hotel's Irish bar, is extremely popular among (largely Irish) guests and locals. The best time to stay at the **Wentworth** is during the Brazilian Street Festival in September, when this Midtown neighborhood comes alive with samba rhythms and Brazilian dancers. The hotel itself is nothing special, but if you like Brazilian food (and Brazilian tourists) this is the place to be. For those who like their ethnic culture world-transforming, the ambience at the **U.N. Plaza-Park Hyatt**, across from the U.N., is highly international, with a multilingual staff and exotic flavors proffered at the Ambassador Grill. International textiles even adorn the hotel walls.

May I get that for you, sir?... The Upper East Side's **Stanhope** specializes in cherubic European clerks who contribute charm and a sense of humor as well as strictly professional service. The **Lowell**'s people are also young, and sweetly earnest about performing well. At **Incentra Village Inn**, you can cozy up in the hotel's small parlor and chat with the owner about places to see and things to do.

Ringing in the New Year... The stylish **Royalton**, near, but not in the center, of Times Square, is a great place to observe the crowds gathered to watch the ball fall; the comfortably priced **Ameritania** will put you at the hub of the action, right on Broadway's Great White Way. Downtown, the **Millenium** will make your heart stop with views of fireworks over New York Harbor. The **Plaza** often offers New Year's specials, as do many other New York hotels. Ask around.

Try these when there's no room... If you're desperate, try **Days Hotel Midtown** on Eighth Avenue. Its location is pretty dreary, and its rooms pure cheap-motel, but at least it has a rooftop swimming pool. **Quality Hotel & Suites Manhattan** on West 47th Street can usually offer Broadway theater-goers a last-minute room at a good price. The **Milford Plaza**, also in the theater district, is so enormous there's got to be space for you. Rooms are motel-like, but at least they have remote-control TV, in-room movies, individually controlled heat, and air conditioning.

$$$$$	Over $400
$$$$	$300–$400
$$$	$190–$300
$$	$110–$190
$	under $110

Algonquin. A $20-million restoration has made this New York landmark liveable again. Redecorated rooms can be small and nightmarishly floral, but the cozy lobby's lovely antiques and literary heat make even Caswell-Massey toiletries bearable for some.... *Tel 212/840–6800, 800/548–0345, fax 212/944–1419. 59 W. 44th St., 10036, B/D/F train to 42nd St. 165 rooms. $$$*

Ameritania. The lobby's silly imitation-Philipe Starck furniture (see Paramount below) fails to mar guests' satisfaction at getting a good deal. Rooms come with cable TV, 24-hour room service, and, in most cases, Broadway views. Two restaurants, a gift shop, and a lobby bar complete the picture—all done in an incongruous Caribbean style, with lite rock wafting over the speakers.... *Tel 212/247–5000, fax 212/247–3316. 1701 Broadway, 10019, B/D/E train to 7th Ave. 250 rooms. $$*

The Barbizon Hotel. A three-year restoration has contributed a pleasant-enough tan-and-pink decor, white tile bathrooms, and pedestal sinks. Downstairs are Restaurant Alexis, featuring French cuisine, and the Star Bar. There's also a fitness center.... *Tel 212/838–5700, 800/223–1020, fax 212/223–3287. 140 E. 63rd St., 10021, N/R train to Lexington Ave. 386 rooms. $$*

Best Western Seaport Inn. A chain mentality surfaces in the slightly cheesy reproduction furniture and the stiff, motelish bedding. No restaurants on the premises, but the South Street Seaport's cafes are steps away. Ask for a room with a view of the Brooklyn Bridge.... *Tel 212/766–6600, 800/HOTEL–NY, fax 212/766–6615. 33 Peck Slip, 10038, 2/3/4/5 train to Fulton St. 65 rooms. $$*

Box Tree. This small luxury hotel, an *Irreverent* favorite, offers some of the city's best dining, at the renowned Box Tree Restaurant, where Continental cuisine is served (jacket and tie required) on Wedgwood china and Lalique crystal. Each bedroom has a different decor (British Empire, Chinese Empire, German Empire—you get the picture), each with working fireplace and a fur throw on the antique, queen-sized bed. There's 24-hour room service and complimentary breakfast.... *Tel 212/758–8320, fax 212/308–3899. 250 E. 49th St., 10017, 6 train to 51st St. 13 rooms. DC not accepted. $$–$$$*

Carlton Arms. All the tenement-type rooms, decorated with wild murals, have sinks; some include a bathroom, while others use toilets and shower rooms down the hall (warning: though they're clean, the demon-head mosaics in the common bathrooms may make it difficult to concentrate). Outrageous ambience at a decent price (students and Europeans get a slight discount).... *Tel 212/679–0680.*

160 E. 25th St., 10010, 6 train to 23rd St. 54 rooms. AE, DC not accepted. $

Carlyle. Nestled among such illustrious neighbors as the Whitney Museum, Central Park, and all the top-of-the-line boutiques and antique shops of Madison Avenue, this Upper East Side hotel exudes the same sophistication and grace as its wealthy patrons. An efficient staff extends every courtesy to movie stars and less-famous guests alike, and the large, private fitness center with sauna, steam room, and massage, is to die for. Downstairs are Bemelman's Bar, decorated with murals by he of the *Madeline* children's books fame; The Carlyle Restaurant, serving classic cuisine among the oil paintings and flower arrangements; and Cafe Carlyle, where Bobby Short still keeps the piano bench warm.... *Tel 212/744–1600, 800/227–5737, fax 212/717–4682. 35 E. 76th St., 10021; 6 train to 77th St. 190 rms. $$$$–$$$$$*

Chelsea Hotel. The service here is friendly if lackadaisical, but a hotel with a history of violence, drug use, and a thousand scary New York stories is not for everyone, even if it has been renovated and the rooms are good-sized. No restaurants on the premises, but the Zig-Zag Bar and Restaurant is half a block away, and the attached El Quixote restaurant serves okay Spanish cuisine.... *Tel 212/243–3700, fax 212/243-3700. 222 W. 23rd St., 10011, 1/9 train to 23rd St. 200 rooms. $$*

Chelsea International Hostel. A very small hostel with coed dorm rooms, a common kitchen, and a garden dining area. Breakfast and linens are provided, and there's a safe for valuables. The cheapest listing here, but you get what you pay for.... *Tel 212/243–4922. 511 W. 20th St., 10011, C/E train to 23rd St. 2 dorms. No credit cards. $*

Chelsea Pines Inn. A bed & breakfast catering exclusively to a gay clientele, located between the West Village and Chelsea. Rooms have refrigerators and in-room sinks; some have private baths, others just showers and a shared hall toilet. The 14th Street location is certainly dreary, but guests aren't likely to mind.... *Tel 212/929–1023, fax 212/645–9497. 317 W. 14th St., 10014–5001, A/C/E train to 14th St. 21 rooms. $*

Days Hotel Midtown. What you'd expect from a motel chain—its one plus is the rooftop pool. Downstairs, the Metro Restaurant and bar serve those too timid to venture out among the sex shops on Eighth Avenue.... *Tel 212/581-7000, 800/572-6232, fax 212/974-0291. 790 8th Ave. 8th Ave. at W. 48th St., C/E train to 50th St. 367 rooms. $$*

The Drake Swissotel. Swiss-owned, it's efficient and impersonal. Every room has a color TV and refrigerator, plus a hair dryer in the beige marble bathrooms. Some offer fax service and voicemail, and there's a business center. The restaurant features Swiss specialties, and the bar can be a happening executive meeting place if you like that sort of thing.... *Tel 212/421-0900, 800/372-5369, fax 212/371-4190. 440 Park Ave., 10022, E/F train to Lexington-3rd Ave. 600 rooms. $$$*

Excelsior Hotel. Spacious rooms and suites with kitchens have been renovated just enough to be respectable, without removing the Art Deco tile in the bathrooms or the fifties linoleum kitchen tables. Choose front rooms for a spectacular view of the Museum of Natural History, rear rooms for children who need silence to sleep.... *Tel 212/362-9200, 800/368-4575, fax 212721-2994. 45 W. 81st St., 10024, B/C train to 81st St./Museum of Natural History. 200 rooms. DC not accepted. $*

Fitzpatrick Manhattan Hotel. As Irish as its name. The rooms are large, with wet bars, trouser presses, terrycloth robes, cable TV, computer and fax outlets, dual-line phones with voicemail, and optional mobile phones, not to mention modern bathrooms, many including whirlpools. No fitness center, but guest privileges at the nearby Atrium Club are available for a small fee.... *Tel 212/355-0100, 800/367-7701, fax 212/308-5166. 687 Lexington Ave., 10022, 4/5/6 train to 59th St. 92 rooms. $$$*

Franklin. This very neat boutique hotel's pleasant rooms have white canopies over the beds, fresh flowers, VCRs, cedar closets, and European-style showers. Breakfast is served in a tiny room off the lobby, where the coffeepot operates around the clock. Good value for the neighborhood.... *Tel 212/369-1000, fax 212/369-8000. 164 E. 87th St., 10128, 4/5/6/ train to 86th St. 53 rooms. DC not accepted. $$*

Four Seasons. Perfect for those who believe too much is not enough. The huge guest rooms have elegant contemporary decor with art deco touches. Blond English sycamore furniture echoes the paneling in the dressing rooms. The subdued 5757 Restaurant and Bar and the Armani-studded Lobby Lounge offer sustenance, a business center provides secretarial services, and, for the body, there's a fitness center and spa.... *Tel 212/758–5700, fax 212/758–5711. 57 E. 57th St., 10022, E/F trains to 5th Ave. 367 rooms. $$$$$*

Gramercy Park Hotel. The rooms are decidedly worn-looking, with nylon bedspreads, a few chips on the furniture, and aged (but clean) bathroom fixtures. The downstairs restaurant is usually empty, and the crooner in the cocktail lounge sings off-key, but the place has a kind of run-down charm—maybe that's why the fashion set has recently moved in. Service is pleasant but slow.... *Tel 212/475–4320, 800/221–4083, fax 212/505–0535. 2 Lexington Ave., 10010, 6 train to 23rd St. 509 rooms. $$*

Holiday Inn Downtown. Near Little Italy, SoHo, TriBeCa, and the Lower East Side, this chain hotel has standard-issue rooms and amenities. Fax machines are available in the lobby, where you can send messages while humming along to the Chinese Muzak—actually a relief from the subway noise.... *Tel 212/966–8898, 800/HOLIDAY, fax 212/966–3933. 138 Lafayette St., 10013, R train to Canal St. 223 rooms. $$*

Hotel 17. Yes, the grimy old building has a certain sordid charm, but the rooms are small, dark, and hot in summer (at least the ceilings are high), with uneven floors and dingy wallpaper. All rooms have phones and cable TV; 15 have baths, the others share toilets and tubs off the hall.... *Tel 212/475–2845, fax 212/677–8178. 225 E. 17th St., 10003, L train to 3rd Ave. 100 rooms. No credit cards. $*

Hotel Wales. This attractive eight-story Victorian hotel's potted ivy, wing-backed chairs, and antique issues of *Country Life* all look very proper. Free breakfast is served in the antique-filled Pied Piper Room, where at tea-time a harpist plays; the popular Sarabeth's Kitchen is next door, as is Busby's Grill. Rear rooms can be dark and small—ask for a front view, unless you loathe street noise.... *Tel 212/876–6000, fax 212/860–7000. 1295 Madison Ave., 10128, 4/5/6 train to 86th St. 92 rooms. DC not accepted. $$*

Incentra Village House. This West Village guest house boasts working fireplaces and lovely antiques. Bathrooms are small and utilitarian; the galley kitchens in every room come with all utensils. Clientele is largely gay and lesbian, but all are welcomed.... *Tel 212/206–0007. 32 8th Ave., 10014, 1/9 train to Sheridan Square. 12 rooms. DC not accepted. $*

Inn at Irving Place. A higher-budget version of the Incentra (see above), with exquisite antiques in every room, along with cable TV, VCRs, remote climate-control, and a very pleasant personal welcome (unless you are under 13, in which case you are not welcome at all). Continental breakfast is included, as well as services like in-room fax machines and laptop computers with Internet access (but who'd want to use them here?).... *Tel 212/533–4600, 800/685–1447, fax 212/533–4611. 54 Irving Pl., 10003, 4/5/6/L/N/R train to Union Square. 8 rooms. $$$*

Jolly Madison Towers Hotel. Popular with Italian vacationers and corporate types, the Jolly, near Grand Central Station, offers standard amenities for a very fair price. The lobby, refurbished in 1994, is hotel modern, the furniture neo-colonial, and the bathrooms awfully small, but you get a minibar, air conditioner, and Italian stations on the cable TV. Health spa, bar, and coffeeshop on premises.... *Tel 212/685–3700, 800/221–2626, fax 212/447–0747. 22 E. 38th St., 10016, 4/5/6/7 train to Grand Central. 225 rooms. $$*

Lowell Hotel. A small and unassuming lobby little prepares one for the wonders above, totally luxurious without ever being stuffy. Rooms have mirrored minibars with fridge, a writing desk, multiline phones with computer and fax hookup, home entertainment centers, even a complimentary umbrella; but if at all possible, choose a suite: they each have a fireplace, Scandinavian comforters, and a garden terrace. The Post House Restaurant is on the second floor; the antique-studded Pembroke Room serves breakfast and afternoon tea. There's a spacious fitness center, and personal trainers are a phone call away.... *Tel 212/838–1400, 800/221–4444, fax 212/319–4230. 28 E. 63rd St., 10021–8088, B/Q train to Lexington Ave. 65 rooms. $$–$$$$*

Malibu Studio Hotel. A buzzer lets you into a turquoise-and-lavender stairway painted with tropical fish and palm trees. In the small second-story lobby you'll find a hardworking

24-hour desk clerk handing out phone messages and trying to answer a phone call in Japanese. Some rooms have kitchenettes, but none offer TV or phones. Still, the bathrooms are spotless, the windows are thermal, and it's better than the Y. No children under 16.... *Tel 212/222–2954, fax 212/678–6842. 2688 Broadway, 10025, 1/9 train to 103rd St. 150 rooms. No credit cards. $*

Mansfield Hotel. Substantially lower-priced than the neighboring Royalton and the Algonquin, the Mansfield is the smart theater-goer's place to stay. The modern lobby adorned with gilt-framed oils seems perennially populated by young Asian girls. The rooms are pleasant enough, with remote TV, VCRs, and hairdryers. Continental breakfast is free.... *Tel 212/944–6050, fax 212/764–4477. 12 W. 44th St., 10036, B/D/F train to 42nd St. 131 rooms. DC not accepted. $$*

The Mark Hotel. Relax in the "neo-classical, English-Italian" lobby and watch Hollywood types make deals. Upstairs, rooms are sharp and elegant, with the usual luxury amenities, including marble bathrooms with large tubs and separate shower stalls. Larger suites have libraries, terraces, and so on. Stop by the intimate Mark's Bar for a cocktail, or dine at the handsome (and expensive) two-tiered restaurant.... *Tel 212/744–4300, 800/223–6800, fax 744–4586. Madison Ave. at E. 77th St., 10021, 6 train to 77th St. 180 rooms. $$$$*

Mayflower Hotel. The Mayflower remains a dependable hotel with a fair price, right on Central Park. Standard rooms have two closets and a kitchenette; there's a small fitness room upstairs. The decor may be early maiden-aunt, but the low-key atmosphere can be a lifesaver.... *Tel 212/265–0060, 800/223–4164, fax 212/265–5098. 15 Central Park West, 10023, 1/9 or A/B/C/D train to Columbus Circle. 577 rooms. $$–$$$*

Michelangelo. Acres of Italian marble downstairs, and upstairs all the upper-crust amenities you'd expect—very large rooms with king-sized beds, stunning Times Square views, marble bathrooms. A small fitness room, lobby bar, and business facilities are on the premises.... *Tel 212/765–1900, 800/237–0990, fax 212/581–7618. 152 W. 51st St., 10019, N/R train to 49th St. 178 rooms. $$$–$$$$*

Milford Plaza. With so much commotion on the enormous first floor, with its gift shops, hairdresser, ATM machine, fax- and copy service, you may wonder why people stay here. (It isn't for the motel-like rooms upstairs.) The answer is cheap package deals of Broadway tickets plus a room. A small fitness center, a gaggle of forgettable restaurants and lounges, and seven conference rooms are available.... *Tel 212/869–3600, 800/221–2690, fax 212/944–8357. 270 W. 45th St., 10036, A/C/E trains to 42nd St. 1,300 rooms. $$*

Millenium Broadway. Huge, muscular, Art Deco frescoes adorn the lobby, while etched mirrors and chrome light the adjoining Restaurant Charlotte, a pleasant place to dine after a play. Sleek, modern rooms feature dual-line phones, TVs, and all the futuristic gadgets you might expect. Then there's that dynamite skyscraper-view of New York.... *Tel 212/768–4400, 800/637–7200, fax 212/768–0847. 145 W. 44th St., 10036, 1/2/3/7/9 and N/R trains to Times Square. 638 rooms. $$$*

Millenium Hotel. Very high-octane Hilton, with tempting weekend rates. Modern furnishings combine with the usual business amenities, fitness room, computerized room service, minibars, terry bathrobes—and, from the higher floors, an absolutely spectacular view of New York Harbor. Taliesin and Grille restaurants offer good American fare, and the Connoisseur Bar has stockbroker decor.... *Tel 212/693–2001, 800/752–0014, ext. 25, fax 212/571–2317. 55 Church St., 10007, N/R train to Cortlandt St. 561 rooms. $$–$$$*

Morgans Hotel. If you are tall, thin, overpaid, and wear only black, you'll fit in at this ultra-discreet little hotel. Rooms lack views but offer down comforters, fresh flowers, and some very high-tech communications capabilities. Room service 5pm–midnight; Continental breakfast is free. There's a bar and cafe downstairs.... *Tel 212/686–0300, 800/334–3408, fax 212/779–8352. 237 Madison Ave., 10016, 4/5/6/7 train to Grand Central Station. 154 rooms. $$$*

New York Hilton and Towers. Expect a standard-issue Hilton room (the glass outer walls are tinted blue), with modern decor; Tower rooms are larger and higher-priced. A multilingual staff, business center, and new exhibit complex keep the Hilton popular with corporate customers; for the rest of us, there's a fitness center, massages, two mediocre restaurants and a pair of lounges, and numerous shops in the lobby.... *Tel 212/586–7000, 800/HILTONS, fax 212/315–1374. 1335 Avenue of the Americas, 10019–6078, B/D/E/F/Q train to 47-50th St./Rockefeller Center. 2,042 rooms. $$–$$$*

New York International American Youth Hostel. The Hilton of hostels offers lodging to travelers of all ages (you have to be an AYH member, but you can join at nominal cost when you register). Most rooms are dormitory style, but some semi-private and family rooms are available. Health-club-style shower stalls and toilets are kept very clean. The community-college ambience extends to the dining area, library, laundry, meeting room, chapel, espresso bar, student travel offices, and sunny garden where a fountain plays. Much cheaper than the YMCA, and lacking only a swimming pool.... *Tel 212/932–3200, fax 212/932–2574. 891 Amsterdam Ave., 10025, 1/9 train to 103rd St. 480 beds. AE, DC not accepted. $*

New York Palace. Reproduction furniture and unexceptional (though luxurious) amenities hit one like a hangover after the glamour of the downstairs bars. Non-smoking floors are offered, as well as 24-hour room service, and same-day laundry and valet, but otherwise the service ain't perfect. A business center and free limousine rides to Wall Street may mollify business travelers. You can dine al fresco in The Courtyard restaurant, in the shadows of St. Patrick's Cathedral.... *Tel 212/888–7000, 800/221–4982, fax 212/355–0820. 455 Madison Ave., 10022, 6 train to 51st St. 963 rooms. $$$*

Off SoHo Suites. Though cheek to jowl with the grim Lower East Side, this place is clean, reasonably priced, and near downtown plays, poetry readings, music, and galleries. The apartment-like suites have phones, color TV, air conditioning, marble baths, and well-equipped eat-in kitchens—very bright and cheery in a Crate and Barrel way. Large basement fitness room and laundry—but maid service is an extra $10 per day.... *Tel 212/979–9801, 800/OFF–SOHO, fax 212/979–9801. 11 Rivington St., 10002, F train to 2nd Ave. 37 suites. DC not accepted. $*

Paramount Hotel. A happening place for the young—check out the very modern lobby, or the Whiskey Bar with its bright, cartoonlike furniture. A mezzanine restaurant lets you watch the show, and you can even leave your kids in a supervised playroom. Rooms are extremely cramped but very stylish. No views, lots of street noise, and a staff that believes looking good should be enough.... *Tel 212/764–5500, 800/225–7474, fax 212/764–5500. 235 W. 46th St., 10036, 1/9 train to 50th St., or 1/2/3/9 to Times Sq. 600 rooms. $$*

The Peninsula Hotel. The bathrooms are to die for—giant marble tubs with plenty of thick, white towels—and the soothing, carpeted bedrooms with accents of peach, green, and gold match any other Manhattan hotel for luxury. And don't forget the 35,000-square-foot health spa, afternoon tea at the Gotham Lounge, meals at Le Bistro, and drinks way up in the Pen-Top Bar and Terrace.... *Tel 212/247–2200, 800/262–4967, fax 212/903–3949. 700 5th Ave., 10019, E/F train to 5th Ave. 242 rooms. $$$$–$$$$*

Pierre Hotel. With an ambience more sophisticated than the Plaza's, yet livelier than the Plaza Athénée's, service less cultlike than the Ritz-Carlton, and architecture less intimidating than the Four Seasons, this is a place to come home to, assuming you have a few million in your pocket. If so, put dibs on a room with a Central Park view and make reservations at the sumptuous Cafe Pierre.... *Tel 212/838–8000, 800/332–3442, fax 212/940–8109. 2 E. 61st St., 10021, N/R train to 5th Ave. 204 rooms. $$$$–$$$$$*

Plaza. Excellent location—but stress when reserving a room that you want one with plenty of space. The ceilings here are high, the beds are firm, and the flowered duvets are actually pretty. Bathrooms have big, thick towels. Service is very casual, though—quick enough, but not particularly deferential.... *Tel 212/759–3000, 800/759–3000, fax 212/759–3167. 768 5th Ave., 10019, N/R train to 5th Ave. 830 rooms. $$$–$$$$*

Plaza Athénée. Rooms are very sophisticated and very French, with soft carpets and delicate antiques, marble baths with Frette robes, Belgian sheets, VCRs, and everything else top-level; the penthouses really let loose, with velvet upholstery, oil paintings, and terraces and glass solariums. Even the hotel's small fitness room has paintings on the walls, and La Régence restaurant, a Louis XV gem, resides downstairs. Yet the Plaza Athénée isn't too grand to offer significant summer savings, so ask for special rates.... *Tel 212/734–*

9100, 800/447–8800, fax 212/722–0958. 37 E. 64th St., 10021, B/Q train to Lexington Ave. 153 rooms. $$$$

Quality Hotel and Suites Manhattan. Owner Sant S. Chatwal, who also owns New York's Bombay Palace restaurants, has restored this rather tired Midtown hotel. Unfortunately, it still looks a bit tired, though not as motel-like upstairs as one might expect. Smallish rooms offer telephones, cable TV, and so on. Proximity to Rockefeller Center, Fifth Avenue shopping, and the theater district give this hotel some legitimacy, but check the Mansfield first.... *Tel 212/768–3700, 800/826–4667, fax 212/768–3403. 157 W. 47th St., 10036, 1/9 train to 50th St. 200 rooms. $$*

Radisson Empire Hotel. The halls are narrow, but who cares when Lincoln Center is just across the way. Chintz is everywhere, the bathrooms compact but sweet. Service is very professional, polite, and alert but understated, not at all stuffy. A good hotel for the price.... *Tel 212/265–7400, 800/333–3333, fax 212/315–0349. 44 W. 63rd St., 10023, 1/9 train to 66th St./Lincoln Center. 373 rooms. $$–$$$*

RIHGA Royal Hotel. A grand, mosaic-tiled and carpeted lobby, the sharp-looking Halcyon Lounge and Halcyon Restaurant, and comfortable beige suites with state-of-the-art business amenities make this a perfect place to meet your clients. Fabulous views of Central Park and the Hudson River, a business center, small fitness center with personal trainer, and—you guessed it—complimentary shoe shine.... *Tel 212/307–5000, 800/937–5454, fax 212/765–6530. 151 W. 54th St., 10019, B/D/E train to 7th Ave. 500 suites. $$$*

Ritz-Carlton New York. A $20-million renovation in 1993, plus some new management, has made this hotel the serious contender it was always destined to be. Service is not only efficient, but intelligent. The Fantino Bar and Restaurant serves enthusiastic locals as well as guests; there's also a small fitness room, a business center, and all the privacy and quiet you could want.... *Tel 212/757–1900, 800/241–3333, fax 212/757–9620. 112 Central Park South, 10019, Q train to 57th St. or A/B/C/D to Columbus Circle. 214 rooms. $$$$$*

Roger Smith. Bright, amusing, and sophisticated, this hotel is a place people come back to. Ignore the colonial-style upstairs bedrooms and spend your time with the other guests in Lily's Restaurant and Bar. Even the clerks here have character, and breakfast is free.... *Tel 212/755–1400, 800/445–0277, fax 212/319–9130. 501 Lexington Ave., 10017, 4/5/6/7 train to Grand Central. 135 rooms. $$–$$$*

Royalton. The Algonquin of the nineties, featuring the 44 Bar and Restaurant where you can study the lifestyles of the rich and famous. Upstairs, the post-modern style is almost scary at times, but fun, with designer Philipe Starck's stark velvet armchairs complementing cherry headboards, thick teal carpets and, in some cases, granite hearths with working fireplaces. There's a 24-hour fitness room, naturally.... *Tel 212/869–4400, 800/635–9013, fax 212/869–8965. 44 W. 44th St., 10036, B/D/F train to 42nd St. 205 rooms. $$$–$$$$*

Shelburne Murray Hill. Most guests here are on long-term corporate stays, living in the workmanlike rooms with full kitchens complete with microwave. Amenities are pretty basic, but you can hook up your laptop and fax machine. Secretarial services, are available downstairs, and there are gym and laundry facilities in the basement.... *Tel 212/689–5200, 800/ME–SUITE, fax 212/779–7068. 303 Lexington Ave., 10016–3104, 4/5/6/7 train to Grand Central. 258 rooms. $$$*

Sherry-Netherland Hotel. The Sherry's lobby includes friezes from the Vanderbilt mansion, the rooms are spacious and grand, and the service is geared to serve every whim. So what's not to like? Some guests never leave, so book early—there aren't as many available rooms as one might think.... *Tel 212/355–2800, 800/247–4377, fax 212/319–4306. 781 5th Ave., 10022, N/R train to 5th Ave. 400 rooms. $$$*

The Stanhope Hotel. Museum Mile gives the Stanhope an artistic flair, and the mood here is almost like a country estate—one where anything might happen. Newly renovated rooms feature Louis XV-style antiques with Asian accents. The perfect place for a mogul who wants out of Midtown.... *Tel 212/288–5800, 800/828–1123, fax 212/517–0088. 995 5th Ave., 10028, 6 train to 77th St. 140 rooms. $$$*

Surrey Hotel. Half a block from the Whitney Museum, with large, comfortable, recently redecorated suites, this place has a lot to recommend it—including full kitchens with surprisingly attractive dining areas. The service is somewhat peevish, but they get the job done. Fitness center, secretarial services, and room service (from Restaurant Daniel, one of the city's best, downstairs) available.... *Tel 212/288–3700, 800/ME–SUITE, fax 212/628–1549. 20 E. 76th St., 10018–1103, 6 train to 77th St. 133 rooms. $$$*

U.N. Plaza-Park Hyatt. This sleek high-rise right near the U.N. gives movers and shakers a raft of furnishings so modern you hardly see them. The rooftop swimming pool, tennis courts, the banquettes in the lobby with custom telephones, and the super-alert desk clerks assure you that you're in the hands of experts. Try the Ambassador Grill for champagne-and-lobster brunch on Sundays.... *Tel 212/758–1234, 800/233–1234, fax 212/702–5051. 1 United Nations Plaza, 10017–3575, 4/5/6/7 train to Grand Central. 427 rooms. $$$*

Urban Ventures, Inc. Mary McAulay and Frances Tesser started this bed-and-breakfast concern in 1979 with only four rooms to offer. They now command 600, nearly all in Manhattan. You'll have a choice of rooms with breakfast or empty apartments without—quality varies wildly, but the two owners have checked out each home and interviewed the hosts. If you like, they'll send you a map with points of interest marked to help you decide which neighborhood you prefer. "Comfort Range" rooms (most with private bath) run $55–85, "Budget Range" (most with shared bath) at $34–50, and entire apartments begin at $60/night.... *Tel 212/594–5650. Box 426, 10024. DC not accepted. $*

Vanderbilt YMCA. The rooms are YMCA quality, but you still get a lot for your buck: the use of the recently renovated fitness club, two pools, and a sauna, plus an excellent and safe East Side location. Rooms are bare, towels are thin, and all the rooms except the $90 suites share showers down the hall. The suites have private bathrooms.... *Tel 212/756–9600, fax 212/752–0210. 224 E. 47th St., 10017, 4/5/6/7 train to Grand Central. 400 rooms. AE, DC not accepted. $*

Waldorf-Astoria. Owned by the Hilton chain and extensively refurbished by them two years ago, the lobby areas bring back New York's best old days. Upstairs, furniture is Hilton reproduction colonial, but the peach carpets are thick and the baths are marble. Some suites have fireplaces. There's a fitness center, a business center, four restaurants (Peacock Alley serves Basque food, the Bull & Bear has steaks, Oscar's Bistro is for light food, Inagiku for Japanese fare), and four lounges. Obviously, this is a big place.... *Tel 212/355–3000, 800/HILTONS, fax 212/421–8103. 301 Park Ave., 10022, 6 train to 51st St. 1,215 rooms. $$$–$$$$*

Washington Square Hotel. The Spanish-style lobby is nice enough, with its wrought-iron gate and tile floors, but the rooms are deadly dreary. Front rooms are supposed to be better, but they're noisy. Continental breakfast included, but the basement restaurant smells like goulash. Cheap, but worth no more than what you're paying. Still, what a location.... *Tel 212/777–9515, 800/222–0418, fax 212/979–8373. 103 Waverly Place, 10011–9194, A/B/C/D/E/F/Q train to W. 4th St. 160 rooms. DC not accepted. $*

Wentworth Hotel. The lobby is long, narrow, and often crowded with chattering Brazilian tourists. Murals depicting views of New York lighten up the place. Otherwise, this is your typical budget-priced hotel, handily near the jewelry district, Rockefeller Center, Midtown shopping, and Broadway.... *Tel 212/719–2300, 800/223–1900. 29 W. 46th St., 10036, B/D/F/Q trains to 47th-50th St./Rockefeller Center. 250 rooms. $*

West Side YMCA. Steps from Lincoln Center and Central Park, the bustling lobby rings with several languages, and there are plenty of opportunities to converse—in the gym, at the pool, the espresso bar, or in the laundry room, for example. Rooms are very basic, with single beds, linoleum floors, and usually no private baths. (Showers are down the hall.)... *Tel 212/787–4400, fax 212/875–1334. 5 W. 63rd St., 10023, 1/9 train to 66th St./Lincoln Center. 430 rooms. AE, DC not accepted. $*

Wyndham. Personal attention from the staff gives this modest place an edge. Smaller than the roughly equivalent Mayflower, the Wyndham has large, apartment-like rooms and suites (some guests are long-term residents), most with modern decor. Downstairs, Jonathan's restaurant is open weekdays except in summer.... *Tel 212/753–3500, 800/257–1111, fax 212/754–5638. 42 W. 58th St., Q train to 57th St. 200 rooms. $$*

Uptown Accommodations

- The Barbizon Hotel **13**
- The Carlyle Hotel **17**
- Excelsior Hotel **3**
- The Franklin **8**
- Hotel Wales **7**
- Lowell Hotel **14**
- Malibu Studios Hotel **1**
- The Mark Hotel **10**
- Mayflower Hotel **6**
- New York International AYH Hostel **2**
- Pierre Hotel **15**
- Plaza Athenee **12**
- Radisson Empire Hotel **4**
- Sherry Netherland Hotel **16**
- The Stanhope Hotel **9**
- Surrey Hotel **11**
- West Side YMCA **5**

Midtown Accommodations

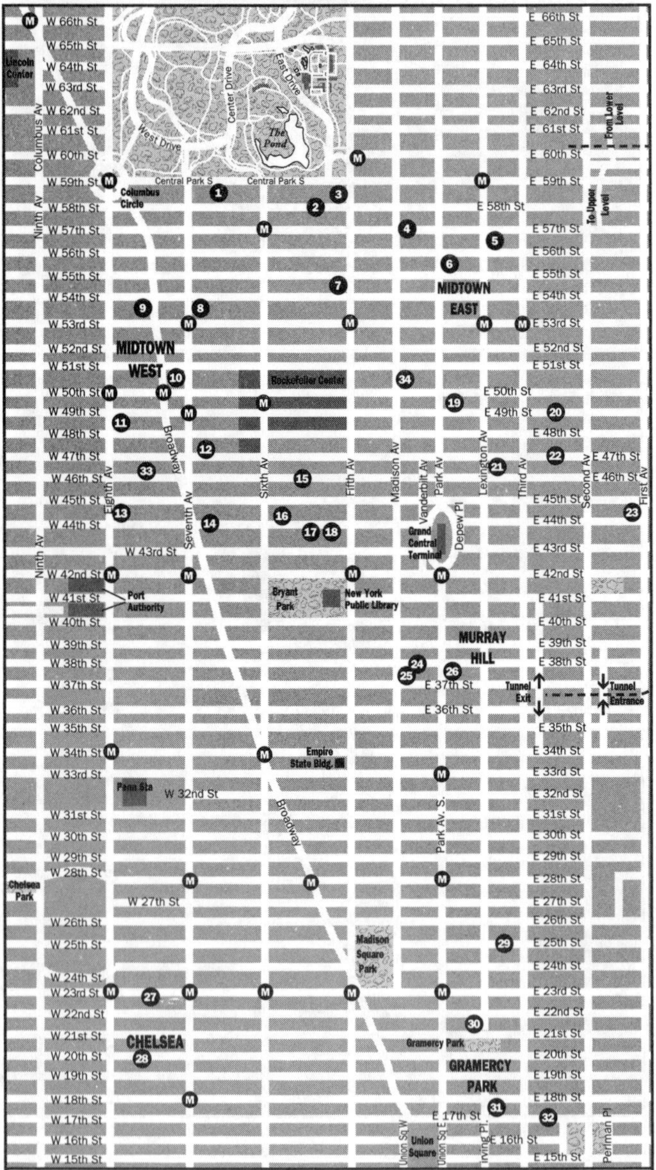

Algonquin **16**
Ameritania **9**
The Box Tree **20**
Carlton Arms **29**
Chelsea Hotel **27**
Chelsea International Hostel **28**
Days Hotel Midtown **11**
The Drake Swissotel **6**
Fitzpatrick Manhattan Hotel **5**
Four Seasons **4**
Gramercy Park Hotel **30**
Hotel 17 **32**
Hotel Macklowe **14**
Inn at Irving Place **31**
Jolly Madison Towers Hotel **24**
Mansfield Hotel **18**
The Michelangelo **10**
Milford Plaza **13**
Morgans Hotel **25**
New York Palace **34**
Paramount Hotel **33**
The Peninsula Hotel **7**
Plaza **3**
Quality Hotel & Suites Manhattan **12**
Royal Hotel **8**
Ritz-Carlton New York **1**
Roger Smith **21**
Royalton **17**
Shelburne Murray Hill **26**
UN Plaza Park Hyatt **23**
Vanderbilt YMCA **22**
Waldorf-Astoria **19**
Wentworth Hotel **15**
Wyndham **2**

Downtown Accommodations

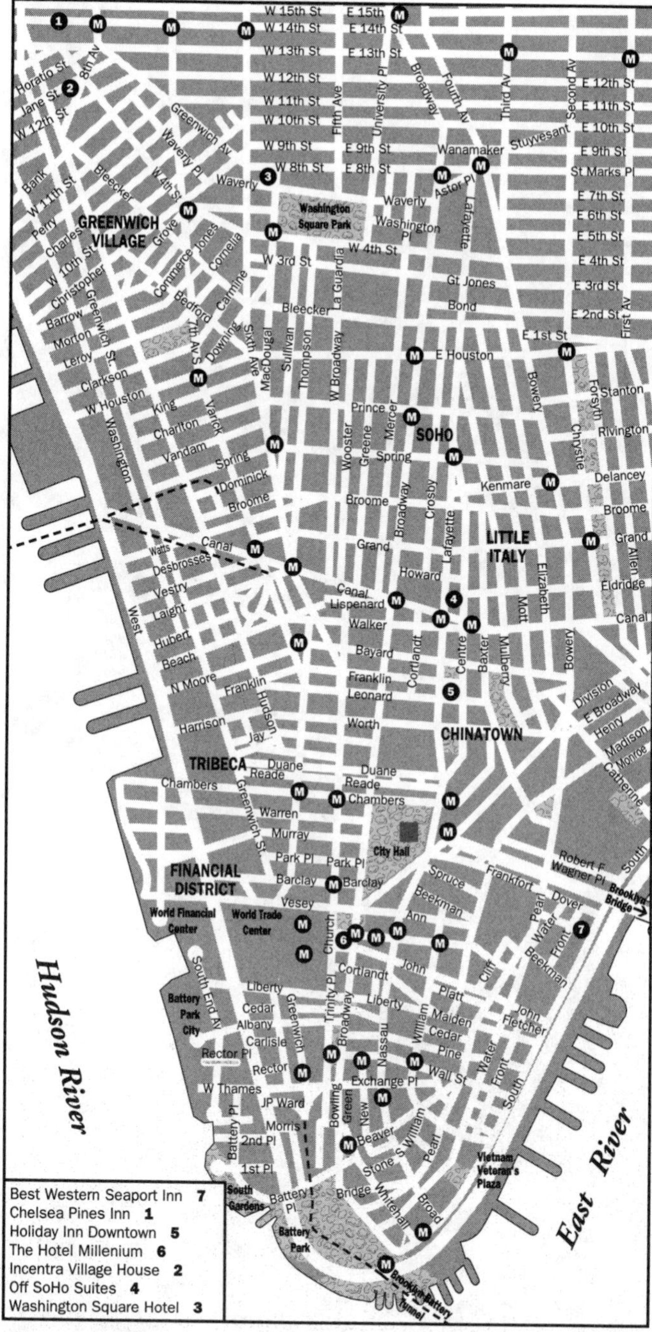

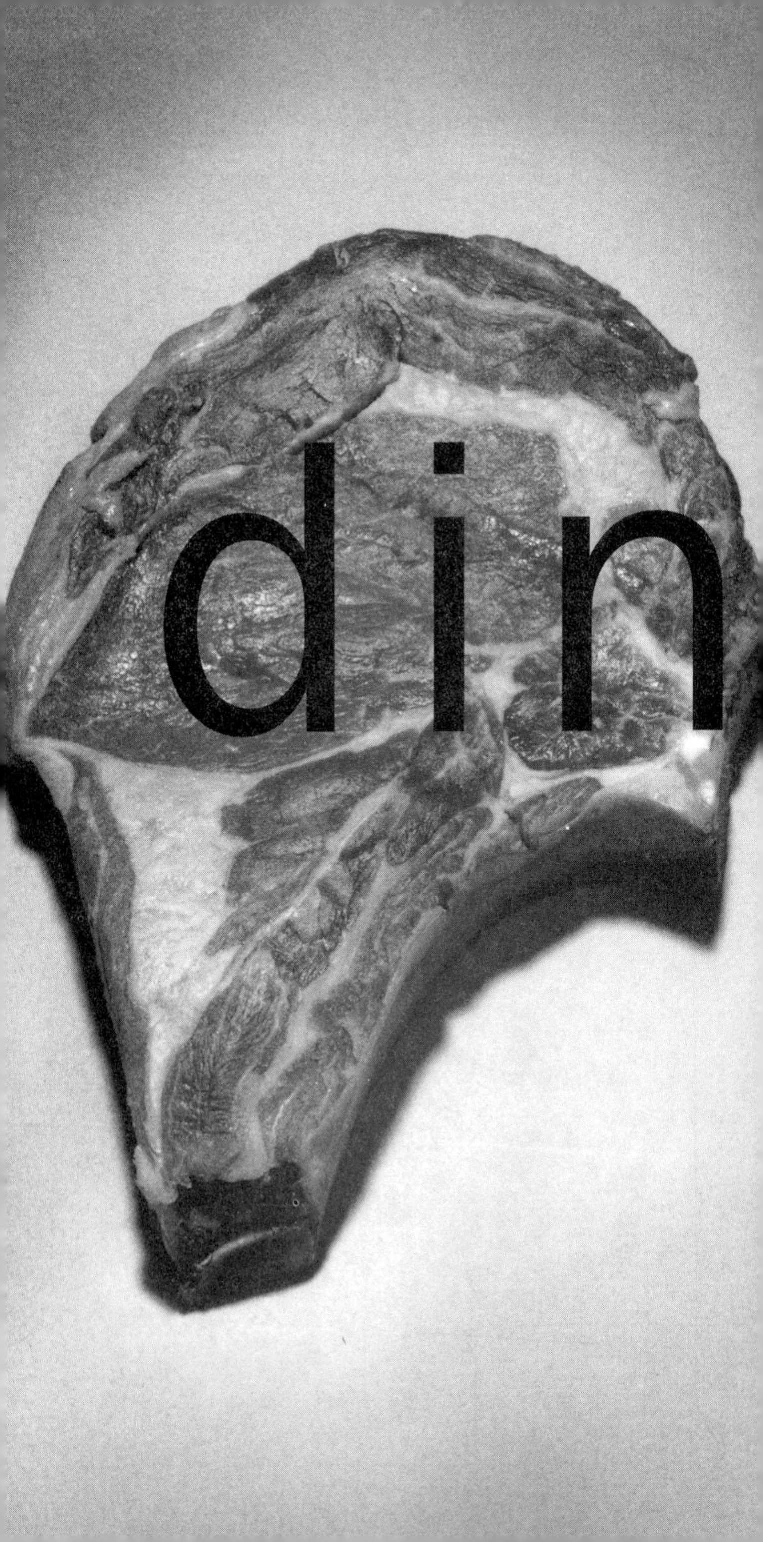
din

2

ing

Some years ago, as a bright young thing, I came to the city because of the theater. When the shine went off that, I dabbled at the fringes of the literary scene. Only now, at long last, have I found my real milieu in New York: restaurants. And my true vocation: eating. I have a sense that this passion will see me through to old age—after all, a day never passes when I don't get hungry, and there's always another restaurant (new, different, and possibly better than all the rest) to try out on just the next block. And considering Manhattan's striving to do things better than they do it anywhere else—be it blini, sushi, California health–nut food, very tall appetizers and desserts (suitable for framing), or bûche de Noël—you've got yourself on the horns of a dilemma. The city's culinary efforts are alternately wildly successful (Manhattan has some of the best French restaurants outside Paris) and baffling (go figure why a Greenwich Village bistro called Chez Ma Tante would specialize in rather good pasta). You can either pay up at a gastronomic shrine like La Côte Basque, or relax your standards and taste your way through the melting pot in the city's countless ethnic storefront cafes. And that's not even counting Manhattan's grazing options: coffee and bagel carts stationed at corners during the morning rush hour, replaced around noon by stands selling those true-blue New York comfort foods, hot dogs and pretzels; Korean salad bars, where the term salad is so broadly defined as to include pasta, spring rolls, and fried chicken along with the roughage, all sold by the pound; free nibbles at gourmet grocery stores and bakeries; a few bona fide American food courts, like the excellent one at South Street Seaport; and, in recent years, an onslaught of designer coffee bars—your Starbucks, Timothy's, and New Worlds—purveying cappuccino, latte, espresso, and muffins heavy enough to serve as ballast.

Only in New York

It's imperative to try a few New York standards: a magnificent **deli** sandwich (generally too big to finish and accompanied by a little cupful of coleslaw); **Chinese** (but mind, Manhattan's come a long way from tired old General Tso's chicken, incorporating the flavors of Thailand, Viet Nam, Burma, and Malaysia in its au courant Asian cuisine); **Hispanic** specialties like rice and beans; pasta (not always quite the way Italians make it, but its own utterly delicious, sui generis self); and **pizza** (created, they say, in New Haven, though on that red-letter day I just know there had to be a New Yorker in the kitchen somewhere).

Getting the Scoop

Recently, the city's restaurant scene has been substantially enlivened by the addition of food critic Ruth Reichl to the staff of the *New York Times*. She came from L.A. but has settled right in, returning time and again to each place she reviews—wearing wigs and other disguises so maitre d's won't guess her M.O. Her restaurant reviews generally run on Fridays and focus as much on the crowd and decor of a place as on its food. For whatever's trendiest, not to mention mouth-watering photos, take a look at the current edition of *New York* magazine; its restaurant critic, Gael Greene, gives reliable advice and more than a few fresh, interesting choices.

What Will It Cost?

A multi-course dinner at one of the city's fanciest eating establishments, including drinks, freely flowing wine, and a tip, can set you back over $100 per person. Lunches at places like The Four Seasons and the Union Square Cafe are somewhat less expensive, and occasionally you'll find prix fixe options—though these seldom include specialty dishes with exotic ingredients. Careful ordering (a glass of wine and an entree, or two appetizers instead of an entree) can help keep the tab down. I often dine at the bar in the swankier joints, where lower-priced menus are sometimes available. In the summer, keep your eye open for special lunch deals (costing the same as the year, for instance $19.95 in 1995) offered as part of a city-wide promotion at some of Manhattan's top restaurants. But you also really can find great meals for under $20 at places with character rather than class, and intensely flavored food rather than subtle haute cuisine. New Yorkers certainly don't spend $100 every time they dine out—and they do so often, believe you me.

Tipping

Service compris is not a concept understood in New York, where restaurant salaries are woefully low and most waiters are only working tables as a means to some other end. (I heard a line in a play that sums it up: At a restaurant table, a man calls out, "Oh actor, actor..."). Dollar bills for coat checkers are standard. When calculating a waiter's tip, many New Yorkers simply double the tax amount on their check (2 x 8.25% = 16.5 %, a reasonable tip). But New York waitpeople work hard for their money, so round it up to 20 % if you can, unless the service is wretched.

Getting the Right Table

I suppose some high-rollers tip maitre d's to get see-and-be-seen tables. Since money talks in New York, I'm sure it works, but the practice strikes many as more than a little gauche. After all, the real way to get a great table is by being a regular. If you're from out of town, a good hotel concierge should have some pull—make your reservations through him or her if you plan to dine at any exclusive restaurants. If you know that you prefer one room in a restaurant over another (for instance, the clubby Grill Room versus the romantic Pool Room at The Four Seasons), ask for it specifically when you make your reservations. Barring that, once you're at the restaurant don't be too timid to request a change if you get put in a spot you don't like and you see better tables empty. Most maître d's will accommodate you, when at all possible. If not, and your assigned seat is simply too miserable, the answer's simple: just get up and go.

When to Eat and How to Dress

I wish it were different—that New York took long lunches (followed by a nap), and then began dinner as late as 10pm, the way they do in Spain, Italy, and Latin America. But Manhattan Island runs on the office clock, lunching from noon to 2, and dining from around 7:30 to 9:30. Unless you just happen to strike it lucky, reservations are required at the kinds of places where they sweep the crumbs off the tablecloth with a little brush; a good general policy is to make a reservation at any place that accepts them, and check on the dress policy when you call. (Listings below note any restrictions that apply at these restaurants.) These days, even top-of-the-line New York restaurateurs recognize the chilling effects of a room full of suits and ties, but the light sure comes to their eyes when hip-looking customers arrive. So if it's a dinner to remember you have in mind, celebrate the occasion by dressing with style.

Where the Chefs Are

David Bouley has vaulted to superstar status with his imaginative French-inspired cooking at his TriBeCa restaurant (named simply Bouley); **Alexander Smalls** puts a nouvelle spin on soul food at Cafe Beulah; **Alfred Portale**, who gave up jewelry designing to apprentice with Michel Guerard, does smoked salmon on a potato galette at the Gotham Bar and Grill; **Charles Palmer**, who owns Aureole, paints masterpieces in dessert sauces; and **Don Pintabona** wears the chef's hat at the TriBeCa Grill. But what really matters is that **André Soltner** has sold that legend among American French restaurants, Lutèce, and retired to a post at the French Culinary Institute. Mr. Soltner spent 34 years in charge of the kitchen at Lutèce, where I once had pigeon in puff pastry I can remember in more detail than my college graduation. While I ate, Mr. Soltner stopped by my table to wish me bon appétit, even though I'd neither been in the restaurant before nor posed for the cover of a glossy magazine. Without a doubt, New York was sad to see him go.

The Lowdown

New York classics... The Four Seasons, La Côte Basque, One if by Land...so the New York restaurant rosary begins. These are legendary places, favored by luminaries, lottery-winners, and regular New Yorkers celebrating very special occasions, with cuisine to match the remarkable settings. The architect Philip Johnson designed the airy Pool Room and dark, woody Grill Room at **The Four Seasons**, where the service is impeccable and the tables so far apart that the Macy's Thanksgiving Day Parade could almost be routed between them. Dover sole, steak tartare, and tuna carpaccio head up the menu, but people have been known to rhapsodize even over The Four Seasons' baked potato, doused in Lungarotti olive oil. **Tavern on the Green** is set in a Central Park bower haunted by topiary beasts, lit up like a diamond tiara at night. Reserve a table in the garden room and order a rack of lamb. The scallops with truffles, frogs' legs, and crème brûlée at **Le Cirque** on the East Side are the stuff of French culinary epiphanies, as are the soufflés and cassoulet at **La Côte Basque**. And if the French fare isn't quite as distinguished at the **Café des Artistes**, the setting is to die for, in the lobby of a grand old Upper West Side apartment building, with murals of naked maidens painted by Howard Chandler Christy. The **Russian Tea Room** is a veritable Fabergé egg of a restaurant, suitable for Romanovs *manqués*. Throughout 1996, it will be closed for renovation. It should reopen in 1997, looking the same as ever—apparently the perpetual Christmasey look is too special to be tinkered with. Prime downstairs red-plush banquettes beside the samovar will still generally be reserved for celebrity types, but they will probably serve the same chicken côtelette à la Kiev and blini stuffed with caviar; someday, I may even work my way through the 17 varieties of Russian vodka offered on the menu. At **Windows on the World** on the 107th floor of the World Trade Center what you get is, above all, a nonpareil Manhattan view; Continental standards like steak-and-veal paillard help elevate the mood, as do vintages from the tome-like wine list. But I'd sell the family jewels for the view of downtown Manhattan from the windows at **The River Cafe**, tucked beneath the eastern end of the Brooklyn Bridge. What's more, new chef Rick Laakkonen has renovated the restaurant's menu, which now features such delicacies as cod-and-lobster risotto and pan-seared baby chicken stuffed with smoked bacon. And if I had enough left over after the jewelry transaction, I'd reserve a table at **One if by Land, Two if by Sea**, where strings of white lights twinkle in the garden and four fireplaces glow warm and mellow. The restaurant occupies a historic carriage house in the West Village, once owned by Aaron Burr, who might have been convinced to quit dueling with Alexander Hamilton had he sampled chef David McInerney's beef Wellington or Cornish game hen in honey-lavender glaze.

Hot spots that won't die... **Bouley** in TriBeCa has managed to keep a high profile by dint of its devilishly handsome dining room and recipes for French-inspired entrees like grilled lobster with artichokes and sturgeon with summer squash. It should be closed through most of 1996 while it moves to a new site, where a cooking school will be appended so other chefs can learn David Bouley's secrets. Also in TriBeCa, there's **Odeon**, encamped in a postmodern stripped-down cafeteria, which provides cassoulet, seafood chowder, roast lamb, and sorbet to the contemporary art crowd; and **TriBeCa Grill**, where the trendy crowd was first lured by the star power of owner Robert DeNiro and then kept on coming for the inventive cooking of chef Don Pintabona. **Aureole**, a relative newcomer in a pretty town house on the East Side with a massive two-story front window, has perfected the art of the dessert, like bittersweet chocolate timbale and crème brûlée. **March**, in another East Side town house, tucks diners away in peaceful little flower-decked nooks, then woos them with chef Wayne Nish's carefully reduced sauces and intriguing pre-appetizer "treats." The menu at the stylish **Union Square Cafe** has been turned into a cookbook—which is only appropriate since this place is a favorite publishing-industry lunch spot. Try the tuna carpaccio in the sunken dining room lined with cherrywood and forest-green wainscoting, followed up with a plate of delectable cookies, or just grab a seat at the bar for oyster slurping and wine sipping. At Midtown's **JUdson Grill** and lower Fifth Avenue's **Gotham Bar and Grill**, the decor and crowds are sleekly handsome, but upstaged by the designer-chic cuisine—salads springing off the plate and desserts that could double as Easter hats.

Bangs for your buck... You can dine at any of the following spots for under $20, easy. What's more, the food is pretty darned good and the atmosphere cheerful. **Aggie's**, a bustling, converted diner on Houston Street, brings home the good-deal honors by dint of its fresh, interesting seafood menu, listed on a blackboard above the counter. **Fanelli** predates most of the other restaurants in SoHo, and never could be called trendy—still, this old–New York tavern packs in the crowds for simple dinners and Sunday brunch. **Eddie's**, in the New York University neighborhood, starts you off with popcorn, followed by delicious burgers and salads; while you eat, listen in as Village scholars deconstruct *Moby Dick*. Twenty-somethings from Wall Street loosen their ties over thick club sandwiches and omelettes at **Boxers,** just off the Sheridan Square Viewing Garden, ogling the cute waitresses and knocking back a few beers. **Blu** is a funky cafe/restaurant serving soups, pastas, and salads to moviegoers with tickets for shows at one of the theaters clustered around Seventh Avenue and W. 23rd Street. **Diane's Uptown** offers 7-ounce burgers for under $4, in modest but comfortable digs. The scene is ever so slightly Parisian at the **Universal Grill**, and the clientele largely gay, but that definitely shouldn't stop straights from stopping into this pleasant spot on Bedford Street in the lower West Village. But my favorite of the lot is the **Cornelia Street Cafe**, which serves very reasonably priced, tasty meals in unpretentiously stylish surroundings. This cafe has been part of the Village scene for ages, and there are always companionable fellow travelers at the bar, not to mention bartenders happy to treat you to a drink if you have the look of a potential regular.

The food's the thing... If they gave out a Tony Award for Best Restaurant, I fear it would seldom go to an establishment in the theater district. There are plenty of eating spots in the neighborhood, of course, and the whole block of W. 46th Street between Seventh and Eighth avenues has come to be called Restaurant Row. **Orso** occupies stylish digs there, and is a notable exception, offering smashing cuisine from the north of Italy, plus famous faces and power-brokers among the clientele. Down the street the sweet, minuscule **Hourglass Tavern** has a different prix fixe menu every night, featuring an international mix of dishes from mesquite-grilled fish to tomato-and-mozzarella salad. The gimmick here is a one-hour time limit when there's a crowd, with hour-glasses on each table to enforce it. On the east side of Times Square there's an inviting bistro called **Café Un Deux Trois**, situated in the airy lobby of an old hotel, with columns and endlessly high ceilings, paper table-cloths and crayons; the menu tends toward unremarkably prepared international standards like salads, steak, fish, and fries, but the place is mobbed before and after the theater. The late Frank Zappa started it and used to be a familiar fixture at the bar. Actors and techies hang out at **Barrymore's**, drawn by a long companionable bar and basic, cheap eats. Right in the middle of W. 44th Street's gaudy marquees and at the back door of the *New York Times*, wood-trimmed **Carmine's** is the nineties version of Mama Leone's, that massive stage-set cliché of a New York Italian restaurant (which, perhaps not coincidentally, closed its doors after this place opened). The difference here is that the food is the real thing, and it's not just for tourists—everybody comes, for simple, tangily delicious southern Italian fare (between this and the Upper West Side branch, Carmine's reportedly goes through 13 *tons* of garlic a year). Down the street is shabby old **Sardi's**, where the red velvet walls groan with hard-to-identify cartoon likenesses of stars and the food is notoriously bad. But for heaven's sake, cut Sardi's some slack. You won't get poisoned if you eat here, and it's a Broadway legend, the scene of countless hit-show openings and big-flop wakes. Besides, the barmen on the second floor produce very credible martinis, and if you go with a card-carrying member of Equity, the thespian's union, you can order from a low-priced "actor's menu."

Little French boîtes... Oysters on the half shell and chardonnay go down smoothly at **Le Pescadou**, where you can sit by the open French doors fronting lower Sixth Avenue, communing with the potted geraniums. Don't count on a bargain meal, but you can be fairly certain of a nice bowl of lobster bisque or bouillabaisse. Small, romantic **Dix et Sept** occupies the ground floor of a West Village town house, where candles flicker on white-clothed tables and Piaf croons. The menu leans towards well-prepared Gallic standards, like good old-fashioned onion soup. Anyone who's ever lived in a turn-of-the-century row house will feel right at home at **Mary's Restaurant**—there are two smallish rooms separated by a wooden sliding door, marble-mantled fireplaces beneath gigantic mirrors, and a window providing a glimpse of the leafy garden in the rear. Though the menu is international by and large, with specialties like roast loin of pork and grilled shellfish, the place is so sweet and cozy it easily qualifies as a boîte. I don't know anyone who isn't crazy about **Tartine**, more a closet than a restaurant, on one of the prettiest blocks in the Village, with an inevitable line outside the door and tables squeezed so close together that by dessert you're generally good friends with the people at the next table. If you can't get in there, saunter over to Greenwich Avenue to **Café de Bruxelle**—not French, obviously, but a kissing cousin. Whenever a "cold November" falls upon my soul, this is where I go, because the small lace-curtained bar is an absolute joy, with a long list of Belgian beers and ever-appealing specialty wines. In the theater district, try **Le Madeleine**, a sweet little lace-curtained cafe with a pretty courtyard—a little bit of the Left Bank on W. 43rd Street, with croque-monsieurs on crusty bread with wonderfully runny cheese. If nothing else, sit at the *petit* bar and have a Kir aperitif.

Like Mama used to make... The **Trattoria Spaghetto** used to be called Mama's, which says precisely what one needs to know about this corner restaurant across the street from Father Demo Square. Tables spill out onto the sidewalk on fair evenings, and once you're seated a waiter sprints over with a basket of Italian bread (which you can butter or dip in olive oil). The pasta is homemade, the offerings just about what you'd find at a trattoria in Rome. Down Bleecker Street is another plain man's Italian eatery, the **Trattoria Pesce Pasta**, with its antipasto beckoning from the front window; order the linguine with clams or the seafood risotto, and you won't be disappointed—though you'll reek of garlic for hours after. **Mappamondo** and its bambino, **Mappamondo Due**, do Italian food the same way, though the clientele tends to be younger and hipper, thanks to the Hudson Street address. Ditto for the East Village's **Cucina di Pesce**, in its cozy basement dining room. If you happen to be on Fifth Avenue in Park Slope, Brooklyn, you'll want to stop for dinner at **Cucina**, in surprisingly stylish digs, with a menu full of pastas and excellent veal. Little Italy is the tourist thing—unabashedly tacky, but fun. You've got to be careful about where you stop for refreshment, though, because the restaurants along Mulberry Street aren't uniformly good. Try **Benito's I** (not II) for simple pasta dishes and delectable fried calamari, or **Puglia**, a real party scene, where you get crammed into long tables with strangers, the plates are passed down to you from the end, and an accordionist squeezes the life out of his instrument. It may not be the best Italian food in town, but if you're out for a rowdy good time, who cares?

Ciao, baby... La cucina classica is raised to brave new heights at **Remi**, in a deliciously airy Midtown dining room lined by Venice's Grand Canal in murals; the risotto takes a while but is marvelously worth the wait, and the ravioli is stuffed with nouvelle sorts of ingredients that would put mama in shock. In the Village, the luscious Italian fare at **Il Mulino** hails from the Abruzzi, while **Bar Pitti** is Florentine all the way, with rustic pastas and sandwiches on hearty country bread. **Po**, a classy new Italian eatery hidden away on little Cornelia Street, has a long narrow dining room, postage-stamp-sized bar, and a menu that plays inventive games with tried-and-true favorites. And then there's the **Grotta Azzurra**, in a Little Italy cellar that evokes Rome's Trastevere, where the waiters warm up to a little good-natured sass. Great quantities of Chianti should be consumed, and it's utterly absurd to ask them to hold the garlic.

China chic... At the swish **China Grill**, the East and West meet right on the plate with dishes like oriental antipasto and grilled beef in soy-cilantro sauce. Jimmy and Wally Chin do nouvelle Chinese (boneless duckling à l'orange, Chinese-Indian lamb stew, and pecan pie) with the spirit of true global villagers at **Chin Chin**, where the walls are lined with pages from the Chin family album. And at **Pig**

Heaven, suckling pork prepared in a glass-lined kitchen gets star billing, along with giveaway cucumber and vinegared cabbage appetizers, garlic-spiked chicken, turnip cakes, and the house Beaujolais Village for $15 a bottle.

And tell me what street compares with Mott Street?... For gustatory adventure, wander down to Chinatown, jammed around the western ramparts of the Manhattan Bridge. Canal Street, a non-stop produce bazaar, is the neighborhood's center; the precariously narrow side streets hold Asian treasures, even if their names (Mott, Hester, Elizabeth, Oliver) bespeak the district's earlier Irish and Italian immigrant days. Restaurant decor tends toward velvet pictures of tigers, and ordering from untranslated menus and non-English-speaking waiters can pose challenges. But what's a meal without a little suspense? Try dunking raw beef, giant clams, un-beheaded shrimp, bean curd, enoki mushrooms, and spinach greens into a bubbling broth hot-pot at the **Triple Eight Palace**, where even the simplest meal turns into a chaotic banquet. The **Oriental Pearl** puts on a splendid, all-you-can-eat dinner buffet for $17.95 per person, featuring over 50 different occasionally hard-to-identify options. Delicacies from the Chao Chow region of China, like black chicken soup, toasted scallops with chives and ginger, and minced pork, clams, and peanuts wrapped in lettuce leaves are the house specialty at the **Chinese Country Kitchen**. **New Hong Kong City** serves such exotic delights as shrimp cakes with walnuts and lemon mayonnaise, duck in pureed taro, and deep-fried sesame Dungeness crab.

Pass the dumplings, darling... Asian appetizers go on parade at Chinatown dim sum restaurants like **Tai Hong Lau**, where you fill out your own orders and then settle in for a taste-fest, starting perhaps with shrimp-filled noodle crêpes, steamed sausage rolls, or perfect pork and sesame pastries. **Jing Fong** is a virtual dim sum packing house, with a walkie-talkie toting hostess and enough room to accommodate 800. The **Shun Lee Cafe** on the Upper West Side does dim sum, too, every night and for weekend brunches, with shark fin dumplings swimming in soup as a favorite.

Chinese on the cheap... Struggling actors, artists, and writers subsist for years on cold sesame noodles and double sauteed pork—especially when such spicy staples come from **Hunan Balcony**, long-term king of the Upper West Side's gaggle of Chinese restaurants. The jam-packed Chinese barbecue heaven, **Big Wong** and sweet **Little Szechuan** in Chinatown, **Ollie's Noodle Shop and Grill** (with outposts in Midtown and the Upper West Side), and **China Fun** on the Upper East Side are all Chinese boomtowns for savvy cheap-eaters. And at **Kelley & Ping** in SoHo, reasonably priced spring rolls, pad thai, and steaming bowls of soba noodles come complete with a cool dash of deconstructed downtown atmosphere.

The pastrami league... Picture an inch and a half of well-marbled pastrami on a kaiser roll, slathered in mustard, accompanied by cauliflower, tomato, and cucumber pickles. I defy you not to salivate. The pastrami sandwich is the standard-bearer for New York Jewish delicatessen food, constructed at coffee shops all over town and at a handful of real, old-fashioned delis, like **Russ & Daughters** on the Lower East Side; so authentic is the scene there that Nora Ephron once called it "the delicatessen I would choose if I had to be married in a delicatessen." Russ & Daughters is, however, strictly for take-out; if you want sit down and eat, **Katz's Deli** just down the block has a pleasingly tacky, vinyl, post–World War II look, cafeteria-style service, brisket, potato knishes, cream sodas, and blockbuster Sunday morning bagels and lox. The **2nd Avenue Delicatessen and Restaurant** is another gold-plate special, serving such classics as noodle pudding, boiled beef flanken, and little salamis called schtickels. Uptown, three revered delis cater to workaday and tourist appetites with the world's largest sandwiches and generally brusque service: the crowded **Carnegie Deli**, renowned for its borscht; the somewhat glitzier **Stage Deli**, where sandwiches bear the names of stars (the "Warren Beatty" is composed of egg salad, anchovies, lettuce, and tomato); and **Wolf's**, where they slice the sturgeon by hand.

Good for the soul... **Sylvia's** of Harlem and the funky little **Pink Teacup** in the West Village used to be the first and last words in Manhattan soul food. Both remain the city's chief suppliers of artery-clogging standards like Crisco-fried chicken, barbecued ribs, and candied sweet potatoes, but a raft of new southern-style restaurants have opened their doors, rewriting Granny's recipe book. **Jezebel 11**, an elegant theater-district spot, has white porch swings, glittering chandeliers, fine napery, and a racially mixed clientele with at least one thing in common—pockets deep enough to afford the seductive entrees on owner Alberta Wright's menu. Leon Ellis, who chefs at sophisticated **Emily's** on Fifth Avenue and 111th Street, can pop open a $200 bottle of champagne as a bubbly accompaniment to his waffles and chicken. Alexander Smalls, a former opera singer who's become the genius behind **Cafe Beulah**, says that his menu is all about "southern revival cuisine based on traditional low-country cooking." Which is what routinely brings in Pulitzer Prize–winning novelist Toni Morrison, and has made this Flatiron spot one of the most chic places in town, with white wainscoting, a long wooden bar, black-eyed pea and arugula salads, Creole steak au poivre, and side orders of lemon candied yams. **Kwanzaa** in SoHo is a history lesson in food, dedicated to the African diaspora, serving everything from Ethiopian chicken to American spareribs, under draped kente cloth and Beninese totem poles; and at **Toukie's**, there's an international tilt to the soul food mix, plus a very cool crowd, gracefully shepherded to tables by supermodel Toukie Smith, former flame of Robert DeNiro and sister of the late fashion designer Willi Smith. Last but not least, a real finger-lickin' barbecue place right in Midtown: **Virgil's Real Barbecue**, which could almost be a clone of Kansas City's fabled Arthur Bryant's and is just about as good as Gotham can do when it comes to smokin' pork. The place does charge a bit steeply to pig out, though—the gargantuan "Rock 'n' Ribs" combo will set you back $37.95—but you get two sides with each entree (dirty rice, mashed potatoes, pickled beets, or collards and rice). Wash it all down with a Rolling Rock and some of Virgil's piquant sauce.

A slice of heaven... The subject of pizza is of deep concern to me. You can get pizza everywhere, from the Battery to the Bronx, by the slice or whole pie, cooked in a coal-fired oven or microwaved, deep-dish (Chicago-style) or thin-crusted (à la New York), topped with everything from kohlrabi to scungilli. But if you want proof of New York's primacy in pies, try **Lombardi's**, scion of the venerable pizza restaurant that opened on this very SoHo location in 1905, with perhaps the best crust in town, fresh hand-cut mozarella, and a delicious specialty—spartan clam pies. The little dining room is a winner too, with a floor made of tiny tiles, red and white tablecloths, and brick walls. **John's Pizzeria** of Bleecker Street serves its pizzas on elevated dishes, and has a reputation for crumbled sausage and classic simplicity; the place is noisy and generally jammed with pizza connoisseurs from outlying colleges. **Two Boots**, with branches in both the East and West Village, specializes in pies with thin crusts and a dusting of cornmeal, topped with Cajun flourishes like jalapeño peppers and crayfish. In poorer days, I used to dress up for drinks at the stylish bar of the Café des Artistes, and then dine at **Vinnie's**, a stellar little pizza joint on Amsterdam Avenue, notable for its sauce.

World food, Part I: Western hemisphere... I need hardly remind you that New York is the immigrant capital of the world. Fortunately, those who came from far away brought along their cuisines, or else racked up a lot of long-distance calls to collect recipes. Among the varied results are quesadillas, tacos, and chimichangas at **Benny's Burritos** and **Tortilla Flats**, two Mexican joints in the West Village where the tab stays low, the Coronas come with lime slices, and the food's satisfyingly filling; as they say out West, all the cakeholes get filled. The Mexican menu at **Mary Ann's** is somewhat more varied; there are spicy fish dishes, along with huge cheese-drenched taco, tortilla, and burrito combo platters on plates hot enough to burn a hole in the table (cool off with a pitcherful of margaritas). Down in SoHo, cheerful little **Lupe's** does a knock-out huevos rancheros for breakfast or brunch. Caribbean and Latin food predominate at a handful of fun, funky spots downtown, like **Boca Chica**, which lines its walls with pictures of the ocean and paper lanterns, and serves up very spicy food and live Latin music way into the night. It's a reggae scene at **Red Strype**, where slumming stylemongers cruise in for Jamaican beer and whatever the day's coconut- or jerk-sauce specialties happen to be. Making less effort to be trendy, **Tasco Porto** does grills, tapas, and sangria the way they make them in Portugal and Brazil, and has a beguiling selection of Portuguese vinho verde, ports, and brandies. And at swank **Patria** the dramatically presented Latin food is wired—how else to explain such mouthful menu offerings as plantain-coated mahi mahi with fufu and lily salad and boneless braised short ribs with Paraguayan *chipa guasu*?

World food, Part II: Eastern hemisphere... Manhattan's top Greek restaurant is **Periyali**, decorated to resemble an Attic farmhouse, with a pricy menu featuring such intriguing dishes as charcoal-grilled octopus and cinnamon ice cream. Moving on across the Aegean to Istanbul, try **Ottoman Cuisine** in a pair of storefronts on the Upper West Side, starting with rice-stuffed dolmas or a white bean salad, and then launching into a lamb shish kebab, or stop in at little **Moustache Pitza** in the shady West Village for a Middle Eastern–style pizza pie. You'll find Japanese restaurants everywhere, serving all-you-can-eat sushi dinners, miso soup, teriyaki, tempura, and the whole nine yards. But sushi in particular is done with real grace at **Japonica**, where they serve a softshell crab maki with a marvelous texture and delicate taste. **Taka** near Sheridan Square is an unpretentious neighborhood place with a female sushi chef who makes her own pottery and is a wonder to watch. Up near Lincoln Center, **Lenge** has a fairly inventive and authentic sushi bar; its wooden booths are often packed with Philharmonic musicians and folks from the nearby ABC studios. Farther up the West Side, tasteful little **Monsoon** brings Vietnamese cooking to a high standard with delectable dishes like *xuong nuong* (divine grilled pork chop slices) and *bo sate* (sauteed beef with peanut sauce). For Thai food, there's Soho's **Kin Khao**, sensuously draped with loads of soft fabrics, right out of *The Story of O*; expect delicious curries, spiced with cilantro, and wonderful prawn dishes. Sixth Street in the East Village is New Delhi central, lined with cheerfully bustling Indian restaurants where low prices prevail. But I favor **Mitali West**, never budging from the tandoori chicken, washed down with Kingfisher beer. If you seek a higher-toned Indian dining experience, try **Darbar** or **Dawat** uptown, both in coolly stylish digs, serving fresh fried breads, lamb, chicken, and a spice rack full of condiments.

Olde New York... Alas, downtown, Delmonico's is gone, but reconstructed Colonial-era **Fraunces Tavern** remains, chiefly as a watering hole for Wall Street types. It was on this site that General George Washington bade farewell to his troops at the end of the Revolutionary War, and the second floor tavern room has been decorated to commemorate that event. The ground-level restaurant serves solid if uninspiring American standards like steaks, pies, and chops. The **Bridge Cafe**, tucked between South Street Seaport and the entry ramp of the Brooklyn Bridge, evokes the mid-to late 1800s; fresh seafood specialties are prepared with imagination and there's a tonic selection of wines by the glass. **Walker's** in TriBeCa, with whirring ceiling fans, a long bar, and pressed tin ceilings, packs in locals at dinner time, when reasonably priced fish and pasta entrees fly out of the kitchen as fast as they can be cooked. The Village has a few old-style eateries, like the **Minetta Tavern**, woody, dark, and favored by off-Broadway playgoers. It's been dishing out Italian food since 1937, and has a long bar perfect for drowning your sorrows in scotch. Manhattan's longest-lived speakeasy remains almost impossible to find, signless and secreted away among 19th-century row houses on Bedford Street in the West Village: To reach **Chumley's**, take the narrow walkway off Barrow Street into Pamela Court, sit yourself down at a table carved with guests' initials, and then order a burger and a draft New Amsterdam. When it's cold outside there's generally a fire in the hearth at **Ye Waverly Inn**, down a flight of brownstone steps on Bank Street, with deep booths and chicken pot pie. And near Macy's, there's **Keens Chop House**, famous for mutton chops since its founding in 1878; the restaurant, where you'll find a vast collection of antique clay pipes, is fancy, with prices to match, but at the bar you can get a good deal on a burger, beer, and oysters on the half shell. In the Lincoln Center area, **O'Neal's** (formerly the long-running Ginger Man) spiffed up its dining room but hung on to the flavor of turn-of-the-century New York. Dinner entrees run toward chops and steaks, and the hamburgers are quite consistent; to the right as you enter is an excellent, very busy bar. And then there's Brooklyn's restaurant gem: **Peter Luger** in Williamsburg, serving what most count as the best steaks in New York. Ten tons of beef shortloins pass through this unreconstructed beer hall every week, dry-aged on the premises, cooked to order, and then served au jus. You'll need to take a cab, but after feasting on a huge slab of steak, German fried potatoes, creamed spinach, and cheesecake, you won't need to eat again for a week.

Vegging out... I'm a flesh-eater myself, but when I start feeling sluggish I go vegetarian at **Pita Cuisine**, an NYU hangout with a pleasant deck overlooking the surprising sights and sounds of LaGuardia Place and marvelous prices on specialties like meatless chili and pita pockets stuffed with what you will. I also love the vegetarian pad thai at the **Little Cafe** in a rather more settled, quiet, and thoroughly unpretentious West Village environment. SoHo eats healthy at the **Spring Street Natural**, but the noise level there can be troubling. The funky **Life Cafe**, an East Village stalwart that has also branched out west, is cozier, serving Tex-Mex veggie specialties while the jukebox spins tunes. Up on the East Side, **Sweet Potato** covers the heath-food field with fresh juices, smoothies, salads, soups, and sandwiches—all dairy- and sugar-free. But real health-food freaks light up at the chance to sup at the elegantly subdued **Zen Palate**, with branches in the theater district and alongside Union Square. The food is Asian and gorgeous, but there's one drawback—the no-drinks policy means no accompanying goblet of wine.

Something fishy... The bivalves are bi-coastal at the **Oyster Bar** in Grand Central Station—hailing all the way from the Olympic Peninsula to Long Island and Chincoteague. But the belly-of-the-train-station setting is so unlovely that I'd suggest something different: **Dock's**, with two branches on the Upper West Side and Midtown, both equally commendable for polished brass fittings, woody bars, and all the ocean's bounty; try the fried seafood platter, with shrimp, scallops, and sole, a steamed lobster, or the New England clambake offered on Sunday and Monday nights. At little **Sloppy Louie's**, an old seamen's cafe in spitting distance from the Fulton Fish Market, you'll have no second thoughts about the bouillabaisse and clam chowder—and since you're here, please order it Manhattan-style (that is, red rather than white).

We never close... New York's classic all-nighters are the **Empire Diner**, an art-deco marvel way west in Chelsea, with live music during the wee hours; **Moondance**, lord of the mushroom burger, in kissing distance from most downtown clubs; Midtown's **Brasserie**, catering to stuffed-shirt workaholics rather than club rats, with a great long bar and eggs Florentine to soak up the excess alcohol in your bloodstream; and **Florent**, in the meat district, where weary club-hoppers change partners before the break of day. For a somewhat less flammable scene, try **Lox Around the Clock** for cafe food in Chelsea, or **French Roast** in the Village, where the food—soups/salads/sandwiches—isn't great but I could swear I once saw Sam Shepard.

If al fresco's your style... What is it that's so satisfying about dining outside? I don't mean restaurants with tables set out on the sidewalk, where street people prey on bleeding-heart diners, exhaust perfumes the air, and you have to scream to be heard over the traffic. I mean eating in a garden, while bees hover in petunia pots and photosynthesis occurs. **I Trulli** is such a place, with fine Mediterranean cuisine and a tiled back patio shaded by a wooden awning; recently, finishing a long lunch there with a plate of figs, I could almost imagine myself on the Italian Riviera. In the same area (Gramercy Park), **Flowers** has an ivy-wrapped rooftop garden with a menu distinct from the one offered inside—grills and barbecues, with an overture of littleneck clams and pancetta, perhaps. Vegetables—yes, there's fertile earth beneath Manhattan's concrete—grow in the rear patio at **Verbena**, where the fare is intriguingly eclectic—for instance butternut squash–filled ravioli, chive popovers, and sweetbreads with celery root hash. The quiet West Village garden at unpretentious **Grove** has roses twining up the fence, plenty of sky, leafy bowers, and a pebble floor. Grove's pastas, salads, fried calamari, and roast chicken are prepared with some little flair, and are reasonably priced. And now that Bryant Park has been renovated in the style of the Left Bank's Luxembourg Gardens, it's become a fitting setting for another green spot, the **Bryant Park Grill**, built onto the back of the New York Public Library and serving pricy entrees like grilled swordfish and cold poached salmon. The place seats 1,000, but hasn't yet figured out how to serve all of them well, and hardy has a restful air. Still, it's green, pretty, and something of a Midtown cynosure.

Counter culture... You can get anything you want at Manhattan's coffee shops, and you can always count on the decor: Formica counters, leatherette booths, and cash registers up front. Multi-paged menus suggest such specialties as Belgian waffles, steaks, pot roast, carrot cake, and spaghetti with meatballs, but what most coffee shops do best is burgers and breakfast. And some positively excel—like E. 61st Street's **Viand**. There are other branches, but I recommend this one, cramped and noisy though it may be, because of its hamburgers—juicy rather than greasy, with the patty in perfect proportion to the bun. Four branches of **Burger Heaven** scattered around the East Side do an invigorating job with burgers as well. **EJ's Luncheonette** is one of the West Side's most convivial breakfast spots, with buckwheat and buttermilk pancakes shouldering out all else. **B&H Dairy** in the East Village is tiny and Ukrainian, with great borscht, blini, and, above all, exquisite homemade challah. And **The Bagel** in the West Village just does everything well, with a counterman so beloved that he's been featured in a few independent flicks made by his almost-famous clientele.

Where the supermodels eat and where they don't... As far as I can tell, the fixation of the moment for dining among supermodels, their stylists, and black-clad photographers started at **The Coffee Shop** on Union Square, named for what it used to be, though the decor's been deconstructed, the menu's flown south to Brazil and the Caribbean, the music's a loud world mix, and the waitresses are so string-bean skinny that you know right away they've got their modeling portfolios stashed in the back. Then came a raft of others, like **Luna Park** virtually next door, which puts on the same fashion wannabe show in a Mediterranean-style courtyard with aluminum tables shaded by Lavazza umbrellas. There's a garden with a ping-pong table behind the **Bowery Bar**, situated in a converted filling station way downtown. It serves tarted-up American cuisine like crab cakes and hot fudge sundaes to hipsters who drink and make merry without seeming to put on a pound. **Live Bait** cooks southern for covergirls and the modeling agency riffraff, and on the first Sunday of every month there's a "Fashion Brunch" at **Marion's**, during which more than a few trendily labeled glad rags are snagged. The joke among the supermodel spots is the **Fashion Cafe**, which just settled into Rockefeller Center. Word has it that Claudia Schiffer, Naomi Campbell, and Elle Macpherson were paid $50,000 each to frequent the place, and now Christy Turlington's signed on, though she calls it "a tacky theme restaurant for tourists." I wouldn't count on actually sight-ing one of them there, but you can order a Christy Veggie Burger or Naomi's Fish and Chips and take in the display of designer wear, ranging from Madonna's bras to Givenchy gowns.

Camping out... Turnover is what keeps Manhattan restaurants in the black, but there are a few places (mostly downtown) that have made their reputations on their willingness to leave guests alone—though sometimes it's rather a matter of benign neglect. **Café Raffaela** near Sheridan Square is like that, serving sandwiches, salads, pastries, and coffee to happy souls left to write novels in sagging old easy chairs. **Scharmann's** of SoHo does much the same sort of food, but in multiple living room sets, with a very European clientele. **Le Gamin** is a crowded little cafe on MacDougal Street just below Houston Street, with benches and tables out front, an espresso machine instead of a hearth, and a slightly snotty attitude. Easier going is the **Bell Cafe** in the no-man's land west of SoHo, for hearty health food and long sitting spells. But my favorite is the **Café Orlin**, which has been serving hummus appetizers and pasta to indolent East Villagers as long as I can remember, and never rushing them out.

The tea ceremony... Coffee, not tea, is the prime caffeine source in the Big Apple. But that doesn't mean you can't get a pot of well-brewed oolong from Ceylon or a lemon verbena tisane, served with the all those perfect little tea accoutrements and a quartet of cucumber sandwiches. My favorite tea spot is **The Rotunda Room** at the Pierre hotel, a darling of a an oval room lined with banquettes and rococo-esque murals, favored by sweet elderly ladies in from the 'burbs. Occasionally the finger sandwiches are a tad stale, but the pastries and scones with Devonshire cream pick up the slack. Farther uptown on the East Side the **Mark** hotel does a high-toned, stuffy tea. A few places downtown do tea—but with a funky spin, of course. **Tea & Sympathy** is an English middle-class tea shop, with a menu full of bangers and mash, too many tables, and not a spot of sherry to be had. Prettier by a mile is **Anglers and Writers**, with antique tables and chairs, flowers, frou-frou, a charming collection of mismatched china, and very buttery cakes, pies, and cookies. And a notable newcomer has recently encamped beneath the SoHo branch of the Guggenheim—the **T Salon,**

Restaurant & Emporium, an exquisitely appointed place with an eclectic menu, tea shop selling pots, leaves, and strainers, paintings by trendy artists, and a companionable bar. But take care, because this place gets packed, especially when there's an art opening under way.

The caffeine scene... Unequivocally speaking, the city's best regular coffee, croissants, brioche, tartlettes, and quichettes are made at the **Patisserie Claude**—if you don't believe me, just ask the folks in the limos who drive down from Connecticut solely to visit this shoebox-sized bit of Gaul in the heart of the West Village. Claude himself presides in a flour-coated apron, speaking French, Spanish, and English as called for, doling out cookies to kids, and leaving the Village bereft when he goes on *vacances* in August. Then I head for **Taylor's**, where the coffee isn't bad at all and the church- social goodies—like brownies topped with cheesecake, called zebras—are so humongous that each slice could serve four; or **Lanciani**, with French, American, and Italian pastries and cakes and blood-thickening espresso. Also in the West Village, the **Bleecker Street Cafe** serves cannoli-craving locals and tourists, while the **Original Espresso Bar** has great Columbian coffee and the world's handsomest gay male clientele. **Chez Laurence** is a reasonably inviting French oasis in the humorless concrete jungle surrounding Grand Central Station.

Kid pleasers... Just about any of the pizza places and dim sum restaurants listed here will be good for youngsters; **Two Boots**, in particular, is a winner with the younger set, and its waiters know how to handle 'em. The **Cowgirl Hall of Fame** is a natural with its Western theme and casual bunkhouse food. **EJ's Luncheonette**'s classic coffee shop menu makes it an ideal stop after the nearby Museum of Natural History. In SoHo, casual **Fanelli** suits kids' tastes, with omelettes, burgers, and fries. **Mary Ann's** has served up many a taco and burrito to neighborhood kids at all three branches and **Hunan Balcony** and **Ollie's Noodle Shop** have trained West Side kids to be Chinese-food fanatics. **Anglers & Writers** may charm children who adore perfect tea parties, while the raucous good cheer and hearty Southern Italian food at **Carmine's** makes this a top Midtown choice for families (but beware: the portions are anything but child-sized).

The Index

$$$$	over $35
$$$	$25–$35
$$	$15–$25
$	under $15

Per person for a three-course meal, not including drinks, tax, or tip.

Aggie's. Big dinners, tangy recipes, and reasonable prices in a bustling converted coffee shop.... *Tel 212/673–8994. 146 W. Houston St., B/D/Q/F train to Broadway/Lafayette. $*

Anglers and Writers. Victoria's Secret decor, high tea, and happy brunches.... *Tel 212/675–0810. 420 Hudson St., 1/9 train to Houston St. No credit cards. $*

Aureole. Fancy French-inspired food in a romantically decorated East Side town house.... *Tel 212/319–1660. 34 E. 61st St., N/R train to Fifth Ave. Jacket and reservations required. $$$$*

The Bagel. Teensy coffee shop, center Village, great clientele.... *Tel 212/255–0106. 170 W. 4th St., A/C/E or B/D/Q/F train to W. 4th St. No credit cards. $*

Bar Pitti. Italian chic with streetside tables in the lower Village.... *Tel 212/982–3300. 268 Sixth Ave., A/C/E or B/D/Q/F train to W. 4th St. $$$*

Barrymore's. Burgers and booze among theater types.... *Tel 212/391–8400. 267 W. 45th St., N/R, 1/2/3/9, or 7 train to Times Sq. $$*

Bell Cafe. Funky sit-around-forever place, with big portions of healthy food.... *Tel 212/334–BELL. 310 Spring St., C/E train to Spring St. $*

Benito's I. Pictures of Vesuvius on the wall, and good old-fashioned Southern Italian fare.... *Tel 212/226-9171. 174 Mulberry St., J/M/Z, N/R, or 6 train to Canal St. or B/D/Q to Grand St. $$$*

Benny's Burritos. Mass-produced Mexican basics in two locations, but noisy and fun.... *Tel 212/633-9210. 112 Greenwich Ave., 1/2/3/9 to 14th St.; tel 212/254-3286. 93 Avenue A, F train to Second Ave. No credit cards. $*

B&H Dairy. Tiny antique Ukrainian coffee shop in the heart of the East Village.... *Tel 212/505-8065. 127 Second Ave., 6 train to Astor Place or N/R to 8th St. No credit cards. $*

Big Wong. Fast, furious, and cheap Chinese barbecue way downtown.... *Tel 212/964-0540. 67 Mott St., J/M/Z, N/R, or 6 train to Canal St. or B/D/Q to Grand St. $*

Bleecker Street Cafe. Chrome, mirrors, crowds, cappuccino, cannoli.... *Tel 212/242-4959. 245 Bleecker St., A/C/E or B/D/Q/F train to W. 4th St. No credit cards. $*

Blu. Eclectic salads and pastas close to the movies.... *Tel 212/989-6300. 254 W. 23rd St., C/E, F, or 1/9 train to 23rd St. $$*

Boca Chica. Fun Latin and Caribbean eating, drinking, and making merry.... *Tel 212/473-0108. 13 First Ave., B/D/Q/F train to Broadway/Lafayette. $$$*

Bouley. Fine downtown French cuisine in a room lined with paintings by the Impressionists. Closed through much of 1996. Call for new address.... *Tel 212/608-3852., 1/2/3/9 train to Chambers St. Reservations required. $$$$*

Bowery Bar. Where the chic meet, play ping-pong, and eat trendy American food.... *Tel 212/475-2220. 358 Bowery, 6 train to Bleecker St. or B/D/Q/F to Broadway/Lafayette. $$$*

Boxers. Lively hetero Village bar scene; hearty salads, sandwiches, and fries.... *Tel 212/633-2275. 186 W. 4th St., A/C/E or B/D/Q/F train to W. 4th St. or 1/9 to Christopher St. $*

Brasserie. Open 24 hours in the heart of Midtown; pretty bar, filling food.... *Tel 212/751-4840. 100 E. 53rd St., 6 train to 51st St. $$$*

Bridge Cafe. Charming, old-fashioned, tucked alongside the Brooklyn Bridge; seafood prevails.... *Tel 212/227–3344. 279 Water St., J/M/Z, 2/3, or 4/5 train to Fulton St. $$$*

Bryant Park Grill. See and be seen in the greenery; pricey Continental fare.... *Tel 212/840–6500. 25 W. 40th St., B/D/Q/F train to 42nd St. or 7 to Fifth Ave. $$$$*

Burger Heaven. Long counter dishing out top-notch burgers.... *Tel 212/755–2166. 20 E. 49th St., E/F train to Fifth Ave. or B/D/Q/F to Rockefeller Center. Also at 54th and Madison, 53rd and Fifth, 41st and Madison, 62nd and Lexington. $*

Cafe Beulah. Nouvelle soul food in elegant digs.... *Tel 212/777–9700. 39 E. 19th St.; N/R, 4/5/6, or L train to Union Sq. $$$$*

Café de Bruxelle. Belgian beer, mussels, salads, and seafood stews, with a stylish dining room and comfortable pocket bar.... *Tel 212/206–1830. 118 Greenwich Ave., A/C/E or 1/2/3/9 train to 14th St. $$$*

Café des Artistes. Intensely lovely and romantic, serving adequate French cuisine.... *Tel 212/877–3500. 1 W. 67th St., B/C or 1/2/3/9 train to 72nd St. Jacket and reservations required. $$$$*

Café Orlin. A quiet, modest East Village cafe for stints with a book or long thoughtful conversations with close friends.... *Tel 212/777–1447. 41 St. Marks Place, 6 train to Astor Place or N/R to 8th St. $*

Café Raffaela. Opera booms, easy chairs invite; soups, pastries, salads in the easy West Village.... *Tel 212/929–7247. 134 Seventh Ave., 1/9 train to Christopher St. No credit cards. $$*

Café Un Deux Trois. Cool, cavernous room; reasonably tasty pre-and post-theater fare.... *Tel 212/354–4148. 123 W. 44th St., N/R, 1/2/3/9, or 7 train to Times Sq. $$$*

Carmine's. Hearty Southern Italian—a good theater district choice. Go for family-style dining—the portions are immense.... *Tel 212/221–3800. 200 W. 44th St., N/R, 1/2/3/9, or 7 train to Times Sq.; tel 212/362–2200. 2450 Broadway, 1/9 train to 86th St. AE only. $$$*

Carnegie Deli. Midtown classic for towering deli sandwiches.... *Tel 212/757–2245. 854 Seventh Ave., B/D/E train to Seventh Ave. $$*

Chez Laurence Patisserie. Brioche, croissants, French pastries, sandwiches, and soups in the atmosphere of the Left Bank.... *Tel 212/683–0284. 245 Madison Ave., 4/5/6 or 7 train to Grand Central. $$*

China Fun. Cheap Chinese eats.... *Tel 212/752–0810. 1239 Second Ave., 6 train to 68th St. $*

China Grill. Chinese with Midtown class.... *Tel 212/333–7788. 60 W. 53rd St., B/D/Q/F train to Rockefeller Center. $$$$*

Chin Chin. Elegant nouvelle Chinese.... *Tel 212/888–4555. 216 E. 49th St., E/F train to Lexington Ave. or 6 to 51st St. $$$$*

Chinese Country Kitchen. Chao Chow specialties in Chinatown.... *Tel 212/966–8899. 194 Grand St., B/D/Q to Grand St. $$$*

Chumley's. An old speakeasy catering to the beer-and-burger college crowd.... *Tel 212/675–4449. 86 Bedford St., 1/9 train to Christopher St. $$*

Coffee Shop. Latin food, big deep booths, loud music, and Ford Agency wannabes as waitresses.... *Tel 212/243–7969. 29 Union Sq. W., N/R, 4/5/6, or L train to Union Sq. $$$*

Cornelia Street Cafe. Laid-back in the Village; well-prepared Continental specialties and a convivial bar.... *Tel 212/989–9318. 29 Cornelia St., A/C/E or B/D/Q/F train to W. 4th St. $$$*

Cucina. Brooklyn's best Italian food, with a Brooklyn-chic dining room.... *Tel 718/262–0909. 256 Fifth Ave., R train to Union St. $$$*

Cucina di Pesce. East Village cellar that does garlicky Italian.... *Tel 212/260–6800. 87 E. 4th St., 6 train to Bleecker St. $$*

Darbar. Uptown Indian, with an entrancing lunch buffet.... *Tel 212/432–7227. 44 W. 56th St., B/Q train to 57th St. or B/D/E to Seventh Ave. $$$$*

Dawat. Northern Indian cuisine, upscale atmosphere.... *Tel 212/355–7555. 210 E. 58th St., 4/5/6 train to 59th St. or N/R to Lexington Ave. $$$$*

Diane's Uptown. A simple little place for fine burgers, fries, and ice-cream sundaes.... *Tel 212/799–6750. 249 Columbus Ave., B/C or 1/2/3/9 train to 72nd St. $*

Dix et Sept. A town house in the Village devoted to all things Parisian.... *Tel 212/645–8023. 181 W. 10th St., 1/9 train to Christopher St. $$$*

Dock's. Seafood in two spiffy settings.... *Tel 212/986–8080. 633 Third Ave., 4/5/6 or 7 train to Grand Central; tel 212/724–5588. 2427 Broadway, 1/9 train to 86th St. $$$*

Eddie's. Great big burgers, omelettes, and salads among NYU coeds.... *Tel 212/420–0919. 14 Waverly Place, N/R train to 8th St. AE only. $*

EJ's Luncheonette. A perfect model of a classic New York coffee shop, uptown and downtown.... *Tel 212/873–3444. 447 Amsterdam Ave., 1/9 train to 79th St. or B/C to 81st St.; tel 212/473–5555. 432 Sixth Ave., A/C/E or B/D/Q/F to W. 4th St. $$*

Emily's. An uptown soul food rival to Sylvia's.... *Tel 212/996–1212. 1325 Fifth Ave., 6 train to 110th St. $$$*

Empire Diner. An art-deco standby that never closes and never fails.... *Tel 212/243–2736. 210 Tenth Ave., A/C/E train to 23rd St. $$*

Fanelli. Clubby, pubby, pastas, steaks, and burgers, and nice Sunday morning reading-the-newspaper atmosphere.... *Tel 212/226–9412. 94 Prince St., N/R train to Prince St. $*

Fashion Cafe. Rockefeller Center's touristy fashion industry theme restaurant.... *Tel 212/765–3131. 51 Rockefeller Plaza, B/D/Q/F train to Rockefeller Center. $$$*

Florent. A hip after-hours haunt in the unprepossessing meat district.... *Tel 212/989–5779. 69 Gansevoort St., A/C/E train to 14th St. No credit cards. $$*

Flowers. Delicious barbecues on a rooftop garden.... *Tel 212/691–8888. 21 W. 17th St., N/R, 4/5/6, or L train to Union Sq. $$$*

Four Seasons. About as elegant as New York gets, with great attention to both diners and food.... *Tel 212/754–9495. 99 E. 52nd St., B/D/Q/F train to Rockefeller Center. Jacket and reservations required. $$$$*

Fraunces Tavern. The oldest pub in New York.... *Tel 212/269–0144. 54 Pearl St., 1/9 train to South Ferry. $$$*

French Culinary Institute. Chefs in training under the masters produce prix-fixe lunches and dinners at its restaurant, L'Ecole, with diners filling out "report cards" afterwards.... *Tel 212/219–3300. 462 Broadway, J/M/Z, N/R, or 6 train to Canal St. $$$*

French Roast. A centrally located 24-hour cafe with a Village clientele.... *Tel 212/533–2233. 458 Sixth Ave., F train to 14th St. or L to Sixth Ave. AE only. $$*

Gotham Bar & Grill. Swank setting, inventive American cuisine.... *Tel 212/620–4020. 12 E. 12th St., N/R, 4/5/6, or L train to Union Sq. $$$$*

Grotta Azzurra. No reservations and long lines at this top spot for garlicky Neapolitan cuisine in Little Italy.... *Tel 212/925–8775. 387 Broome St., B/D/Q train to Grand St. No credit cards. $$*

Grove. Continental fare and a pretty garden out back.... *Tel 212/675–9463. 314 Bleecker St., 1/9 train to Christopher St. $$$*

Hourglass Tavern. Pre-theater in 60 minutes or they boot you out, but a comforting fixed price.... *Tel 212/265–2060.*

373 W. 46th St., N/R, 1/2/3/9, or 7 train to Times Sq. No credit cards. $

Hunan Balcony. Efficient, reliable Chinese Upper West Sider with a huge menu; eat in or take out.... *Tel 212/865–0400. 2596 Broadway, 1/2/3/9 train to 96th St. $*

Il Mulino. Top-flight Italian, via Abruzzi.... *Tel 212/673–3783. 86 W. 3rd St., B/D/Q/F train to Broadway/Lafayette. $$$$*

I Trulli. Nouvelle Italian with a lovely tiled patio out back.... *Tel 212/481–7372. 122 E. 27th St., 6 train to 28th St. $$$$*

Japonica. Sushi to die for.... *Tel 212/243–7752. 100 University Place, N/R, 4/5/6, or L train to Union Sq. $$$*

Jezebel 11. Pork chops and collard greens as if at the Ritz.... *Tel 212/582–1045. 630 Ninth Ave., A/C/E train to 42nd St. AE only. $$$$*

Jing Fong. Dim sum reigns.... *Tel 212/964–5256. 20 Elizabeth St., J/M/Z, N/R or 6 train to Canal St. or B/D/Q to Grand St. $*

John's Pizzeria. Thin crusts, sauce, fresh mozzarella cheese, crumbled Italian sausage all in near-perfect proportion.... *Tel 212/243–1680. 278 Bleecker St., A/C/E or B/D/Q/F train to W. 4th St. Also at 408 E. 64th St. and 48 W. 64th St. No credit cards. $*

JUdson Grill. Take-your-breath away dining room and egotistical American specialties.... *Tel 212/JU2–5252. 152 W. 52nd St., B/D/Q/F train to Rockefeller Center. No shorts. $$$$*

Katz's Deli. Come in a little pink waitress uniform and you'll feel right at home—then order the little pink lox and you'll transcend (but only on Sundays).... *Tel 212/254–2246. 205 E. Houston St., F train to Second Ave. $*

Keens Chop House. Old-style New York, old recipes, mutton chops.... *Tel 212/947–3636. 72 W. 36th St., A/C/E or 1/2/3/9 to 34th St. $$$*

Kelley & Ping. Asian noodles, SoHo-style.... *Tel 212/228–1212. 127 Green St., N/R train to Prince St. $*

Kin Khao. Haute Thai for those who understand funky elegance.... *Tel 212/966–3939. 171 Spring St., C/E train to Spring St. $$$*

Kwanzaa. The African diaspora in food.... *Tel 212/941–6095. 19 Cleveland Place, 6 train to Spring St. $$$*

La Côte Basque. Lots of stars, attitude, and splendid classic French fare.... *Tel 212/688–6525. 60 W. 55th St., E/F train to Fifth Ave. Jacket, tie, and reservations required. $$$$*

Lanciani. West Village cafe, excellent pastries.... *Tel 212/929–0739. 271 W. 4th St., 1/9 train to Christopher St. AE only. $*

Le Cirque. Same deal as La Côte Basque, and a knock-out wine list.... *Tel 212/794–9292. 58 E. 65th St., 4/5/6 train to 59th St. or N/R to Lexington Ave. Jacket, tie, and reservations required. $$$$*

Le Gamin. Funky upper SoHo espresso, etc. spot.... *Tel 212/254–4678. 50 MacDougal St., B/D/Q/F train to Broadway/Lafayette. No credit cards. $*

Le Madeleine. French bistro fare before and after the theater.... *Tel 212/256–2993. 403 W. 43rd St., N/R, 1/2/3/9, or 7 train to Times Sq. $$$*

Lenge. Reasonably priced and consistently good sushi and Japanese food.... *Tel 212/799–9188. 200 Columbus Ave., 1/9 train to 66th St./Lincoln Center; tel 212/535–9661. 1465 Third Ave., 4/5/6 train to 86th St. $$*

Le Pescadou. Sweet setting, succulent French seafood.... *Tel 212/924–3434. 18 King St., 1/9 train to Houston St. $$$*

Life Cafe. Tex-Mex vegetarian in the Village.... *Tel 212/477–8791. 343 E. 10th St., L train to First Ave. or 6 to Astor Place; tel 212/929–7344. 1 Sheridan Sq., 1/9 train to Christopher St. AE not accepted. $*

Little Cafe. Thai food, pastas, and vegetarian specials, all freshly and healthily-prepared.... *Tel 212/242–1058. 183 W. 10th St., 1/9 train to Christopher St.; tel 212/988–9006. 1439 Second Ave., 4/5/6 train to 86th St. $$*

Little Szechuan. A Chinatown closet off the beaten track, but love those steamed dumplings and whole pan-fried fish.... *Tel 212/349–2360. 31 Oliver St., J/M/Z, N/R, or 6 train to Canal St. or B/D/Q to Grand St. $$*

Live Bait. Food from south of the Mason-Dixon line, served by would-be covergirls.... *Tel 212/353–2400. 14 E. 23rd St., N/R train to 23rd St. $$$*

Lombardi's. Classic pizza pies since 1905.... *Tel 212/941–7994. 32 Spring St., N/R train to Prince St. No credit cards. $*

Lox Around the Clock. Souped-up diner with a bar that stays open all the time; slightly overpriced.... *Tel 212/691–3535. 676 Sixth Ave., F train to 23rd St. AE only. $$*

Luna Park. Models wait tables alongside Union Square; Mediterranean cuisine.... *Tel 212/475–8464. 29 Union Sq. W., N/R, 4/5/6, or L train to Union Sq. $$$*

Lupe's. Mexican via East L.A., nice crowd, cold Coronas.... *Tel 212/966–1326. 110 Sixth Ave., C/E train to Spring St. No credit cards. $*

Lutèce. For decades, the source of New York's best French food, but recently sold to a restaurant chain called Ark; so, status pending.... *Tel 212/752–2225. 249 E. 50th St., E/F to Lexington Ave. or 6 to 51st St. Jacket, tie, and reservations required. $$$$*

Mappamondo and Mappamondo Due. West Village pasta places, with fair prices and a neighborhoody feeling.... *Tel 212/675–3100. 11 Abingdon Sq.; tel 212/675–7474. 581 Hudson St. 1/9 train to Christopher St.*

March. Innovative French cuisine by master chef Wayne Nish, in a romantic East Side town house.... *Tel 212/838–9393. 405 E. 58th St., N/R train to Lexington Ave. or 4/5/6 to 59th St. $$$$*

Marion's. Chic downtown dive that does a "fashion brunch".... *Tel 212/475–7621. 354 Bowery, F train to Second Ave. $$$*

The Mark Hotel. Nice lobby teas, if a tad stiff.... *Tel 212/879–1864. 25 E. 77th St., 6 train to 77th St. $$$*

Mary Ann's. Hearty Mexican in three locations.... *Tel 212/633–0877. 116 Eighth Ave., A/C/E train to 14th St.; tel 212/249–6165. 1503 Second Ave., 6 train to 77th St.; tel 212/877–0132. 2452 Broadway, 1/9 train to 86th St. AE, D, DC not accepted. $$*

Mary's Restaurant. American and Continental cuisine in a cozy Village row house.... *Tel 212/741–3387. 44 Bedford St., 1/9 train to Christopher St. $$$*

Minetta Tavern. Southern Italian cuisine in an old-fashioned pub setting.... *Tel 212/475–3850. 113 MacDougal St., A/C/E or B/D/Q/F train to W. 4th St. $$$*

Mitali West. Tandoori, biryani, poori, and more from the subcontinent.... *Tel 212/989–1367. 296 Bleecker St., 1/9 train to Christopher St. $$$*

Monsoon. Vietnamese newcomer, spicy and smart.... *Tel 212/580–8686. 435 Amsterdam Ave., 1/9 train to 79th St. or B/C to 81st St. $$*

Moondance. Lower Sixth Avenue diner that stays open always.... *Tel 212/226–1191. 80 Sixth Ave., C/E train to Spring St. $*

Moustache Pitza. Middle Eastern specialties in a crowded little West Village spot.... *Tel 212/229–2220. 90 Bedford St., 1/9 train to Christopher St. $*

New Hong Kong City. Chinese delicacies until 4am every day.... *Tel 212/431–1040. 11 Division St., B/D/Q train to Grand St. $$$*

Odeon. By now an institution in chic; delicious American cuisine.... *Tel 212/233–0507. 145 W. Broadway, 1/9 train to Franklin St. $$$$*

Ollie's Noodle Shop. Filling, low-priced Chinese.... *Tel 212/362–3111. 2315 Broadway, 1/9 train to 86th St. Also at 190 W. 44th St. and 2957 Broadway (116th St.). $*

One if by Land, Two if by Sea. Continental cuisine served with many flourishes in a historic Greenwich Village carriage house.... *Tel 212/228–0822. 17 Barrow St., A/C/E or*

B/D/Q/F train to W. 4th St. Jacket and tie advised. Reservations required. $$$$

Oriental Pearl. Where all the world's a Chinese banquet.... *Tel 212/219–8388. 103 Mott St., J/M/Z, N/R, or 6 train to Canal St. or B/D/Q to Grand St. $$$*

The Original Espresso Bar. Regular and specialty coffees, sandwiches, and muffins.... *Tel 212/627–3870. 82 Christopher St., 1/9 train to Christopher St. No credit cards. $*

Orso. Very Tuscan, very good; an oasis in the theater district.... *Tel 212/489–7212. 322 W. 46th St., N/R, 1/2/3/9, or 7 train to Times Sq. Reservations required. $$$$*

Ottoman Cuisine. The cousin of a place in Istanbul.... *Tel 212/799–6363. 413 Amsterdam Ave., 1/9 train to 79th St. $$$*

Oyster Bar. Oysters from everywhere ordered from a chalkboard; basement train-station setting; whopping wine list.... *Tel 212/490–6650. Grand Central Terminal, 4/5/6 or 7 train to Grand Central. $$$$*

Patisserie Claude. Fabulous French pastries and cakes, for eating in or taking out.... *Tel 212/255–5911. 187 W. 4th St., A/C/E or B/D/Q/F train to W. 4th St. No credit cards. $*

Patria. Latin at its most chic.... *Tel 212/777–6211. 250 Park Ave. S., N/R, 4/5/6, or L train to Union Sq. $$$$*

Patsy's Pizza. Really great pizza just across the Brooklyn Bridge.... *Tel 718/858–4300. 19 Old Fulton St., 2/3 train to Clark St. No credit cards. $*

Periyali. Chic Greek.... *Tel 212/463–7890. 35 W. 20th St., F train to 23rd St. $$$$*

Peter Luger. The best steaks in town—but way out in Brooklyn.... *Tel 718/387–7400. 178 Broadway, J train to Marcy Ave. House credit card only. $$$$*

Pig Heaven. Chinese suckling pork and all the Chinese trimmings on the Upper East Side.... *Tel 212/744–4333. 1540 Second Ave., 6 train to 77 St. MC, V not accepted. $$$*

Pink Teacup. Little Village cafe that specializes in down-home cookin'.... *Tel 212/807–6755. 42 Grove St., 1/9 train to Christopher St. No credit cards. $*

Pita Cuisine. Where NYU eats healthy.... *Tel 212/254–1417. 535 LaGuardia Place. B/D/Q/F train to Broadway/Lafayette. $*

Po. Inventive Italian in a handsome but unpretentious Village dining room.... *Tel 212/645–2189. 31 Cornelia St., A/C/E or B/D/Q/F train to W. 4th St. $$$*

Puglia. Garlicky Italian in loud, lusty, close quarters.... *Tel 212/966–6006. 189 Hester St., 6 train to Spring St. $$*

Red Strype. Named for a Jamaican beer, with Jamaican cuisine to go along.... *Tel 212/274–9565. 35 Crosby St., J/M/Z, N/R, 6, or A/C/E train to Canal St. No credit cards. $*

Remi. Homage to Venice in the form of risotto and pasta.... *Tel 212/581–4242. 145 W. 53rd St., B/D/Q/F train to Rockefeller Center. $$$$*

The River Cafe. Christmas lights on the East River, stellar kitchen, companionable bar.... *Tel 718/522–5200. Fulton St. Landing, 2/3 train to Clark St. $$$$*

Rotunda Room. Tea with all the trimmings and a fanciful neo-Baroque setting in the posh Pierre Hotel.... *Tel 212/940–8185. 2 E. 61st St., N/R train to Fifth Ave. $$*

Russ & Daughters. Classic deli food, lower East Side.... *Tel 212/475–4880. 179 E. Houston St., F train to Second Ave. AE, D, DC not accepted. $*

Russian Tea Room. A New York classic, currently closed for expansion, famous for star sightings and Russian caviar.... *Tel 212/265–0947. 150 W. 57th St., B/Q or N/R train to 57th St. $$$$*

Sardi's. The theater district classic, still worth a visit.... *Tel 212/221–8440. 234 W. 44th St., N/R, 1/2/3/9, or 7 train to Times Sq. $$$*

Scharmann's. Cool, European SoHo cafe.... *Tel 212/219–2561. 386 W. Broadway, C/E train to Spring St. No credit cards. $$*

Shun Lee Cafe. Chinese generalists, but also dim sum.... *Tel 212/595–8895. 43 W. 65th St., 1/9 train to 66th St./Lincoln Center. $$$*

Sloppy Louie's. Seafood by the docks.... *Tel 212/509–9694. 92 South St., J/M/Z, 2/3, or 4/5 train to Fulton St. $$$*

Spring Street Natural. SoHo on tofu.... *Tel 212/966–0290. 62 Spring St., 6 train to Spring St. $$$*

Stage Deli. Uptown Jewish deli, with big sandwiches named for stars.... *Tel 212/245–7850. 834 Seventh Ave., B/D/E train to Seventh Ave. $$$*

Sweet Potato. Upper East Side eats to live forever.... *Tel 212/535–8423. 1466 2nd Ave., 6 train to 77th St. No credit cards. $*

Sylvia's. The Harlem soul food standard.... *Tel 212/996–2669. 328 Lenox Ave., 2/3 train to 125th St. No credit cards. $$$*

T Salon, Restaurant & Emporium. Teas for every palate from the world over, below the SoHo Guggenheim.... *Tel 212/925–3700. 142 Mercer St., C/E train to Spring St. $$*

Tai Hong Lau. Dandy Chinatown dim sum.... *Tel 212/219–1431. 70 Mott St., J/M/Z, N/R, or 6 train to Canal St. or B/D/Q to Grand St. $*

Taka. Neighborhood Japanese in the West Village.... *Tel 212/242–3699. 61 Grove St., 1/9 train to Christopher St. $$$*

Tartine. Pretty West Village spot for French cuisine.... *Tel 212/229–2611. 253 W. 11th St., 1/9 train to Christopher St. $$$*

Tasco Porto. Brazilian steaks, port wine, sangria.... *Tel 212/343–2321. 535 Broome St., C/E train to Spring St. $$$*

Tavern on the Green. The Central Park classic.... *Tel 212/873–3200. Central Park W. at W. 67th St., 1/9 train to 66th St./Lincoln Center. Jacket advised. Reservations required. $$$$*

Taylor's. American muffins, British scones, pasta salads, brownies—all in gargantuan proportions.... *Tel 212/645–8200. 523 Hudson St., 1/9 to Houston St.; tel 212/366–9081. 228 W. 18th St., 1/9 train to 18th St. No credit cards. $*

Tea & Sympathy. Tea shop, Manchester-style.... *Tel 212/807–8329. 108 Greenwich Ave., 1/2/3/9 train to 14th St. No credit cards. $*

Tortilla Flats. Mexican basics for filling up before hitting the clubs.... *Tel 212/243–1053. 767 Washington St., A/C/E train to 14th St. AE only. $*

Toukie's. Mostly soul food, but some mix; in SoHo, but the feeling of Harlem in the thirties.... *Tel 212/255–1411. 220 W. Houston St., 1/9 train to Houston St. $$$*

Trattoria Pesce Pasta. Very garlicky southern Italian, West Village neighborhoody.... *Tel 212/645—2993. 262 Bleecker St., A/C/E or B/D/Q/F train to W. 4th St. $$$*

Trattoria Spaghetto. Best homemade pasta dishes in town.... *Tel 212/255–6752. 232 Bleecker St., A/C/E or B/D/Q/F train to W. 4th St. $$$*

TriBeCa Grill. Robert DeNiro's place, and très chic.... *Tel 212/941–3900. 375 Greenwich St., 1/9 train to Franklin St. Reservations required. $$$$*

Triple Eight Palace. Bustling joint, splendid Chinatown Chinese.... *Tel 212/941–8886. 78 E. Broadway, F train to E. Broadway. $$$*

Two Boots. Pizza with a Cajun twist, with great ability to please kids...*Tel 212/505–2276. 37 Avenue A, F train to Second Ave.; tel 212/633–9096. 75 Greenwich Ave., 1/2/3/9 train to 14th St. AE only. $$*

Union Square Cafe. Knock-out American cuisine, with French and Italian flourishes.... *Tel 212/243–4020. 21 E. 16th St., N/R, 4/5/6, or L train to Union Sq. Reservations required. $$$$*

Universal Grill. Contemporary Continental, unobtrusive gay scene.... *Tel 212/989–5621. 44 Bedford St., 1/9 train to Christopher St. $$$*

Verbena. Fresh American dishes in a vegetable garden.... *Tel 212/260–5454. 54 Irving Place, N/R, 4/5/6, or L train to Union Sq. $$$*

Viand. Classic coffee shop, unsurpassed hamburgers.... *Tel 212/751–6622. 673 Madison Ave., 4/5/6 train to 59th St. or N/R to Lexington Ave. No credit cards. $$*

Vinnie's. Upper West Side pizza specialist.... *Tel 212/874–4382. 285 Amsterdam Ave., 1/2/3/9 train to 72nd St. No credit cards. $*

Virgil's Real Barbecue. Ribs, sausage, and chicken accompanied by stuffed jalapeño peppers, mashed potatoes, kale, corn relish, and subs in Bubba-sized portions.... *Tel 212/921–9494. 152 W. 44th St., N/R, 1/2/3/9, or 7 train to Times Sq. $$$*

Walker's. A lively downtown pub, with commendable pasta and fish.... *Tel 212/941–0142. 16 N. Moore St., 1/9 or A/C/E train to Canal St. $$$*

Windows on the World. The last word in view restaurants, reopening after renovation in December 1995.... *Tel 212/938–1111. 1 World Trade Center, N/R or 1/9 train to Cortlandt St., 2/3 to Park Place, or C/E to World Trade Center. Jacket, tie, and reservations required. $$$$*

Wolf's Sixth Avenue Delicatessen and Restaurant. Pile-'em-high deli sandwiches and prize sturgeon.... *Tel 212/586–1110. 101 W. 57th St., B/Q train to 57th St. $$$*

Ye Waverly Inn. Colonial-style eatery in the West Village.... *Tel 212/929–4377. 16 Bank St., 1/2/3/9 to 14th St. $$$*

Zen Palate. Asian health food.... *Tel 212/582–1669. 663 Ninth Ave. N/R, 1/2/3/9, or 7 to Times Sq.; tel 212/614–9291. 34 Union Sq. E., N/R, 4/5/6, or L train to Union Sq. $$$*

Uptown Dining

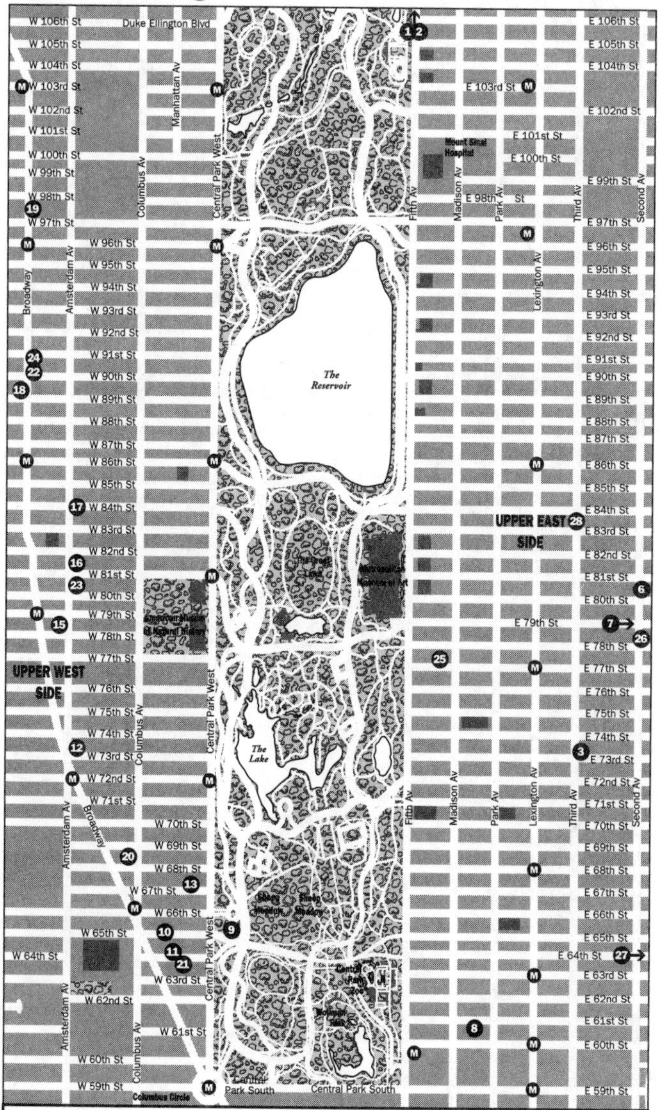

- Aureole **8**
- Cafe des Artistes **13**
- Carmine's **22**
- Diane's Uptown **14**
- Dock's **18**
- EJ's Luncheonette **16** & **3**
- Emily's **2**
- Hunan Balcony **19**
- John's Pizzeria **21** & **27**
- Lenge **20** & **28**
- The Mark Hotel **25**
- Mary Anne's **24** & **26**
- Monsoon **23**
- O'Neal's **11**
- Ollie's Noodle Shop **17**
- Ottoman Cuisine **15**
- Pig Heaven **6**
- Popover Café **4**
- Shun Lee Cafe **10**
- Sweet Potato **7**
- Sylvia's **1**
- Tavern on the Green **9**
- Vinnie's **12**

Midtown Dining

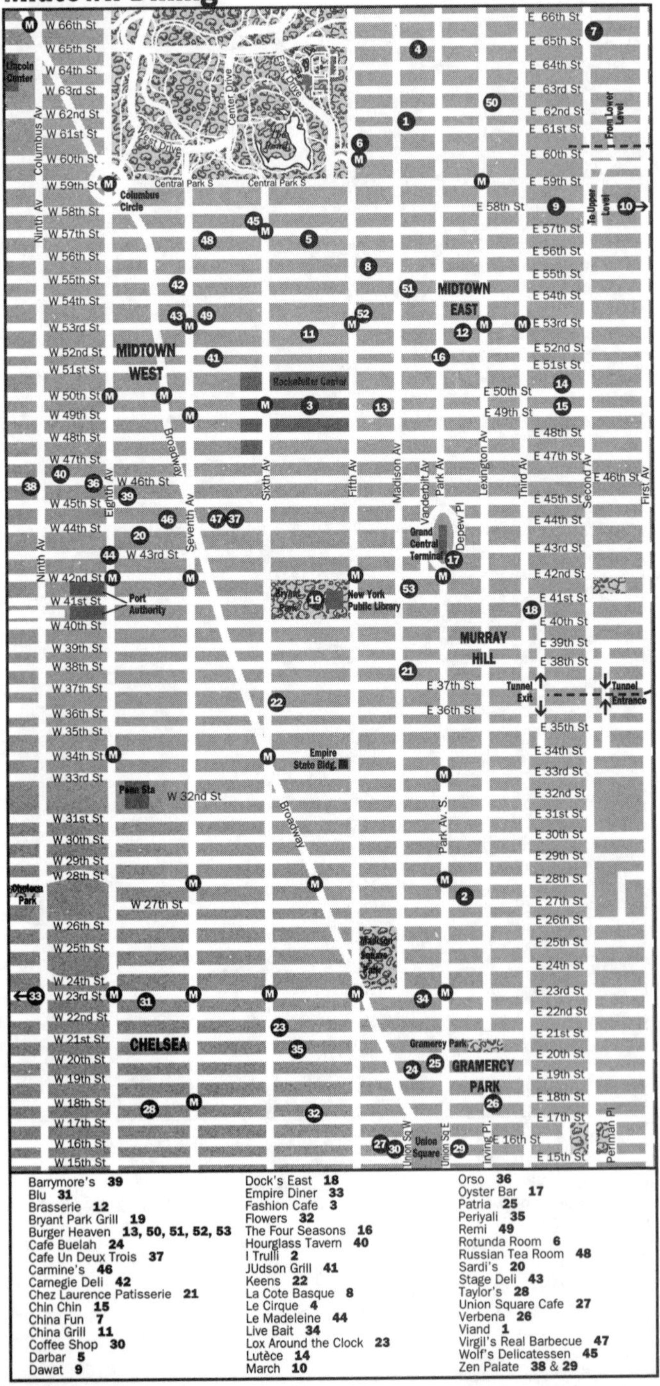

Barrymore's 39
Blu 31
Brasserie 12
Bryant Park Grill 19
Burger Heaven 13, 50, 51, 52, 53
Cafe Buelah 24
Cafe Un Deux Trois 37
Carmine's 46
Carnegie Deli 42
Chez Laurence Patisserie 21
Chin Chin 15
China Fun 7
China Grill 11
Coffee Shop 30
Darbar 5
Dawat 9
Dock's East 18
Empire Diner 33
Fashion Cafe 3
Flowers 32
The Four Seasons 16
Hourglass Tavern 40
I Trulli 2
JUdson Grill 41
Keens 22
La Cote Basque 8
Le Cirque 4
Le Madeleine 44
Live Bait 34
Lox Around the Clock 23
Lutèce 14
March 10
Orso 36
Oyster Bar 17
Patria 25
Periyali 35
Remi 49
Rotunda Room 6
Russian Tea Room 48
Sardi's 20
Stage Deli 43
Taylor's 28
Union Square Cafe 27
Verbena 26
Viand 1
Virgil's Real Barbecue 47
Wolf's Delicatessen 45
Zen Palate 38 & 29

Greenwich Village Dining

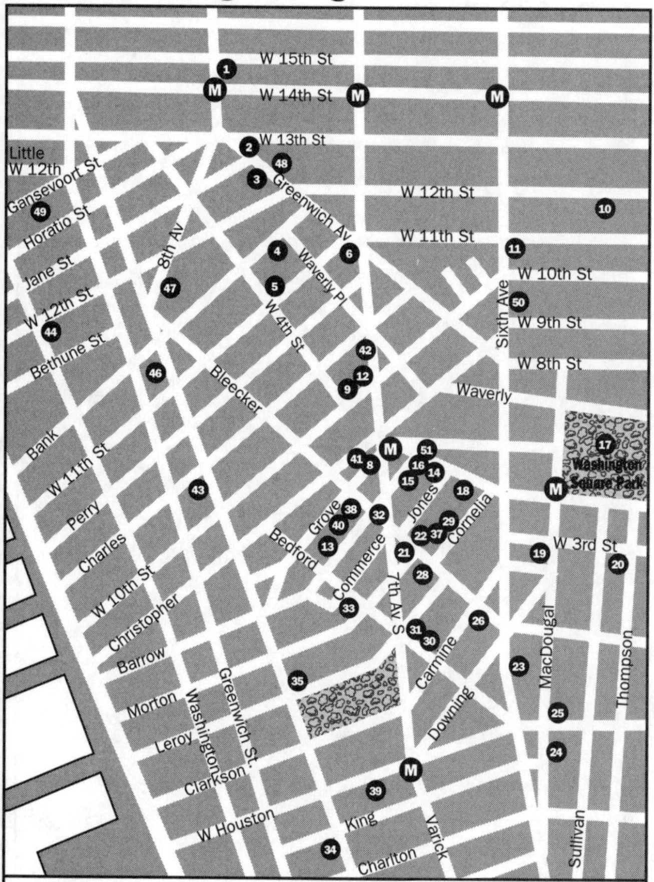

Aggie's **25**
Anglers & Writers **35**
The Bagel **18**
Bar Pitti **23**
Benny's Burritos **3**
Bleecker St. Cafe **21**
Boxers **16**
Cafe de Bruxelle **2**
Chumley's Café **13**
Cornelia St. Cafe **29**
Dix et Sept **12**
EJ's Downtown **50**
Florent **49**
French Roast **11**
Gotham Bar & Grill **10**
Grove **38**
Il Mulino **20**
John's Pizzeria **22**
Le Gamin **24**
Le Pescadou **34**
Life Cafe West **51**
Little Cafe **9**
Luna Park **17**
Mappamondo **47**
Mappamondo Due **46**
Mary Anne's **1**
Mary's **30**
Minetta Tavern **19**
Mitali West **32**
Moustache Pitza **33**
One if by Land . . . **15**
The Original Espresso Bar **41**
Patisserie Claude **14**
Pink Teacup **40**
Po **37**
Raffaela's **42**
Taka **8**
Tartine **5**
Taylor's **43**
Tea & Sympathy **48**
Tortilla Flats **44**
Toukie's **39**
Trattoria Spaghetto **26**
Trattoria Pesce Pasta **28**
Two Boots **6**
Universal Grill **31**
Ye Waverly Inn **4**

East Village Dining

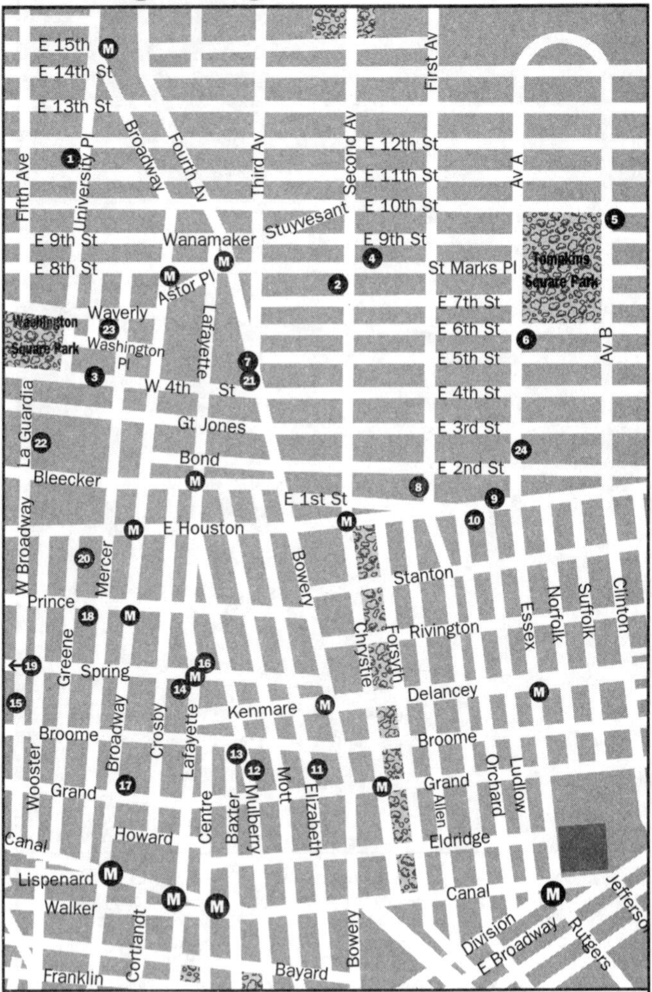

B&H Dairy **2**
Benito's I **12**
Benny's Burritos East **6**
Boca Chica **8**
Bowery Bar **21**
Cafe Orlin **4**
Cucina di Pesce **3**
Eddie's **23**
Fanelli **18**
French Culinary Institute **17**
Grotta Azzurra **13**
Japonica **1**
Jing Fong **11**
Katz's Deli **9**
Kelley & Ping **20**
Kin Khao **19**
Kwanzaa **16**
Life Cafe East **5**
Marion's **7**
Pita Cuisine **22**
Russ & Daughters **10**
Scharmann's **15**
Spring St. Natural **14**
Two Boots **24**

Downtown Dining

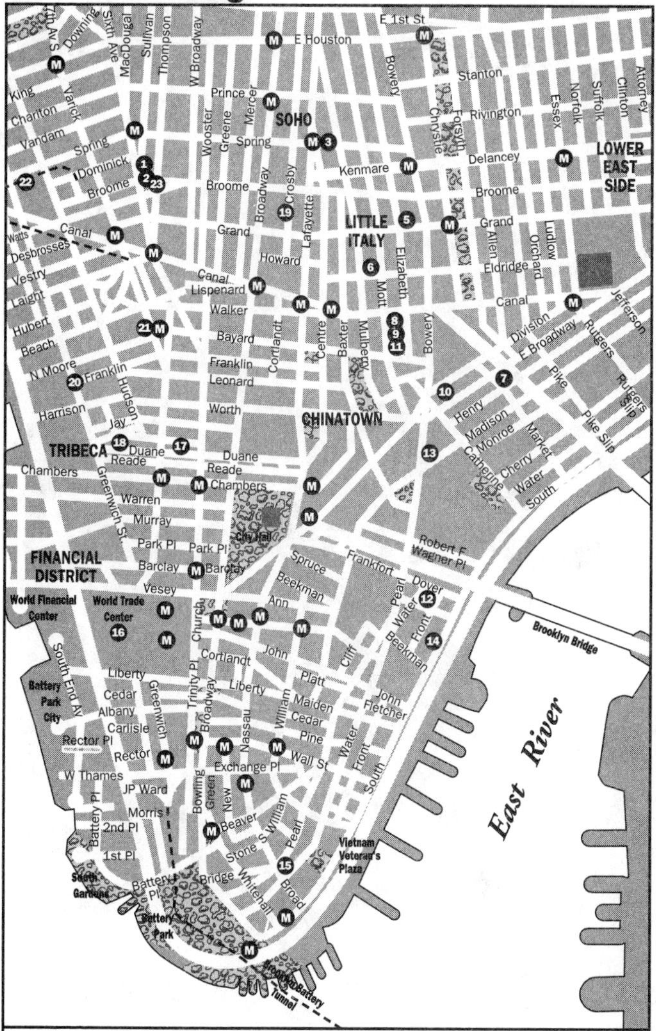

Bell Cafe **22**
Bouley **18**
Big Wong **9**
Bridge Cafe **12**
Chinese Country Kitchen **5**
Fraunces Tavern **15**
Little Szechuan **13**
Lombardi's **3**
Lupe's **1**
Moondance **2**
New Hong Kong City **10**
Odeon **17**
Oriental Pearl **8**
Puglia **6**
Red Strype **19**
Sloppy Louie's **14**
Tai Hong Lau **11**
Tasco Porto **23**
TriBeCa Grill **20**
Triple Eight Palace **7**
Walker's **21**
Windows on the World **16**

diver
THOMAS

3

sions

New York Harbor
and Miss Liberty,
Times Square, the
Empire State
Building, the
Brooklyn Bridge—
that's the short

list of New York City's must-sees. The unabridged list would take up volumes, not even counting city sights that are totally ephemeral—city squares mantled in snow and icicles, bike messengers flying like dervishes down the avenues, subway musicians playing at a certain stop one day and then gone the next... Taking in everything could drive a person to distraction. So make it easy on yourself by picking out one or two top attractions to visit each day. After you visit them, roam around the neighborhoods where they lie, taking the distinct pulse of the place by simply sitting on a park bench or in a café. Then wander on, preferably by foot. As novelist Elizabeth Bowen wrote of Rome, "to be anything but walking is estrangement." It's just as true of New York.

Getting Your Bearings

The kingdom of New York is composed of five boroughs: Staten Island (which is always agitating to secede from the union), the Bronx, Queens, Brooklyn, and the island of Manhattan, 13.5 miles long and 2.3 miles across at its widest point. The population is 7.3 million, with 1.5 million packed into Manhattan's high-rise apartment buildings, rowhouses, and fire-escape-filigreed tenements, lining 504 miles of streets. Access to the island is provided by three tunnels, some 12 bridges, the Staten Island ferries, and Roosevelt Island's aerial tram. From 14th Street all the way up to the northern tip of Manhattan, getting the lay of the land is a cinch, because, in 1811 urban planners laid the city out on a virtually unvarying grid. Numbered avenues run north and south. Sixth Avenue is also known as the Avenue of the Americas. Between Fifth and Third lie three named avenues—Madison, Park, and Lexington (Park turns into Fourth Avenue below 14th Street)—and east of First Avenue you'll find York and East End Avenue uptown, while the Upper West Side confuses everything by renaming its avenues: Central Park West, Columbus, Amsterdam, West End. Numbered streets run east and west—though traffic moves alternately east or west, since most streets are one-way, except for the major cross-streets: 14th, 23rd, 34th, 42nd, 57th, 72nd, 79th, 86th, and 96th. Broadway cuts across the grid on one sweeping, 17-mile northwest diagonal. Fifth Avenue is the city's "Continental Divide" in terms of addresses; east and west of it, cross-street addresses start at zero, and are prefixed by an E. or W. (Hence 240 E. 37th Street or 315 W. 53rd Street.) Avenue addresses baffle everybody—while 633 Third Avenue is at 40th Street, 633 Madison Avenue is at 59th. It's all based on a complicated formula—there's a chart in the front of the phone book—but to know where you're going, just call and ask what the nearest cross street is. Piece o' cake, right?

But now for the bad news. Figuring out where you are is a lot harder downtown. Take a look at a map and you'll see why—the street grid looks like it's gone through a Cuisinart. I still get lost in parts of the Village and Lower East Side, and am always (delightedly) coming upon streets I had never heard of before, like Weehawken, Attorney, and Lispenard. Back in the old days, streets were laid out along property lines, and useless marshlands covered large swatches of the littoral; the Village grew up as a jumbled tent encampment for refugees during the yellow fever epidemic of 1822, and strong, straight major arteries like Seventh Avenue weren't even extended south of 14th Street until 1911. This explains the loony, skewed, logic-defying layout of downtown.

You could just stay uptown—but wouldn't that be sad! So venture into the maze, remembering that the farther south you go, the closer together everything is (you can walk from the West Village to SoHo or from South Street Seaport to the World Trade Center in a handy 10 minutes). Hang onto the lifeline of Broadway, and think of downtown in three parts, from north to south: The Village lies between 14th and Houston streets; SoHo is sandwiched between Houston and Canal streets (the name comes from "south of Houston," in fact); and everything below Canal Street is downtown, including the financial district, TriBeCa (the "triangle below Canal"), Chinatown, and the Lower East Side. Heritage Trails of New York has marked off four prime sightseeing routes in the lower Manhattan area

Talk City

If you write ahead for free tickets, you can sit in on a taping of one of three talk shows shot in New York: The Geraldo show, *the* Late Show with David Letterman, *or the* Rush Limbaugh Show. *You'll have to be at least 16 years old (18 for Rush Limbaugh). Letterman tickets are a hot commodity—send a postcard requesting tickets six months in advance. Limbaugh tickets can be ordered by phone, two months ahead; for Geraldo, send a letter (with a self-addressed, stamped return envelope) one month in advance.* (You tell me *why Geraldo tickets are the easiest to snag.)* ***Geraldo****. Tapings Tues–Thur, 1 and 4....* Tel 265–8520. 524 W. 57th St., NY, NY 10019. ***Late Show with David Letterman****.* Tapings Mon–Fri 5:30pm.... Tel 212/975–5853. Ed Sullivan Theater, 1697 Broadway, NY, NY 10019. ***The Rush Limbaugh Show****. Tapings Mon–Thur 5pm....* Tel 212/397–7367. 515 W. 57th St.

by painting more than 4 miles of dots on the sidewalks. The green route meanders between Wall Street and Battery Park; the blue starts at the Chase Manhattan Plaza; the red explores the City Hall area; and the orange winds from the American Stock Exchange to the World Financial Center. But if you see red footprints on the pavement, watch out, because there's a phantom painter on the loose downtown, whose markings lead you nowhere in particular and then mysteriously peter out.

The Lowdown

Partytime in Gotham... Back in New York's Dutch days, folks got crazy on the eve of Lent by playing an unsavory sort of game that, as far as I can make out, involved mutilating the greased carcass of a goose. I'd like to claim we've come a long way since then, but that wouldn't be just, considering the drunken brawling that goes on during the St. Patrick's Day Parade (March 17). The stomach is feted and then sated at the Ninth Avenue International Food Festival (mid-May), when Ninth Avenue from W. 57th to 42nd streets turns into one giant global-village smorgasbord; booths purvey everything from empanadas to Thai spring rolls. Gay Pride Week (in mid-June) culminates in another wild ride of a parade (generally on Sunday morning), with guys in such exquisite drag it would put RuPaul to shame. All day long on the Fourth of July firecrackers can be heard going off everywhere in the city, but the big pop happens at around 9pm on the waterfront between Battery Park and South Street Seaport, with a fireworks show full of displays to remember, gorgeously mirrored in the water. The West Village, which has a significant population of émigrés from France, celebrates Bastille Day (July 14) with games of petanque (the French version of boccie) played by the city's top French chefs on MacDougal Street, and the cast of Les Misérables doing the can-can on Gansevoort Street. Mid-August brings Harlem Week, with celebrations centering around 125th Street. Come September, Brooklyn is the scene of the West Indian American Day Carnival, when the air along Eastern Parkway is so thick with hot Afro-Latin music that you could cut it with a machete. Count on New York to put a few twists in the old recipe for fun, which it does in spades during the Greenwich Village Halloween Parade (October 31, after nightfall, of course), which winds up Sixth Avenue from Spring to 23rd streets. This is New York's version of Mardi Gras, with great attention paid to costumes. More wholesome by a mile is the Macy's Thanksgiving Day Parade (November 24), when kids zipped up into warm winter coats line the curbs of Central Park West and Broadway from W. 77th Street to Herald Square, growing rosy-cheeked and enchanted at the sight of celebrity-laden floats and gigantic helium-filled balloon effigies of Mickey Mouse and all their favorite cartoon characters. Or you could just happen to strike it lucky and land in the city for a tickertape parade, which is how New York celebrates great civic and national events, on Broadway from Battery Park to City Hall.

The king of Museum Mile, and his minions... Sticklers note that Museum Mile actually runs a mile and a half along Fifth Avenue from the Frick Collection at E. 65th Street to **El Museo del Barrio** at E. 105th Street. Over a score of museums line this stretch of wide pavement, making it something of a magic carpet for art lovers. But only one of them occupies a site on the western, Central Park side—the vast **Metropolitan Museum of Art**, which lies above E. 82nd Street. The Met's encyclopedic collection includes over three million works of art from all ages and corners of the globe, purchased or donated by Rockefellers, Sacklers, Lehmans, and other wealthy patrons and housed in myriad mazelike wings. The Met can seem daunting. In a long half day you might be able to cruise past most of its hits, like the Assyrian Nimrud Ivories dating from the 13th to the 7th century BC, Botticelli's 1490 *Annunciation*, the Dogon sculptures from the western Sudan, the Temple of Dendur, Degas's gemlike *Dancing Class*, and Picasso's portrait of Gertrude Stein, not to mention some 40 sculptures by Rodin. I've done this once or twice, but it's really better to limit yourself to a handful of wings—maybe the half acre of 19th-century European Paintings, masterpieces from the Neo-Classicists to the Impressionists; or the Rockefeller Wing, featuring "primitive" art from Africa, Oceania, and South America; the tombs and reliquaries of pharoahs in the Egyptian Wing; or the Greek and Roman Galleries. For Orientalists there's the Ming Dynasty-era Astor Chinese

Garden Court; the stunning American Wing picks up long before the Whitney Museum starts, with Duncan Phyfe furniture, handsome portraits by John Singer Sargent, and a painstakingly recreated Frank Lloyd Wright room. Before leaving, climb up to the rooftop sculpture garden, if only to see the city skyline fringing Central Park. Many masterworks from the Met's medieval collection aren't in the Met at all, but way up on Manhattan's west side, in Fort Tryon Park: **The Cloisters** holds, among other treasures, the Unicorn Tapestries, an illuminated manuscript called *Les Belles Heures du Duc de Berry*, and the 12th-century Bury St. Edmunds Cross. But many will find the Cloisters most memorable for its dramatic Hudson River cliffside setting and bizarre composition, a Frankenstein-like amalgamation of medieval architecture from all over Europe: a Romanesque chapel, a 12th-century Spanish apse, portions of cloisters from five different monasteries. Back on Museum Mile, above the Met, you'll find the **Museum of the City of New York**, with fine historical interiors; the **International Center of Photography**; and the **Cooper-Hewitt National Design Museum**, overseen by the Smithsonian Institution. Of the three, I'd chose the Cooper-Hewitt in a flash, partly because it occupies a mansion built by Andrew Carnegie in 1901, and because its rotating displays of decorative arts—from Japanese kimonos to Bauhaus chairs—never fail to beguile. Unfortunately, it'll be closed for restoration until September 1996; in the meantime, you can stroll around the splendid garden out back. But to my mind the **Frick Collection** is the apogee of Museum Mile, a lovely, intimate place for some of life's transcendent moments. Among all the famous paintings hanging on museum walls in New York, the one I care for most is at the Frick—Whistler's stunningly pink *Valerie, Lady Meux*, who eyes the viewer with the subtlest sort of come-on, while a signature Whistler butterfly floats in front of her.

I know what I like, and I like modern art... Go directly to the **Museum of Modern Art** (MoMA), which covers all of contemporary art beginning with the Post-Impressionists. MoMA opened in 1929 on Fifth Avenue, but then moved to new International-style digs on W. 53rd Street 10 years later, with its Philip Johnson-designed sculpture garden. The collection consists of

100,000 paintings and sculptures, 10,000 films, and 100,000 books—but numbers don't tell the MOMA story at all, because this museum has more masterworks by late 19th- and 20th-century artists than any other in the world. You will stop, all agog, by Vincent Van Gogh's *Starry Night*, Henri Rousseau's *Sleeping Gypsy*, Piet Mondrian's *Broadway Boogie-Woogie*, and Pablo Picasso's *Desmoiselles d'Avignon*. The **Whitney Museum** is a logical stop for contemporary art lovers, housing a collection of American painting, sculpture, and graphic arts in styles as various as Pop, Conceptual, Social and Magical Realist. The permanent collection contains works by George Bellows, Edward Hopper, Andy Warhol, Jasper Johns, and Louise Nevelson; and Whitney Biennial shows are considered the last word in cutting-edge art. Way west in Chelsea, you can sit on the rooftop at the **Dia Center for the Arts**, and then wander into sculptor Dan Graham's glass and metal "reflective experience." SoHo has three important modern art forums in the **Alternative Museum**, dedicated to works with a social or political agenda; the **New Museum of Contemporary Art**, featuring such whimsical curios as Jimbo Blachly's *Unperturbed Abstraction*, a streetside window installation which the artists often enter for stints of performance art; and the **Guggenheim Museum SoHo**, with a rotating schedule of exhibits shown in a bare loft space with towering ceilings. But when I have a spare Sunday afternoon, the museum I visit is the **Solomon R. Guggenheim Museum**. The permanent collection contains Chagalls, Matisses, Van Goghs, Picassos, and Kandinskys till the cows come home, and there's always some intriguing special exhibit; the last time I was there huge piles of penny candy were on display—an exhibit I tried hard to contemplate before stashing some pieces in my purse (don't worry, this was allowed). But forget all that, it's the building that provides transcendent moments. Frank Lloyd Wright was the architect, and in the Guggenheim he sought to suggest the ziggurat. It's one immense concrete spiral, with a seven-story tower alongside, ascended via a half-rounded elevator. You zoom to the top, then cruise slowly on foot down a long spiral ramp, past the artworks.

Coming to America... Technically speaking, nearly all Americans are immigrants—no matter how long ago their ancestors made the trip. But the greatest wave lasted from about 1890 to 1950, when 12 million people arrived from places like Eastern Europe, Russia, Ireland, and Italy, with the crest coming in 1907. What they first saw upon entering New York Harbor was the **Statue of Liberty**, still perhaps the city's most stirring sight. Copper-coated Miss Liberty, standing 150 feet from base to torch, was designed by Frederic-Auguste Bartholdi, Alexandre-Gustave Eiffel, and Richard Morris Hunt. Take a ferry to the statue from Battery Park; an elevator whisks you to the top of the pedestal, from which it's a 12-story climb to the crown. The ticket booth is, appropriately, at Battery Park's **Castle Clinton**, an old fort that served as the city's prime disembarkation point for immigrants until 1892, when the federal government opened new processing facilities on **Ellis Island** (also reached by ferry from Battery Park). The Great Hall has been carefully restored; displays of immigrant memorabilia can be toured and a film is shown. The American Immigrant Wall of Honor outside, skirting the waterfront, is moving to behold, with the names of 420,000 immigrants inscribed. When newcomers finally reached Manhattan, most carried their baggage up Broadway, then veered right to the Lower East Side, a neighborhood of tenement buildings and sweatshops that spans 4 square miles from Broadway east to the river, between Houston and Canal streets. Italians, Irish, Chinese, and Jews lived in close, squalid quarters there, with Hispanics joining them more recently. **Sara Delano Roosevelt Park**, running along Chrystie Street between Houston and Canal streets, remains the district's center, the scene of a bustling open-air bazaar. Just east lies the Jewish commercial hub of Orchard Street and the **Lower East Side Tenement Museum**, housed in an 1868 tenement, with dioramas that reveal the rigors of life in a cramped railroad apartment, with a bathtub in the kitchen and a toilet down the hall.

New York stories... Great poets have left their marks all over New York, beginning with that dauntless American oracle, **Walt Whitman**, raised in a house on **Cranberry Street** across from Plymouth Church in Brooklyn Heights. As a reporter for the *Brooklyn Eagle* he roamed far and wide, drinking in New York and its people, resulting in his poetic masterpiece *Leaves of Grass*, which he set at a printshop once located at **170 Fulton Street**. Master of the macabre **Edgar Allen Poe** had a hard time settling down in any one place for long, but we know he helped to run a boarding house at **113 1/2 Carmine Street**, was treated for a head cold in 1837 at the **Northern Dispensary** (Christopher and Waverly streets), and retreated with his invalid wife to a farmhouse on the Upper West Side (on the site of a tenement at **206 W. 84th Street**) where he finished *The Raven*. In the years before the Great War, a rooming house at **61 Washington Square South**, which has since been demolished to make way for the classrooms of New York University, had so many poets and novelists living there (including **Lincoln Steffens** and **Edwin Arlington Robinson**) that it came to be known as the "House of Genius." After the war, another light shone bright in the Village—**Edna St. Vincent Millay**, she of the flaming red hair and green eyes, who bedazzled legions of suitors, and finally married a Dutch coffee merchant named Eugen Boissevain. They lived at **75 1/2 Bedford Street**, a rowhouse just nine-and-a-half-feet wide in the green bower of the West Village. (One of her relatives recovered from a dire illness at St. Vincent's Hospital, at Seventh Avenue and W. 11th Street, hence her middle name.) The modernist **e.e. cummings** grew old, crusty, and reclusive at **4 Patchin Place**, a secretive little mews off 10th Street west of Sixth Avenue; **Bob Dylan** haunted clubs around the intersection of **Bleecker** and **MacDougal streets**. Welsh poet **Dylan Thomas** became a permanent fixture at the **White Horse Tavern**, at the southwest corner of Hudson and W. 11th streets, where you can still down a beer and imagine his sonorous voice; he spent his last bleerily alcoholic days at the the Victorian Gothic **Chelsea Hotel** (222 W. 23rd Street), also inhabited at various times by **Tennessee Williams**, **Yevgeni Yevtushenko**, and **Arthur Miller**. In the East Village, kind-hearted **W.H. Auden** lived for many years above a bar at **77 St. Marks Place**, today marked by a plaque bearing this line of his verse: "If equal affection cannot be, let the more loving one be me." Beat poet **Allen Ginsberg** hung out at the **St. Mark's Church-in-the-Bowery**. It remains headquarters for other younger poets, who join in weekly readings at the long-running Poetry Project. A more recent addition to the East Village scene is the **Nuyorican Poets Cafe**, featuring poetry slams and rap. But if all you want to do is cuddle up with a book of verse, stop by the **Poets House**, started in 1985 by Stanley Kunitz and Elizabeth Kray, where there are deep easy-chairs and 30,000 volumes of poetry.

Beautiful buildings, Downtown... "Look up!" exclaims the estimable *American Institute of Architects Guide to New York City*. This is the only way to appreciate Manhattan's grand, gorgeous buildings, though with so much to absorb at street level, it's easy to pass them by. So make a special trip to the **Woolworth Building** at 233 Broadway just below City Hall, a 60-story skyscraper with enchanting Gothic embellishments and known as the "Cathedral of Commerce" when dimestore magnate F.W. Woolworth had it erected (paying $13.5 million in cash) in 1913, employing Cass Gilbert as architect. I know of no finer lobby in the city—go inside and gaze at the marvelous glass-mosaic vaulted ceiling, where you'll find a gargoyle-ish likeness of Mr. Woolworth counting coins at the top of a crossbeam on the south side. Step over to City Hall Park to view it from a distance, then turn to note the fine neo-classical Federal lines of **City Hall**, itself, and the handsome twin towers of the **Park Row Building** across the traffic island to the south (at 15 Park Row between Ann and Beekman streets), Manhattan's tallest edifice from 1899 to 1908. The foyer of the **American Telephone and Telegraph Building** (195 Broadway), a fascinating forest of columns, nearly rivals the Woolworth lobby. There was little chance that **Jefferson Market Courthouse** (now a branch of the New York Public Library, at Sixth Avenue and 10th Street) would start an archectural trend when it went up in 1876, because the building is simply too bizarre—but delightfully so. With its red brick, myriad gables, slender arched windows, and towers, it is one part Bavarian castle, one part Venetian palazzo.

Beautiful buildings, Midtown... Everyone stops short when they come upon the **Flatiron Building**, which rises in an awesome wedge at the skinny triangular meeting of Broadway, Fifth Avenue, and 23rd Street. It went up in 1902, and boasts one of the city's earliest structural steel frames. In 1930, the 1,048-foot-tall **Chrysler Building** (405 Lexington Avenue at 42nd Street) surpassed the Woolworth Building in height. To get a good view of this Art Deco landmark, find a spot on Lexington Avenue in the high Forties and look downtown, marveling above all at the building's outlandish crown, composed of six levels of brilliant stainless steel arches topped by a dramatically lit lancet spire. Closer up you'll find brickwork designs inspired by automobile hubcaps, and a Jazz Age fantasy in African marble in the lobby. The Chrysler Building only held onto the world's tallest title for a few months, until the **Empire State Building** (Fifth Avenue and 34th Street) opened its doors. Just down the street from the Chrysler Building you'll find another architectural wonder from 1930, the **Daily News Building** (220 E. 42nd St.), with a powerful red-and-black-striped composition; check out the huge globe and weather instruments in the lobby, but don't look for the newspaper, because the *Daily News* moved to cheaper digs in 1995. Another rival to the Woolworth Building's lobby is the extravagantly ornamented lobby of the **Fred R. French Building** (551 Fifth Avenue). The **Helmsley Building**, completed in 1929, sits astride Park Avenue at East 46th Street, with a golden pyramidal roof; and the dignified Edwardian **Plaza Hotel** at Fifth Avenue and 59th Street (see Accommodations), made of white brick topped by a slate mansard roof, overlooks Central Park. Two stone lions greet visitors on the broad stone steps of the **New York Public Libaray** (Fifth Avenue and 42nd Street), where there are al fresco cafes and plenty of shady spots for brown-bag lunches. This 1911 building is New York Beaux Arts at its best, with a grand, airy lobby, Romanesque arches, and two sweeping side staircases. Those who favor modern architecture should stop by the **Seagram Building** (375 Park Avenue), designed in the International Style by Mies van der Rohe in 1958, with interiors (including the lobby-level Four Seasons restaurant—see Dining) by Philip Johnson. This simple, black-mirrored rectangle looms powerfully, fronted by a plaza—actually one of the first introduced in the high-rent district of Midtown. Equally impressive is **Lever House**, completed in 1952, which opened up the whole block of Park Avenue between East 53rd and 54th streets; one stainless-steel-and-glass slab sits on columns occupying the site horizontally, while another rises at the north end, creating one gigantic, backwards L. The **Citicorp Center** (Lexington Avenue between 53rd and 54th streets) shot up in 1978, cantilevered over St. Peter's Lutheran Church, with two lower-level shopping and eating arcades and a height of 900 feet; its top 130 feet have been sliced diagonally, yielding the building's signature angled crest. One final modernistic landmark lies at 909 Third Avenue: New Yorkers call it the "**Lipstick Building**," due to its tall, rounded shape. John Burgee and Philip Johnson were the architects, which must have been convenient for Johnson, since he lived virtually around the corner at 242 E. 52nd Street, in a shockingly contemporary townhouse he designed, now the **Museum of Modern Art Guesthouse**.

On the square... In the last ten years or so, many of New York's finest squares, containing parks, have undergone dramatic restoration. Once the domain of junkies, pushers, and the homeless, Midtown's **Bryant Park** (Sixth Avenue between 40th and 42nd streets) now seems a little patch of Versailles, with pebbled paths, very Continental green iron folding chairs, clean restrooms, a wide central lawn, and a stage hosting free midday concerts and free Monday night movies in summer. Fashion designers set up runways there for showings of their newest collections, and recently the **Bryant Park Grill** (see Dining) settled in. **Union Square** (Broadway and Park Avenue South, 14th to 16th streets) isn't bordered by buildings of great architectural distinction (indeed, the atmosphere is busy and rattling), but it has an interesting red-tinted past: In the thirties, orators held forth on soapboxes here, stirring up the city's Left Wing sensibilities. Now a splendid **greenmarket** takes over the concrete flats at the north end of the square, open for business on Monday, Wednesday, Friday, and Saturday, and a chic cafe called **Luna Park** (see Dining) has blossomed in the center of it all. **Stuyvesant Square** (bisected by Second Avenue, between 15th and 17th streets) lies amid the Beth Israel Medical Center complex, with a fine brownstone church at the western end; sedate **Gramercy Park** (20th to 21st streets, at the foot of Lexington Avenue) is surrounded by a distinguished residential neighborhood, where the townhouses are decorated with New Orleans-style wrought-iron porticoes and porches. But there's a fence with a locked gate around Gramercy Park; only residents have keys.

Mixed nuts... Tompkins Square Park is, in many ways, the heart of the **East Village**. At the turn of the century

Eastern European immigrants settled in, leaving behind pleasing traces like **B & H Dairy** (see Dining) and the **Russian and Turkish Baths**, where you can sip borscht, sizzle in the Russian room, or sweat out your toxins in the Turkish Room. When the wild sixties rolled in, the East Village was transformed into New York's Haight-Ashbury, with avant-garde artists bunking in communal apartments, flower children wandering freely, and artistic meccas like the innovative theater **LaMama E.T.C.** (74 E. 4th Street) and the **St. Mark's Church in-the-Bowery Poetry Project**. East of Tompkins Square Park, **Alphabet City** (so named because the avenues bear letters not numbers) sprawls toward the East River, a dodgy urban netherland with a large Hispanic population and fearless Gen-X homesteaders. In the **West Village**, where Seventh Avenue South crosses W. 4th and Christopher streets, little **Sheridan Square** (historically, Christopher Park, founded in 1837) saw violence of a different kind in 1967, when homosexual protestors clashed with cops in the Stonewall Riot, sparking the beginning of the country's gay activism. The **General Philip H. Sheridan monument** strikes an odd note there, with white-wrapped lifelike statues of gay and lesbian couples taking up bench space below him. Drunks, bums, and gay prostitutes make it a rest stop, no longer badgered by the NYPD. In fact, the precinct house in the West Village now has so many homosexual officers that it's locally known as "Fort Bruce." If you stop in only one square during your visit to New York, make it **Washington Square**, where Fifth Avenue dead-ends at 10th Street with a grand triumphal arch designed by Stanford White. A trout stream ran through this area in the 18th century, and in the early part of the 19th, wealthy denizens from downtown moved up to its environs—including Henry James's grandmother, who owned a now-demolished rowhouse at 19 10th Street. James would be amazed to see it now, because Washington Square Park is a veritable circus. The wide fountain is the city's top stage for street performers; its fenced-in dogwalk yields canine shows; chess is the park's prime sport, played at stone tables at the southwest corner; and NYU students use the place for a quad (indeed, it's the scene of the university's commencement ceremonies every spring). Certainly, there are streetpeople, pickpockets, and pushers, too—but not in disproportionate numbers. The Village mixes here, generally with a very positive attitude.

Knockin' on heaven's door... With so much of New York's art lining the walls of museums, most tourists don't venture into the city's churches, unless maybe to go to a gospel service up in Harlem (see "Way Uptown," below). During the week, however, Manhattan churches remain deeply peaceful places, where one can sit, breathe, and think. **St. Patrick's Cathedral** (Fifth Avenue and 50th Street) is a cavernous edifice designed by James Renwick in the mid-19th century, skirted by wide stone steps and pinnacled by twin 330-foot Gothic spires. Also in Midtown, **St. Bartholomew's Episcopal Church** (Park Avenue at 51st Street), built in 1918, has grand Romanesque vaulting, Byzantine decorations, and, being a socially responsible sort of congregation, a homeless shelter in the foyer. A little farther east, tucked beneath the northwest corner of the Citicorp Center (Lexington Avenue and 54th Street), is **St. Peter's Lutheran Church**, often the showcase for Off-Off Broadway theatrical productions; the miniscule **Erol Beker Chapel** at the north side is what really makes it worth a stop—pure white, and designed by Louise Nevelson. Uptown, the **Church of St. John the Divine** (Amsterdam Avenue at 112th Street) still struggles toward completion. It was started in 1892, and conceived on an incredibly grand scale—indeed, when the last gargoyle is finally sculpted and set, it will be the biggest cathedral in the world (though on a technicality, since St. Peter's in Rome is larger but not officially a cathedral). Byzantine-Romanesque is the style originally intended, but this behemoth has been in the works for so long that French Gothic and Gothic Revival have come into play too, resulting in a huge, glorious hodgepodge. Graceful, Gothic **Riverside Church**, over at 120th Street and Riverside Drive, was a hotbed for Viet Nam War opposition, fueled by the wise, reasoned voice of the Reverend William Sloane Coffin. You can ascend its belfry for a peaceful refuge 392 feet high, with sweeping views of the Hudson River and New Jersey beyond; the carillon has 74 bells weighing 100 tons, and chiming daily at noon and on Sundays at 3pm. On the south side of Washington Square sits **Judson Memorial Church**, its strawberry-blond stone shimmering and Italian campanile towering over the park. Built in 1892 by the prominent design firm of McKim, Mead & White, and paid for by John D. Rockefeller, Sr., it served impoverished immigrants who settled downtown at the end of the 19th century. On lower Broadway, at the end of Wall Street, the first **Trinity Church** was built in 1696. But the original church was burned down by British General Howe in 1776; the lovely Gothic gem that stands here now was completed in 1846, with huge bronze doors designed by Richard Morris Hunt and a bucolic colonial-era cemetery wrapped around it. One of Trinity's chapels, **St. Paul's** (at Broadway and Vesey Street), survives as the city's only pre-Revolutionary War structure, built in 1766 with Scotsman Thomas McBean as architect. The heart of the building is a modest Georgian hall, topped 30 years later by a somewhat ostentatious spire. Inside you'll find the pew where George Washington worshipped from 1789 to 1790, when New York briefly served as the nation's capital.

Reel to reel... The movie industry started in the New York area (New Jersey, to be exact, where Thomas Edison had his lab), and so many films and televison shows have used the city for a backdrop that walking around here gives many folks a disconcerting sense of déjà vu. Christopher Reeve and Margot Kidder posed at the entrance to the **Daily News Building** (220 E. 42nd Street) in the 1978 film version of *Superman*; the **New York County Courthouse** downtown (Centre and Pearl streets) served in 1957 as the opening setting for *Twelve Angry Men*, which starred Henry Fonda; a white townhouse at **171 E. 71st Street** was Audrey Hepburn's East Side digs when she wasn't window-shopping at 57th and Fifth in *Breakfast at Tiffany's*; the **New York Public Library** was de-spooked in 1984's *Ghostbusters* (the ghostbusters operated out of a firehouse in TriBeCa at 14 Moore Street). **Tom's Restaurant** at 112th and Broadway is the hangout for Jerry and his pals on TV's *Seinfeld*; an apartment building at the **corner of Grove and Bedford streets** in the West Village is supposed to be home base for the characters of *Friends*. Above all, though, New York is a movie*going* town. Lots of big Hollywood flicks make their debuts in Manhattan theaters, with the stars in attendance and the whole glitzy nine yards. Most of the grand old theaters from the 1920s and 1930s are gone or have been subdivided into multiplexes, leaving the **Zeigfeld** (141 W. 54th Street) as the city's best big screen for restored classic epics like *Spartacus*, along with first-run blockbusters. **Radio City Music Hall**, that grand Art Deco auditorium in Rockefeller Center, presents live shows and concerts rather than films these days, but the backstage tour gives a unique glimpse into the old movie palace. The **Ed Sullivan Theatre** (Broadway at 53rd Street) holds powerful memories of the days when Sullivan's Sunday-evening variety show presented everyone from Elvis to the Beatles to an Italian mouse puppet named Topo Gigio; today it's home to CBS's *The Late Show with David Letterman,* which has made celebrities of every small-business proprietor on the block (Mujibar and Sirajul work up the block at a store called Rock America, Rupert Gee at the Hello Deli around the corner). The **Museum of Television and Radio** in Midtown, founded by CBS titan William S. Paley, has 30,000 old television programs and 7,000 vintage radio shows in its stacks, which can be checked out for sampling at custom-built consoles. (Most requested tape: The 1964 Ed Sullivan Show introducing the Beatles to American audiences.) The museum also mounts displays and organizes special screenings, and has a fun gift shop on its first floor. Out in Queens, near the old but still functioning Kaufman Astoria Studios, is the **Museum of the Moving Image**, a classily put-together place for movie addicts to indulge themselves. It has a theater, screening room, changing exhibits, complete sets from famous films, and 60,000 pieces of movie memorabilia.

Crossroads of the world... **Times Square**, situated at the giant X-shaped intersection of Broadway, Seventh Avenue, and 42nd Street, is Gotham's theater district, Sodom, and Gomorrah all rolled into one, where you'll be jostled and hustled and blinded by the colossal, ever more sexually explicit billboards. Avoid it at all costs on the evening of December 31, when the giant ball drops, ringing in the New Year—pickpockets ply their trade, drunks brawl, and the NYPD tries (without succeeding) to turn the square into a police state. The rest of the year it's the electric, kinetic soul of the city, safe enough during the workday and before curtain time. There are some 35 theaters scattered east and west of Broadway between 42nd and 51st streets, interspersed with grubby fast-food joints and peep shows; the lovely little **Lyceum** on Shubert Alley (which cuts between 44th and 45th streets just west of Times Square) is the oldest. Redevelopment of the

Times Square area has been in the works for ages, but at last it seems as if something's really going to happen. The Walt Disney Company is renovating the old **New Amsterdam Theatre** on the most wretched block of 42nd Street, where in the fall of 1996 it will begin staging blow-out musicals like the hit *Beauty and the Beast*; across the street, a Toronto-based production company plans to turn the ramshackle **Lyric and Academy Theatres** into one 1,850-seat venue, also for splashy musicals, and **Madame Tussaud's** of London has signed onto the 42nd Street renovation project as well. Clearly, by the dawning of the 21st century Times Square will be utterly changed—which is why it's a good idea to see it now while all its hyperbolical honky-tonk is still unabashedly intact.

Park it here... Riverside Park, which runs alongside the Hudson River from W. 76th to 129th streets, and **Prospect Park** in Brooklyn, considered the masterwork of the the 19th-century landscape design team of Frederick Law Olmsted and Calvert Vaux, are two emeralds in the city's treasure trove. But **Central Park** is indisputably the diamond, if only because it's so... well, so *central.* Stretching from 59th to 110th streets, it occupies 840 acres of prime Manhattan real estate, but if the city ever tried to sell it off the populace would revolt. It's crowded as a circus on weekends, when it becomes everybody's backyard. Always in need of renovation or trash collection somewhere, and dangerous in the off-hours, all in all it's dearly beloved. The city bought the marshy, rock-strewn property for the park in 1851; at the time one newspaper reporter called it "a pestilential spot where miasmic odors taint every breath of air." But then Olmsted and Vaux took over, filling the lowlands, extracting boulders, erecting rustic stone bridges and Beaux Arts lampposts, and running four major crosstown arteries (65th, 79th, 86th, and 96th streets) through it—though due to the clever way they've been engineered, the park's integrity remains unspoiled. The designers' goal was to create not a formal greenspace but a rich natural landscape, where urban denizens could briefly forget they lived in a city. The sweeping greenswards of the 22-acre **Sheep Meadow** (north of 65th Street) and the 36-acre **Great Lawn** (midpark between 79th and 86th streets) were seeded, 58 miles of pedestrian paths were laid, and wonderful architectural follies rose, like **Belvedere Castle** overlooking **Turtle Pond** (now housing a children's learning center and U.S. Weather Service Station, just above 79th Street). The Victorian Gothic **Dairy** (midpark at 65th Street) currently serves as the park's information center and rents queens, kings, and pawns for those who want to test their skill in the **Chess House** nearby. Woodland sections like **the Ramble** (lining the northern shores of the **Lake**) and the **Ravine in the North Woods** (midpark around 103rd Street—go here only on weekend days, and never alone), were left intact, and have since become rest stops for flocks of migrating birds. Of course, the park has changed since Olmsted and Vaux's time. In 1880 the **Metropolitan Museum of Art** moved into a site on the east side at 82nd Street. Around 1950 another urban planner put his own imprint on the park—Robert Moses, the city's tireless highway builder, who cut tennis courts, playgrounds, recreation centers, and baseball diamonds into the greenswards. And more recently the Sheep Meadow and Great Lawn have become great open-air stages for the Metropolitan Opera, rock singers like Paul Simon, the New York Philharmonic, and (on those rare occasions when he comes to visit) the Pope. Begin by entering at 59th Street and Fifth Avenue, where paths winding to your left take you along the placid **Pond**, **Wollman Skating Rink**, the Dairy, and a delightful 1903 **Carousel**. Or walk straight into the small though engaging **Central Park Zoo** (there's another entrance at 64th Street and Fifth Avenue), where snow monkeys, polar bears, and red pandas roam in natural settings. Just north of the zoo entrance, an archway leads under the fanciful **Delacorte Clock**; on the hour two monkeys strike a bell, an elephant plays the accordion, goats pipe, penguins drum, and hippos fiddle. South of 72nd Street lies **the Mall**, lined with statues of great men like Robert Burns, Shakespeare, and Christopher Columbus, and great Rollerbladers, who've claimed this as their turf. **Bethesda Terrace**, one of the only formal settings in Central Park, graces the central sector above 72nd Street, with the "Angel of the Waters" fountain, sculpted by Emma Stebbins in 1870; rowboats from the **Loeb Boathouse** (which has a snack bar) ply the waters of the lake below. **Strawberry Fields**, Yoko Ono's garden tribute to John Lennon, is at 72nd Street and Central Park West. On the north side of the Lake, mid-park at 79th Street, the **Delacorte Theatre** presents two Shakespeare plays every summer. Tickets are free, but in great demand—so you must line up at the box office as early as noon on the day of a performance. Runners follow the jogging path around the **Jacqueline Kennedy Onassis Reservoir**, midpark from 87th to 95th streets, with the **Tennis House** northwest of that. Contrary to popular fears, the northern reaches of the park can be navigated safely on weekend afternoons—they hold seldom-visited glories like the **Great Hill** (on the west side at 106th Street), a popular picnic spot; the recently renovated **Harlem Meer**, stocked with fish; and the **Conservatory Garden**, perhaps my favorite place in Central Park. Enter through the Vanderbilt Gate (taken from the Vanderbilt mansion downtown) at 105th Street and Fifth Avenue; stroll along the crabapple allées with overarching bows and shady benches; stop for a moment in the Japanese wisteria pergola, decked with blooms in the spring; gaze at the delightful *Three Maidens* statue in the French Garden; and then find your way to the Secret Garden on the south side, where heliotropes, snapdragons, hollyhocks, phlox, butterflies, and bumblebees run riot on hot summer days.

Way uptown... Harlem is the vast area north of Central Park, stretching from 125th to 168th Street, with **Spanish Harlem** occupying a lower eastern portion from 96th to 125th streets and Fifth Avenue to the East River. Dutch farms and roadside taverns were scattered across it in New York's early years, but in the 1890s it was developed as a semi-suburban getaway for affluent whites. By the 1920s black New Yorkers, driven out of Midtown by high rents, moved up (and all but a very small number of whites bailed out). Harlem blossomed thereafter, with jazz spiraling out of clubs like the **Apollo Theatre** (happily, still open), Small's, and the Cotton Club, where Josephine Baker danced and the floor shows were swank—though, ironically, only white patrons were allowed. Meanwhile, however, poverty spread in Harlem and housing projects rose up; the sixties brought racial protests, crystallized around the mesmerizing figure of Malcolm X. It is a sad fact that most white New Yorkers never venture into Harlem, and can't quite figure out why so many foreign visitors wish to do so. (Most make the trip with an organized tour. I'd suggest **Harlem Your Way Tours Unlimited, Inc.,** or

Harlem Spirituals, Inc.) And in truth, most of Harlem is desperately rough. Change is coming, though, but slowly. Recently Robert DeNiro bought the old Minton Playhouse, with plans to refurbish and reopen it, and the Harlem Chamber of Commerce is at work renovating numerous blocks. From the subway stop at 125th Street and Lenox Avenue (also known as Malcolm X Boulevard), Harlem's main commercial drag, the skyline of downtown Manhattan looks like a mirage. The cultural heart of Harlem is the **Schomburg Center for Research in Black Culture** (a branch of the New York Public Library, at Lenox Avenue and 135th Street), where you can see the collection of Puerto Rican-born Arturo Alfonso Schomburg (1874–1938). Taught in school that blacks had no history, Schomburg spent his life amassing a library that proves the lessons false. Just down the block is the **Liberation Bookstore** (tel 212/281–4615, 421 Malcolm X Blvd.), a friendly, packed little place; west on 135th is the **Harlem YMCA**, where Harry Belafonte and James Baldwin studied. The **Abyssinian Baptist Church**, on 138th Street between Lenox Avenue and Adam Clayton Powell Jr. Boulevard, is where all the Sunday morning tour groups stop to hear gospel voices raised. **Londel's**, around the corner (tel 212/2324–6114, 2620 Frederick Douglas Blvd. [Eighth Avenue]), is a good place to stop for soul food before heading on to **Strivers' Row**, actually two rows of fine houses on 138th and 139th streets between Adam Clayton Powell Jr. Boulevard and Eighth Avenue. These are known as the richest blocks in Harlem. In **Hamilton Terrace**, another high-rent Harlem neighborhood, you'll find **Hamilton Grange**, a yellow frame house that would look at home on Maryland's Eastern Shore. It was briefly the summer home of Alexander Hamilton, first Secretary of the Treasury (he's the guy on the $10 bill). Born in the West Indies, Hamilton is thought to have been part black, which makes it a fitting coincidence that this house should be one of Harlem's crown jewels.

On the waterfront (and on the water)... There's water, water everywhere around Manhattan, though highways and railroad tracks block access to it in many places, alas. A move is under way to encircle the island with a thin ribbon of parks, which will probably be a long time in coming, given the city's tight budget. Until then, folks in the know find ways to take in the waterfront, beginning way up north in **Washington Heights** at the new **Pier and Marina in Inwood**. Situated at the eastern foot of Dyckman Street, it has a snack bar selling fried calamari and shrimp, and at the moment just 12 private boats moored here. But there are fine views up toward **Fort Tryon Park** and the treacherous confluence of the Hudson and Harlem rivers, dubbed **Spuyten Duyvil** by the Dutch. Moving on down the west side, you'll find the salty little houseboat colony at the **79th Street Boat Basin in Riverside Park**. At **The Intrepid–Sea–Air–Space Museum**, occupying a World War II aircraft carrier permanently berthed at the end of W. 46th Street, you can climb a gun turret, board a submarine, and learn about great sea disasters of the past. The *Lusitania* once docked at the foot of W. 23rd Street, which is now home to the **Chelsea Piers Sports and Entertainment Complex**; lining the Hudson River from piers 59 to 62 (see Getting Outside), it's now the embarkation point for **Spirit Cruises**. Down at Christopher Street, West Villagers encroach on rattletrap piers to sunbathe, or Rollerblade, bike, and jog on **Hudson River Park**'s concrete waterfront path (which after nightfall becomes the realm of transvestite hookers). Romantics favor a little pocket of shorefront turf known as **South Cove**, tucked into **Battery Park City**. But the **Circle Line** is uncontestably the best way to take to the water in New York, on three-hour daytime sightseeing cruises. You round the southern tip of the island, sampling nonpareil views of the harbor and Statue of Liberty, cruise past Brooklyn and right under the Brooklyn Bridge, then head up the East River to glimpse the United Nations, cutting to port at the Harlem River, and so back into the Hudson River's broad, deep channel. Amplified commentary is provided, along with plenty of snack food—and, on a bright summer day, possibly a sunburn. Down at **Battery Park**, on the island's southern tip, you'll feel as if you're perched at the prow of a gigantic ship headed out into New York Harbor. Seagulls cry, vendors sell hot dogs, soft drinks, and souvenirs, and benches line the waterfront. From the park's southeast corner, you can catch a ride on the ***Petrel***, a 76-foot yacht with teakwood decks, formerly owned by John F. Kennedy, cruises last about 45 minutes. The **Staten Island Ferry Terminal** sits at the far end of the park (at the foot of Whitehall Street); pay a mere 50 cents and head over the waves to the little community of St. George on Staten Island, passing Governor's Island, Miss Liberty, and the Brooklyn container port. Farther out, you get a sterling view of the Verrazano Narrows Bridge, which connects Staten Island to Brooklyn, near Coney Island. The round-trip takes 50 minutes. **South Street Seaport** is a veritable shrine to matters nautical, situated at the foot of stone-paved Fulton Street, where the old Fulton Ferry landed from 1814 until 1883, when the Brooklyn Bridge opened. The riverside block of Fulton Street, lined with shops, restaurants, and pubs, turns into one giant Wall Street frat party after the financial markets close on Friday night. The visitors center for the South Street Seaport Museum lies halfway down a row of early 19th-century buildings on the south side of Fulton Street—note their handmade brick, stonework details, and imperfect old glass. The museum encompasses five historic seaport blocks of Fulton, Water, Front, and South streets, but above all, a handful of antique ships berthed at Pier 16: the *Peking*, the largest sailing ship ever built; a fishing schooner from 1891; and the *Ambrose*, a lightship built in 1907. **Liberty** and **Pioneer schooner cruises** can be booked here, as well. The Seaport's handsomely restored Pier 17 has more shops and restaurants, concerts on summer nights, and, at the north end, a fine Brooklyn Bridge vantage point, from which you can just make out Brooklyn's **Fulton Ferry Landing**, illuminated by the white Christmas lights of the **River Cafe** (see Dining).

In bloom... At almost any time of year, a trip to the **Brooklyn Botanical Garden** is most highly recommended, but when spring comes, what a blooming wonderland this 50-acre park becomes! The Beaux Arts administration building is lined with lily ponds and beds of tulips. Nearby there's a sweet swelling of the earth called "Daffodil Hill." Down the path, a wooden teahouse sits beside a gemlike pond with a bright red *torii* gate near the far shore; this is the landmark Japanese Garden, a favored backdrop for wedding pictures. Then it's on to the cherry esplanade, which blossoms in late April; the Rose Garden hits its prime in June. Recently renovated greenhouses, a renowned collection of fabulously gnarled bonsai, and a nice little al fresco cafe complete the picture. Five times as large, the **New York Botanical Garden** in the Bronx is easy to reach; it's the first stop on Metro North's Hudson Line. Enter via the Enid A. Haupt Conservatory, a series of graceful domed glass houses built in 1901 to recall the Great Palm House in England's Kew Gardens. A bit of a hike will take you through a hemlock forest, native plant garden, and rhododendron valley—with perhaps a final stop at the Old Lorillard Snuff Mill, built in 1840, where terraces overlook the Bronx River and there's a pleasant tea service. In Midtown, at the **New York Horticultural Society**, much smaller displays of spring blooms, roses, and autumnal chrysanthemums are mounted. And if you have a bit of time on your hands, venture north to **Wave Hill**, a 28-acre 1840s estate in **Riverdale** (an hour by subway from Midtown), with a lawn sloping down toward the Hudson River and carefully planted gardens everywhere. Previous owners of the estate include Teddy Roosevelt, Arturo Toscanini, and Mark Twain; now it's managed by the city, which charges no admission on weekdays.

Getting high... Make your way to the **Empire State Building** on Fifth Avenue at 34th Street, occupying the site of two old Astor family mansions. Call me old-fashioned, but I still prefer this 1,250-foot skyscraper to the much taller **World Trade Towers**. This is, after all, where a big gorilla held in one gargantuan paw a delightfully writhing Faye Raye in the 1933 flick *King Kong*. Get there early, because later on the lines wind all the way around the block. The **World Trade Towers** down in the financial district top the Empire State Building by 100 feet. These plain, black, rectangular twin giants were built between 1966 and 1976, with a wide, windy plaza skirting them. Tourists zip upward via elevator (in 58 ear-popping seconds) to the observation deck on the 107th floor of building number two. Tower one is home to **Windows on the World**, a pricey restaurant, also on the 107th floor (see Dining); drinks and nibbles with a view are available at the **Hors d'Oeuvrerie** next door. I've done my duty now, and told you the city's two prime view spots. But frankly, I prefer someplace where you can sit down civilly, and order a gin and tonic. The **Beekman Tower Hotel** on the East Side, just above the U.N., is my favorite such place, at the not-too-pretentious restaurant/lounge on the 26th floor called the **Top of the Tower**; when the weather is fair, you can sit outside, viewing midtown Manhattan from the starboard side. Others favor the **Rainbow Room** (see Nightlife) on the 65th floor of Rockefeller Center, with a Promenade Bar overlooking Manhattan south, or the **Top of the Sixes** at 666 Fifth Avenue (tel 212/757–6662), where people used to have power lunches, and the view is still powerful. Uptowners sometimes take in the sights from the **Terrace Restaurant** (tel 212/666–9490, 400 W. 119th Street) atop Butler Hall on the Columbia University campus. But if all you really want is cocktails and a smattering of NYC lights, try the rotating bar in the **Marriott Marquis Hotel** (tel 212/398–1900, 1535 Broadway) overlooking Times Square. It's gimmicky, and the service has been known to be despicable, but the view is great at nightime, and unbeatable on New Year's Eve, when you can watch the action on the square without coming too close to the riff-raff.

Art where you least expect it... Not so long ago I took a shortcut through the lobby of the **Equitable Center** at 797 Seventh Avenue, never expecting to encounter two marvelous large-scale murals by Roy Lichtenstein and Thomas Hart Benton; I made myself late for an appointment admiring the latter, a sweeping paean to Jazz Age New York. The lobby is actually one of several outposts of the Whitney Museum (another one occupies the lower level of the **Philip Morris Building** at 120 Park Avenue), but the beauty part is that entrance is free. Stop into the **Church of the Ascension** on Fifth Avenue and 10th Street to take a gander at the elaborate marble altar by Augustus Saint-Gaudens and the vast altarpiece behind it, painted by John La Farge. Up the street lies another surprising free gem, the **Forbes Magazine Galleries**, housing a warren-like exhibition of eccentricities collected by the late publishing magnate Malcolm Forbes—golden panels from the ocean liner *Normandie*, 12,000 toy soldiers struggling against opponents in wonderfully detailed dioramas, delightful model yachts, antique Monopoly gameboards, and 12 glorious Fabergé eggs. And way downtown, beneath the stunning oval rotunda of the **United States Custom House** at One Bowling Green, you'll find Reginald Marsh's cheering rendering of the history of the city, commissioned by the WPA (the Depression-era Work Projects Administration). The beautiful Beaux Arts building, designed by Cass Gilbert in 1907, is more impressive that the museum it houses: the **National Museum of the American Indian** (overseen by the Smithsonian Institution), with rotating exhibits of evocative Native American art, some of it contemporary and some of it from the past. Here, too, admission is free.

Secret gardens... For a moment put aside any notions of picnicking in Central Park, and instead imagine yourself coming upon a green place full of flowers and bees where it ought not to be—for instance, at Houston Street and Second Avenue in the lower East Village. Houston Street is blighted there, and nearby the Bowery begins, known for its boozy bums (these days we call them streetpeople). But in the **Liz Christy Garden** you can sit on a wooden bench amid rose bushes and snapdragons and feel apart from the city, fantasizing yourself in Stratford, England, or York. It's the work of a marvelous group of urban pioneers called the **Green Guerillas**, who make little patches of earth bloom all over town; they also have delightful gardens on **W. 89th Street** between Columbus and Amsterdam avenues and on **W. 48th Street** between Ninth and Tenth avenues. **Hudson River Park**, just north of the World Financial Center, has the unbeatable benefit of fronting directly onto the Hudson River; on weekends people jog or blade down to this park along a concrete path that starts on the riverfront near Christopher Street, where they play volleyball, drink bottled water, then strip down to teeny-weeny bathing suits (at least the gay men do) to soak up a few rays. **City Hall Park** (lower Broadway, at Fulton Street and Park Row) is entirely more demure, frequented by lunching secretaries during the workweek, but almost no one on the weekends. **Clement Clark Moore Park** on W. 22nd Street brightens up Chelsea, and happens to lie just across the street from the **Empire Diner** (see Dining). Up on the West Side, you can take a moment to smell the natural perfume at the **W. 91st Street Flower Garden**, along the esplanade in **Riverside Park**. In springtime, I have often contemplated jumping the wrought-iron fence of the **Sheridan Square Viewing Garden** (on W. 4th Street at Barrow Street); instead I content myself by wending my way back behind the church of **St. Luke's in the Field** (Hudson and Grove streets) to its private garden (behave circumspectly and no one should mind your intrusion).

Summertime brings a rich, peonied hush to this place, and perhaps because St. Luke's is Episcopalian, I always find myself thinking of C.S. Lewis there. The **Vale of Cashmere** in Brooklyn's **Prospect Park** is where I go for rhododendrons, blooming in the late springtime in a deep valley much cherished and manicured by park volunteers. But don't go there at nighttime, since it's a strut for gay hookers—don't they have taste!

The commute... Every day, millions commute in from the environs, and the experience is well worth sampling, though not at rush hour. Besides, you get to begin your excursion at **Grand Central Terminal** (E. 42nd Street and Park Avenue); of course, you could go to Long Island or New Jersey from the concrete barnlike **Pennsylvania Station**, but that place is just no fun. Grand Central, however, is an urban epiphany, with a vast main concourse 275 feet long, 120 feet wide, and 125 feet high; the clock in the center is the city's prime rendezvous point. The facade is part Art Nouveau, part Viennese Secessionist, and an even bigger part Beaux Arts, with the whole colossal hulk of the building lying over a cavernous train shed with 10 unique loop tunnels, sending inbound trains right back out again. (Technically it's not a station but a terminal, at the end of numerous lines.) The terminal, which opened in 1913 and has a "kissing gallery" at its western end for farewell embraces, was described in a 1937 radio broadcast as the "crossroads of a million private lives! Gigantic stage on which are played a thousand dramas daily." Plenty of wraithlike homeless people now live in the tunnels below: don't expect comfortable sitting areas or the sort of perfect renovation one encounters at Washington, D.C.'s Union Station. This is a working terminal, with no time for anything but frantic comings and goings.

Utter childishness... Kids must have a special kind of radar for **F.A.O. Schwarz** (see Shopping); whenever they pass near the renowned toy store (as seen in the movies *Big* and *Home Alone 2*), they've got to go in, entering via a veritable zoo of stuffed animals. There are real zoos in the metropolitan area, too, or rather Wildlife Conservation Centers, as the correct term is these days: the **Central Park Wildlife Center** at the southeast corner of Central Park, and Brooklyn's **Prospect Park Wildlife**

Center, which used to be such a decrepit old place, (I once plotted a mystery novel that began with the finding of a corpse there). It has since been beautifully renovated with children in mind, and just southeast of it there's a vintage carousel that still works, with dashing horses from Coney Island. The **Bronx Zoo** is something of a schlep from Manhattan, though it can be reached via subway. Its 4,000 animals live in naturalistic environments spread over 265 acres—younger kids may find it's too much to walk. But they can ride camels, cruise over 38-acre Wild Asia on a monorail, spy on nocturnal animals in the World of Darkness display, and walk through Jungle World, a tropical rain forest environment. In Central Park, marionettes cavort at the **Swedish Cottage Theatre**, and the **Conservatory Garden** (Fifth Avenue and 105th Street) has a delightful statue of Mary and Dickon (from *The Secret Garden* by Frances Hodgson Burnett) standing over a lily pond. But frankly, it's the long-extinct creatures at the **American Museum of Natural History** that thrill young ones most. This world-famous repository of fossils, minerals, and anthropological material just refurbished its two spectacular dinosaur halls, which hold wonders like a 65-million-year-old T-Rex skeleton. Mechanized skulls of Triceratops and Anatotitan demonstrate how the behemoths chewed, and at computerized video Lifeline Stations kids can time-travel to three ages when the dinosaurs lived, viewing what their home turf looked like. Downstairs in the Teddy Roosevelt Rotunda there's a five-story-high cast of Barosaurus. The Naturemax theater here shows films on a giant IMAX screen, and the attached **Hayden Planetarium** has some great star shows aimed at various age levels, with themes from *Sesame Street* to *Star Trek*. But what I really love here are the extraordinarily detailed dioramas in which stuffed grizzlies and gorillas and gnus pose like flies trapped in amber, their entire ecosystems lovingly recreated. Sure beats studying this stuff in science class.

Must-sees for second-time visitors from Peoria... Sorry to be proscriptive, but there really are a few must-see sights in New York. Foremost of these is the **Brooklyn Bridge**, designed by John Roebling, whose toes were crushed by a ferryboat while he was surveying along the waterfront (he eventually died from tetanus in 1869). The Brooklyn Bridge lies south of the Williamsburg and

Manhattan bridges, closest to the East River's confluence with New York Harbor. A long ramp near City Hall in lower Manhattan provides access to the pedestrian walkway, perhaps the city's finest promenade of all. It will take you less than an hour to cross the bridge, stopping often to take in the exquisite views. When you reach the Brooklyn side, turn right on Cadman Plaza West, and right again on handsome Clark Street to reach the **Brooklyn Heights Promenade**, cantilevered over the Brooklyn-Queens Expressway. Here you can see the great bridge you just traversed, the spires of downtown, and the harbor in all their splendor. At the very heart of midtown Manhattan lies 21-acre **Rockefeller Center**, a virtual city-within-a-city, composed of 18 office buildings, two shopping concourses, Radio City Music Hall, the Channel Gardens, and the glorious Lower Plaza, where skaters glide beneath a brilliant golden statue of Prometheus, and the flags of U.N. member nations fly. The whole sweeping complex was the brainchild of John D. Rockefeller, who built the center during the Great Depression. The Art Deco, 70-story **GE Building**, formerly the home of RCA, fronts on Rockefeller Plaza, which runs between West 48th and 51st streets; this is where the the holiday season begins with the raising and lighting of the city's colossal Christmas tree. Down the block, on Sixth Avenue, marvelously sleek and neon-lit **Radio City Music Hall** celebrates the season on into January with its famous Christmas Spectacular, in which cartoon characters romp and the Rockettes kick high. (You can tour both Radio City and the NBC studios in the GE Building, or stop by the information booth at the east entrance of the GE Building to get Rockefeller Center walking tour brochures.) On Fifth Avenue at 82nd Street lies the magnificent **Metropolitan Museum of Art**, the largest museum in the U.S. and the fourth largest in the world: The little aluminum button that proclaims you paid to enter the Met is a true badge of Manhattan. If there's a snowstorm or a hurricane on the way, you might find this museum empty; otherwise there's always a crowd, even during Friday and Saturday evening hours. The **United Nations Center**, which presides over the East River between 42nd and 49th streets, remains a striking complex, even if the mandate of the U.N. has been rendered ambiguous of late. Tours depart from the north entrance, where there's an excellent gift shop, and a lovely garden wraps around the

U.N., with a half-mile esplanade overlooking the East River. Downtown's premier attraction is the **New York Stock Exchange** on Wall Street between New and Broad streets. George Post designed the building's colonnaded facade in 1903; to the left is a modern addition, where you can enter for an interesting trip to the visitor's gallery above the frenzied trading floor. **Lincoln Center** lies on on a 15-acre site on Columbus Avenue between West 62nd and 65th streets. Opened in 1962, it includes **Avery Fisher Hall**, where the New York Philharmonic performs, the **Metropolitan Opera House**, the **Vivian Beaumont and Mitzi E. Newhouse Theatres**, and the **New York State Theatre**, home to the New York City Ballet and School of American Ballet (see Entertainment). Catching a performance at one of these beauty spots is well-nigh mandatory; even when the major companies are on break, artistic activity never lulls. Even if you don't get a ticket for a performance, stroll through the wide plaza, where there's a cafe and a reflecting pool surrounding a statue by Henry Moore. At dusk, as well-dressed crowds swarm towards brightly lit lobbies, it's magical indeed.

Abyssinian Baptist Church. Everybody's favorite Sunday morning gospel service, up in Harlem.... *Tel 212/862-7474. 132 W. 138th St., 2/3 train to 135th St. Sun service at 11am. Donation suggested.*

Alternative Museum. Avant-garde art in SoHo.... *Tel 212/966-4444. 594 Broadway, E/F train to Prince St., 6 train to Spring St. Open Tues–Sat 11–6. Donation suggested.*

American Museum of Immigration (Statue of Liberty and Ellis Island). Reached by ferries that depart from

Battery Park and Liberty Park in New Jersey.... *Tel 212/363–3200; ferry information 212/269–5755. Open daily 9:30–5 (until 7 in summer), first ferry departs 9:15. Admission charged.*

American Museum of Natural History. The last word in rocks, fish, mammals, birds, and bones—plus knock-out dinos.... *Tel 212/769–5100. Central Park West at 79th St., B/C train to 81st St. Open Sun–Thur 10–5:45, Fri–Sat 10–8:45. Donation suggested.*

American Museum of the Moving Image. An interesting museum all about the movies, located on the site of Paramount Pictures' original New York home.... *Tel 718/784–0077. 36—01 35th Ave., Astoria, Queens, R/G train to Steinway St. Open Tues–Fri 12–5, Sat–Sun 11–6. Admission charged.*

Apollo Theatre. The Harlem Jazz Age landmark, reopened in 1978, with popular amateur nights on Wednesdays.... *Tel 212/749–5838. 253 W. 125th St., 2/3 train to 125th St. Call for schedule. Admission charged.*

Beekman Tower Suite Hotel. Way east in Midtown, with an untouristy rooftop-view bar and restaurant.... *Tel 212/355–7300. 3 Mitchell Pl., 4/5/6/7/S train to Grand Central.*

Bronx Zoo. Largest city zoo in the U.S.... *Tel 718/367–1010. 185th St. and Southern Blvd., 2 train to Pelham Parkway, Metro North to Fordham Rd. (then Bx9 bus), or BxM11 Liberty Line bus (tel 212/652–8400). Open daily 10–5. Admission charged (pay what you wish Wed).*

Brooklyn Botanic Garden. Fifty acres of flora in the heart of Brooklyn.... *Tel 718/622–4433. 100 Washington Ave., D train to Prospect Park. Open Tues–Fri 8–6, Sat–Sun 10–6 (closes at 4:30 Oct–Mar). Admission free.*

Castle Clinton National Monument. A fort, then immigrant processing center, then music hall—but now an historical museum and ticket booth for Statue of Liberty and Ellis Island trips.... *Tel 212/344–7220. Battery Park at Broadway, 1/9 train to South Ferry, N/R to Whitehall St. Open daily 9–5, closed Jan–Feb. Admission free.*

Central Park. 840 green acres in the heart of Manhattan; the visitors center is at the Dairy, midpark at 65th St.... *Tel 212/794–6564. For information on park events and Urban Park Ranger walking tours call 800/201–PARK.*

Central Park Wildlife Conservation Center. Beautiful though small zoo right in Central Park.... *Tel 212/439–6500. 5th Ave. at 64th St., N/R train to 5th Ave. Open Mon–Fri 10–5, Sat–Sun 10:30–5:30. Admission charged.*

Circle Line. Circumnavigations of the island of Manhattan, a city classic.... *Tel 212/563–3200. Pier 83 at W. 42nd St., 1/2/3/9/7/S to Times Square, or A/C/E to Port Authority. Call for schedule. Admission charged.*

The Cloisters. The Metropolitan Museum of Art's Fort Tryon branch, given over to medieval art.... *Tel 212/923–3700. Fort Tryon Park, A train to 190th St. Open Tues–Sun 9:30–4:45 (until 5:15 Mar–Oct). Admission charged.*

Cooper-Hewitt National Design Museum. The decorative arts in Andrew Carnegie's uptown mansion; re-opening September 1996.... *Tel 212/860–6868. 2 E. 91st St., 4/5/6 train to 86th or 96th St. Open Tues 10–9, Wed–Sat 10–5, Sun 12–5. Admission charged.*

Dia Center for the Arts. Contemporary art studio/museum in new West Chelsea digs.... *Tel 212/989–5912. 548 W. 22nd St., A/C/E train to 23rd St. Open Thur–Sun 12–6, closed July–Aug. Donation suggested.*

Ellis Island. See **American Museum of Immigration**, above.

El Museo del Barrio. Hispanic art, with a Puerto Rican emphasis.... *Tel 212/831–7272. 1230 5th Ave., 6 train to 103rd St. Open Wed–Sun 11–5. Donation suggested.*

Empire State Building. Glassed-in observation deck on the 102nd floor, open-air on the 86th.... *Tel 212/736–3100. 5th Ave. and 34th St., 4/5/6 train to 33rd St. or B/D/F/N/R/Q to 34th St. Open daily 9:30–midnight. Admission charged.*

Forbes Magazine Galleries. Toy soldiers, model yachts, Monopoly gameboards, and other intriguing collectibles....

Tel 212/206–5549. 62 5th Ave., 4/5/6/N/R train to Union Square. Open Tues–Sat 10–4. Admission free.

Frick Collection. A turn-of-the-century palace on Fifth Avenue containing gems by the likes of Gainsborough, Turner, Titian, and Whistler.... *Tel 212/288–0700. 1 E. 70th St., 6 train to 68th St. Open Tues–Sat 10–6, Sun 1–6. Admission charged.*

Solomon R. Guggenheim Museum. Frank Lloyd Wright's ziggurat, marvelous special exhibits, and lots of contemporary old favorites.... *Tel 212/423–3500. 1071 5th Ave., 4/5/6 train to 86th St. Open 10–6 (until 8 Fri and Sat), closed Thur. Admission charged (pay what you wish on Fri).*

Guggenheim Museum SoHo. Downtown outpost of famed Museum Mile star, with a rotating exhibit schedule.... *Tel 212/423–3500. 575 Broadway, N/R train to Prince St. Open 11–6 (until 8 on Sat), closed Mon–Tues. Admission charged.*

Hamilton Grange National Memorial. A fine yellow clapboard house once occupied by Alexander Hamilton, in the distinguished Hamilton Terrace neighborhood of Harlem.... *Tel 212/283–5154. 287 Convent Ave., A/C/D train to 145th St. Open Wed–Sun 9–5. Admission free.*

Harlem Spirituals, Inc. Gospel, jazz, soul food, and sightseeing tours up in Harlem.... *Tel 212/757–0425. 1697 Broadway, Suite 203, 1/9 train to Columbus Circle. Call for schedule. Admission charged.*

Harlem Your Way! Tours Unlimited. Walking tours of Harlem, meeting at a turn-of-the-century rowhouse.... *Tel 212/690–1687. 129 W. 130th St., 2/3 train to 125th St. Call for schedule. Admission charged.*

Heritage Trails of New York. Walking tour brochures of lower Manhattan, available at the visitors information center at Federal Hall National Memorial.... *Tel 212/767–0637. 26 Wall St., 2/3/4/5 train to Wall St. Open weekdays 9–5. Admission free.*

International Center of Photography. Rotating photographic exhibits and an interesting permanent collection.... *Tel 212/860–1777. 1130 5th Ave., 4/5/6 train to 96th St.*

Midtown branch: *Tel 212/768–4680, 1133 6th Ave., 1/2/3/7/9/N/R to Times Square. Open 11–6 (until 8 Tues), closed Mon. Admission charged.*

Intrepid Sea–Air–Space Museum. A great World War II aircraft carrier displays its gun turrets, batteries, hangers, and fighter bombers.... *Tel 212/245–2533. Pier 86, W. 46th St. at 12th Ave., A/C/E train to 42nd St. Open Wed–Sun 10–5. Admission charged.*

Jewish Museum. Jewish history, religion, culture, and art in a Gothic-French chateau on Museum Mile.... *Tel 212/423–3200. 1109 5th Ave., 4/5/6 train to 96th St. Open 11–5:45 (until 8 Tues), closed Fri–Sat. Admission charged.*

Lower East Side Tenement Museum. An immigrant walk-up displaying life as poor, ethnic New York lived it at the turn of the century.... *Tel 212/431–0233. 90 Orchard St., F train to Delancey St., J/M to Essex St. Open Tues–Fri 11–4, Sun 12–5. Donation suggested.*

Metropolitan Museum of Art. The big house, in terms of NYC art.... *Tel 212/535–7710. 5th Ave. at 82nd St., 4/5/6 train to 86th St. Open 9:30–5:15 (until 8:45 Fri–Sat), closed Mon. Admission charged.*

Museum of Modern Art. The world gone abstract, in masterworks; nice Garden Cafe and lobby bookstore; exquisite Sculpture Garden.... *Tel 212/708–9480. 11 W. 53rd St., E/F train to 5th Ave. Open Sat–Tues 11–6, Thur–Fri 12–8:30. Admission charged.*

Museum of Television and Radio. Displays and thousands of vintage shows on tape.... *Tel 212/621–6600. 25 W. 52nd St., E/F train to 5th Ave. Open 12–6 (until 8 Thur), closed Mon. Admission charged.*

Museum of the City of New York. Famed NYC interiors, vintage firefighting equipment, toys, theatrical memorabilia, and more.... *Tel 212/534–1672. 5th Ave. at 103rd St., 6 train to 103rd St. Open Wed–Sat 10–5, Sun 1–5. Admission charged.*

National Museum of the American Indian. Rotating displays of Native American art; Old Custom House setting, with

Reginald Marsh murals in the dome.... *Tel 212/668–6624. One Bowling Green, 5 train to Bowling Green. Open 10–5. Admission free.*

New Museum of Contemporary Art. Videos, installations, and exhibitions of artists at work now in the city.... *Tel 212/219–1355. 583 Prince St., E/F train to Prince St., 6 to Spring St. Open 12–6 (until 8 Sat), closed Mon–Tues. Admission charged.*

New York Aquarium. Whales, electric eels, hogfish, zebra fish, piranha, and much activity among the sea lions at feeding time.... *Tel 718/265–FISH. W. 8th St. and Surf Ave., Brooklyn, D train to W. 8th St./Coney Island. Open 10–5 (until 7 in summer). Admission charged.*

New York Botanical Garden. 250-acre botanical park and renowned horticultural research center.... *Tel 718/817–8705. 100th St. and Southern Blvd, the Bronx, Metro North from Grand Central to Botanical Gardens station. Open 8–6 (until 7 Apr–Oct), closed Mon. Admission free.*

New York Horticultural Society. Small floral displays, classes, garden tours.... *Tel 212/757–0915. 128 W. 58th St., E/F train to 5th Ave. Open Mon–Fri 10–6. Admission charged.*

New York Public Library. The great research library on Fifth Avenue, where you read "between the lions".... *Tel 212/340–0849. 5th Ave. at 41st St, B/D/F/7 train to 42nd St. Open Mon and Thur–Sat 10–6, Tues–Wed 11–7:30. Admission free.*

New York Stock Exchange Center. Down on Wall Street, of course, with displays explaining how the market works, how to read a stock table, etc. Plus an Exchange viewing gallery.... *Tel 212/656–5168. 20 Broad St., 2/3 train to Wall St. Open Mon–Fri 9:15–3:30. Admission free.*

Nuyorican Poets Cafe. East Village poetry haunt.... *Tel 212/505–8183. 236 E. 3rd St., F train to 2nd Ave. Call for changing schedule. Admission charged.*

Petrel. A sleek 1938 racing yacht sailed by John F. Kennedy, offering daytime and sunset cruises.... *Tel 212/825–1976.*

Battery Park, R train to Battery Park, 4/5/6 to Bowling Green, 1 to South Ferry. Mid-May–mid-Oct. Admission charged.

Poets House. A poetry library in SoHo.... *Tel 212/431–7920. 72 Spring St., N/R train to Prince St., 6 to Spring St. Open Tues–Fri 11–7, Sat 11–4, closed Sun–Mon. Admission free.*

Prospect Park. Olmsted and Vaux's big Brooklyn park, and a real beauty.... *Tel 718/788–0055. Bounded by Eastern Parkway, Flatbush Ave., Parkside Ave., and Prospect Park West; 2/3/4 train to Grand Army Plaza, F to 15th St./Prospect Park, D/Q to Prospect Park.*

Prospect Park Wildlife Center. A children's zoo grows in Brooklyn.... *Tel 718/965–6560. Prospect Park Willink Entrance (off Flatbush Ave.), B/D/Q train to Prospect Park. Open 10–4:30. Admission charged.*

Radio City Music Hall. 6,000 seats, gorgeous Art Deco flourishes, and the Rockettes. Tours available.... *Tel 212/632–4041. 6th Ave. at 50th St., B/D/F train to Rockefeller Center. Call for schedule. Admission charged.*

Russian and Turkish Baths. An old-fashioned hothouse, where you can drink borscht, take wet or dry heat, and chill in a Swedish shower. Swimming suits required, communal setting.... *Tel 212/674–9250. 268 E. 10th St., 6 train to Astor Pl. Open 9–5 (Tues, Fri, and Sat coed; Thur and Sun men only, Wed women only). Admission charged.*

Schomburg Center for Research in Black Culture. Programs, exhibitions, and library facilities for scholars—all on black history and culture.... *Tel 212/491–2265. 515 Malcolm X Blvd. (Lenox Ave.), 2/3 train to 135th St. Open Mon–Wed 12–8, Thur–Sat 10–6, Sun 1–5. Admission free.*

Seaport Liberty Cruises. Jaunts into New York Harbor, embarking from the Seaport.... *Tel 212/630–8888. Pier 16 Ticket Booth, South St. Seaport, 2/3/4/5 train to Fulton St. Call for schedule. Admission charged.*

South Street Seaport. Historic ships to tour, antique buildings to stroll by, cobblestones beneath your feet.... *Tel 212/669–9424. 12 Fulton St., 2/3/4/5 train to Fulton St. Open 10–5. Admission charged.*

Spirit Cruises. Lunch, brunch, cocktail, dinner, and moonlight cruises around the island; somewhat more intimate than the Circle Line.... *Tel 212/727–7768. Pier 62 in Chelsea, A/C/E train to W. 23rd St. Call for schedule. Admission charged.*

St. Marks Church-in-the-Bowery. Historic East Village church with a long-running poetry program.... *Tel 212/674–0910. 131 E. 10th St., 6 train to Astor Pl. Admission charged to poetry readings.*

Statue of Liberty. See **American Museum of Immigration**, above.

Swedish Cottage Theatre. Marionette theater in Central Park.... *Tel 212/988–9093. Mid-park at 81st St., B/C train to 81st St. Performances Tues–Fri 10:30 or noon, Sat noon or 3pm, reservations required. Admission charged.*

United Nations Center. Le Corbusier's Secretariat and General Assembly buildings, overlooking the East River. Tours available.... *Tel 212/963–7539. 1st Ave. between 42nd and 48th Sts., 4/5/6/7/S train to Grand Central. Open 9:15–4:45. Admission charged for tours.*

U.S. Customs House. See **National Museum of the American Indian**, above.

Wave Hill. Manor house and gardens overlooking the Hudson River in the Bronx.... *Tel 718/549–3200. W. 248th St. and Independence Ave., Metro North to Riverdale. Open Tues–Sun 10–4:30. Admission charged weekends only.*

Whitney Museum of American Art. Contemporary American specialist.... *Tel 212/570–3600. 945 Madison Ave., 6 train to 77th St. Open Wed, Fri–Sun 11–6, Thur 1–8. Admission charged.*

World Trade Center. Observations of New York from the 107th floor deck of building number two.... *Tel 212/435–4170. W. Church, Vesey, and Liberty Sts.; 1/9 train to Cortlandt St. Open 9am–9:30pm. Admission charged.*

Uptown Diversions

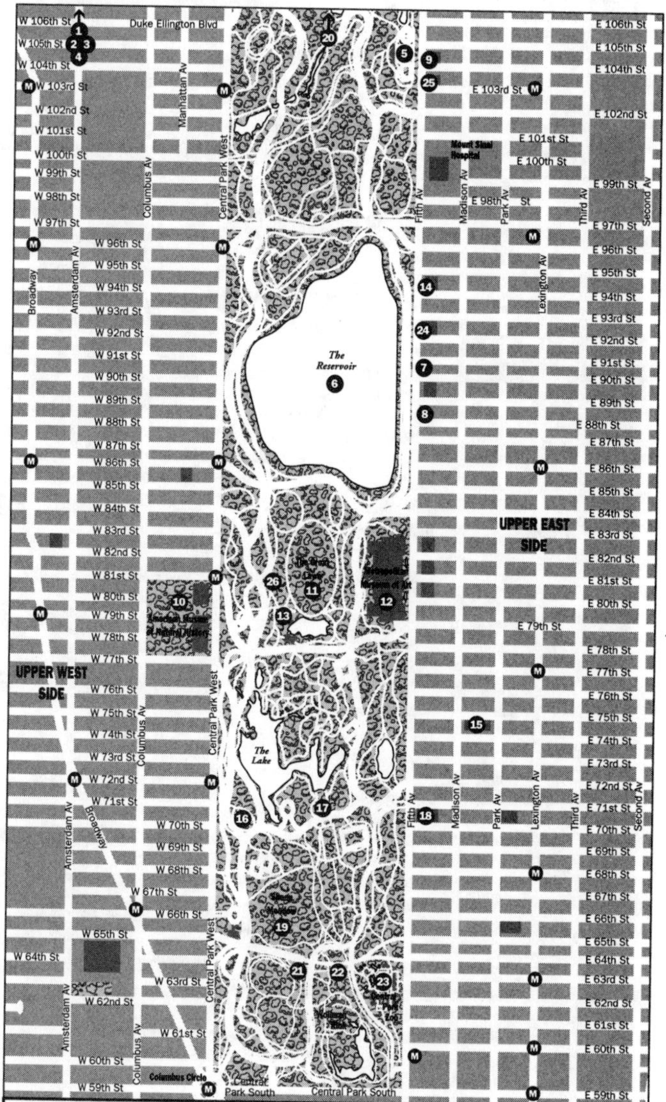

Abyssinian Baptist Church **1**
American Museum of Natural History **10**
Apollo Theatre **3**
Central Park
- Bethesda Terrace **17**
- Carousel **21**
- Conservatory Gardens **5**
- Dairy **22**
- Delacorte Theatre **13**
- Great Lawn **11**
- Jackie O. Reservoir **6**
- Sheep Meadow **19**
- Strawberry Fields **16**
- Swedish Cottage **26**
- Zoo **23**

The Cloisters **4**
Cooper/Hewitt National Design Museum **7**
El Museo del Barrio **9**
Frick Collection **18**
Guggenheim Museum **8**
Hamilton Grange National Monument **2**
International Center of Photography **14**
Metropolitan Museum of Art **12**
Museum of the City of New York **25**
Schomberg Center **20**
Whitney Museum of American Art **15**

Midtown Diversions

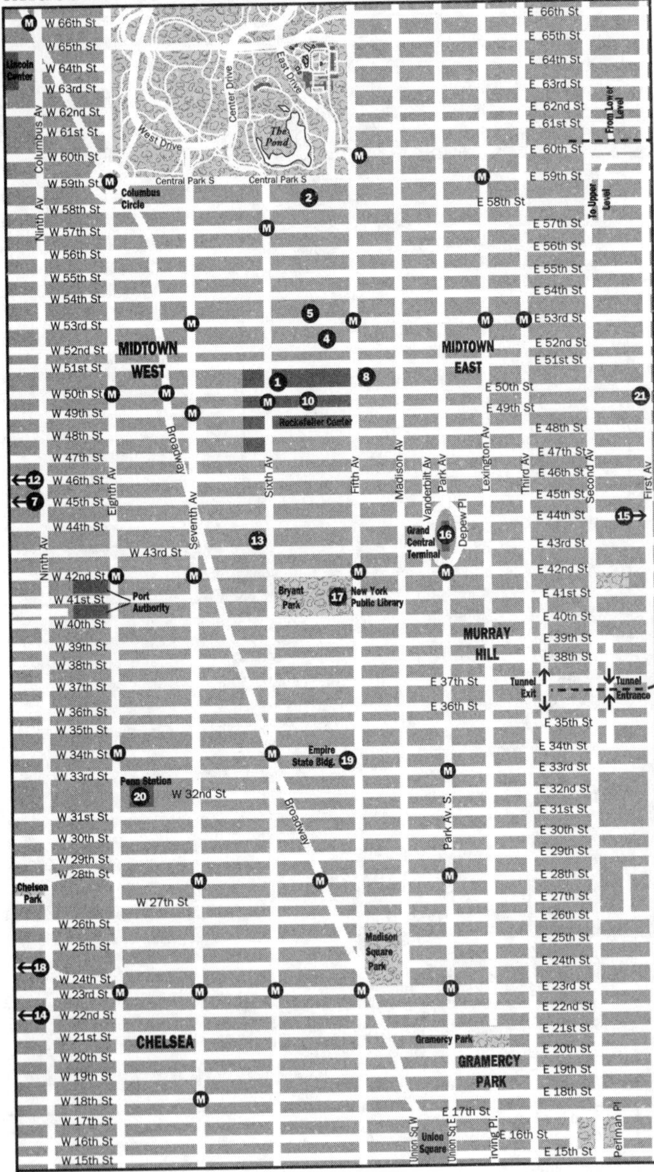

Beekman Tower Suite Hotel **21**
Circle Line **7**
Dia Center for the Arts **14**
Empire State Building **19**
Grand Central Station **16**
International Center of Photography **13**
Intrepid Sea-Air-Space Museum **12**
MoMA **5**
Museum of Television & Radio **4**
New York Horticultural Society **2**
New York Public Library **17**
Pennsylvania Station **20**
Radio City Music Hall **1**
Rockefeller Center **10**
St. Patrick's Cathedral **8**
Spirit Cruises **18**
United Nations **15**

Downtown Diversions

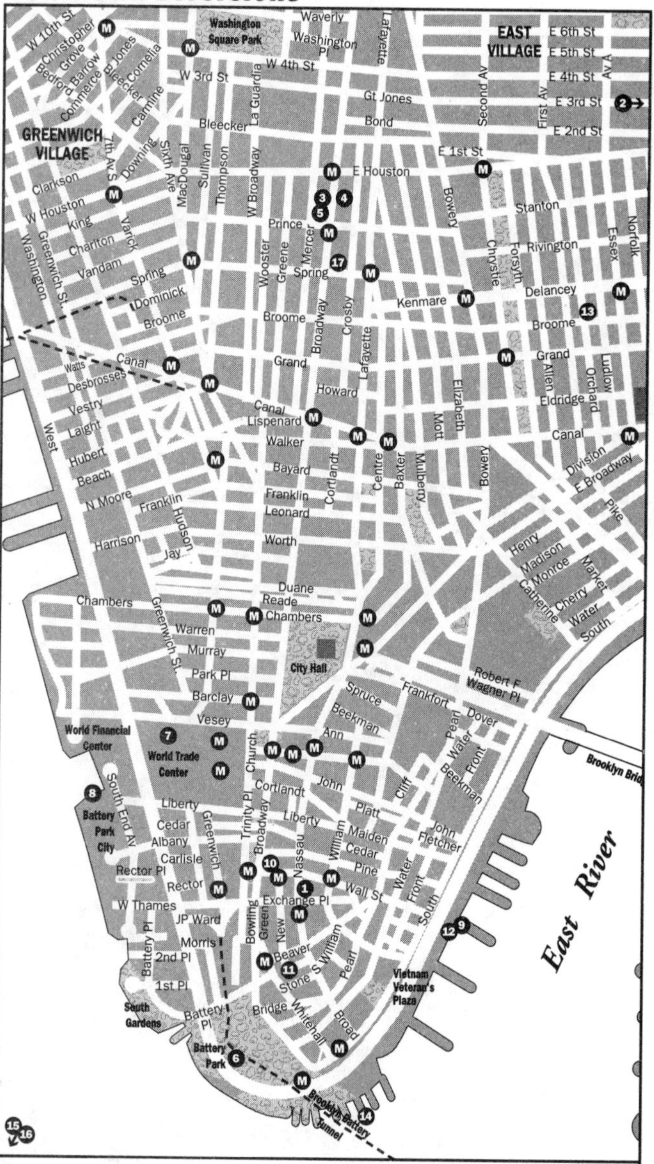

- Alternative Museum **4**
- Castle Clinton National Monument **6**
- Ellis Island **15**
- The Guggenheim Museum SoHo **5**
- Lower East Side Tenement Museum **13**
- National Museum of the American Indian **11**
- New Museum of Contemporary Art **3**
- New York Stock Exchange Center **1**
- Nuyorican Poets Cafe **2**
- Petrel **8**
- Poets House **17**
- South Street Seaport **9**
- Staten Island Ferry Terminal **14**
- Statue of Liberty **16**
- Trinity Church **10**
- World Trade Center **7**

getting

4

outside

Despite rumors that Americans are returning to their La-Z-Boy recliners in legion numbers, that's one trend New

Yorkers aren't buying. Workaholics chained to their desks for 10–hour days strive to keep in shape whenever they can grab an hour to run on busy streets or ply the Stairmasters in sleek health clubs, watching MTV on monitors above. The exercise obsession is further fueled by the need to stay beautiful and young forever in this very vain city, not to mention the desperate hope of meeting a cute, trim mate at the Nautilus machine. The city boasts parks aplenty for pick-up softball games, running, cycling, and blading (all pursued with hyper-intensity, of course). Chief among them is Central Park, of course, but long skinny Riverside Park on the West Side and Prospect Park in Brooklyn are also top sports spots.

The Lowdown

Born to run... The extraordinary popularity of the New York City Marathon every November is a testament to New Yorkers' penchant for running, which they pursue in heavy traffic, in fair or foul weather, on hard, uneven surfaces, and despite never-ending streetside diversions. Serious runners join the **New York Road Runner's Club** (tel 212/860–4455), which sponsors a Central Park Safety Patrol, a year-long schedule of races, and clinics in all five boroughs (including marathon prep and a New Year's Eve run), and more loosely organized Central Park runs twice a night, at 6:30 and 7:15pm, and at 10am on weekends (meet at club headquarters, 9 E. 89th Street, a block from the 90th Street entrance to Central Park and to the newly renamed Jacqueline Kennedy Onassis Reservoir). You see runners puffing their way around just about every park in the city, from the Battery to Washington Square to Carl Schurz on the Upper East Side. But without a doubt, the best place to run in Manhattan is **Central Park**, where you can chalk up distances; the Outer Loop of the park's circular drive is 7.02 miles, the Middle Loop 4.04 miles (enter the park at 72nd Street and follow the drive around the south end of the park), and the soft-surface path around the Reservoir, 1.57 miles. Safety can be an issue here; unaccompanied women should run only at peak times and stay on the path, at least on the northern stretches. **Riverside Park** lines the Hudson River for 4 miles beginning at West 72nd Street, providing knock-out views for runners;

there's also a quarter-mile, open-air track near the 72nd Street entrance. A jogging path along the **East River** can be caught near Sutton Place and followed all the way to the mayor's digs at Gracie Mansion. Out in Brooklyn's **Prospect Park** (take the 2 or 3 subway train to Grand Army Plaza), a gem of a landscape designed by the same 19th-century team who laid out Central Park, the big interior circuit passes shady woods and a colony of swans on the Lullwater, running approximately 3.5 miles in all. The New York dream of creating a narrow belt of parkland all around Manhattan is far from being realized, but a start has been made between **Hudson River Park** and the fenced-off piers at the foot of Christopher Street in the West Village; there's little green, but a 2-mile running/skating/biking path assumes the air of a carnival on sunny afternoons.

A bicycle built for one... Bikes can be rented for cruises through Central Park at the **Loeb Boathouse** (near W. 74th St., tel 212/517–2233), but you'll get equipment in better condition from **Metro Bicycles** (midtown shop at 360 W. 47th St., tel 212/581-4500, and five other locations around town). Wear a helmet, ride on the right with traffic, clearly claim space in a lane as opposed to riding on the side of the street where you can get hammered by opening car doors—and as a favor to me, watch out for pedestrians. Most of the running paths mentioned above, with the exception of the reservoir in Central Park, are fine for reasonably carefree biking. But for some wild and woolly urban treks, try the **Lafayette Street bike lane**, which runs north only from Houston Street to 14th Street at Union Square; cross the East River on the **Brooklyn Bridge bike lane**, a steep but scenic 1-miler; catch the bike lane just north of South Street Seaport that leads through parking lots **under the FDR Drive** and some monster puddles; or take the aerial tramway at E. 60th Street to Roosevelt Island and then bike through **Lighthouse Park**, watching for speed bumps as you go. If you've got several hours, take a tour to the outer boroughs—or at least Brooklyn—cruising along the city's oldest dedicated bicycle path, which accompanies **Ocean Parkway** from Prospect Park's Church Avenue entrance all the way to Coney Island; study the shifting demographics of this once-grand boulevard as you pedal along.

It's okay to take bicycles on the subway, but if you're headed farther afield you'll need to get a pass for trips on the Long Island, New Jersey Transit, and Metro North railroads. The **New York City Cycle Club** (tel 212/886–4545) sponsors group rides and training clinics, while the **Century Road Club Association** (tel 212/222–8062) is particularly keen on racing.

Pounding the pavement... **Fifth Avenue** and **Broadway** are virtual yellow brick roads, fine especially on Sundays for hikes all the way from the south end of Central Park to the Battery (I've done this walk in a little over two hours—the great thing about walking in New York is that there's so much to see en route, you forget how far you've tramped). **Upper Broadway** takes you right through the fascinating heart of the Upper West Side, and there's nothing prettier than a springtime ramble up the East Side's **Park Avenue**, when banks of flowers bloom in the neatly planted median strip and you can peer under canopies into the lobbies of luxury co-ops. **Riverside Park** has some wonderful riverview promenades, both in the park and along shady **Riverside Drive**. If you want to be led by the hand, not to mention edified by a trivia-nut tour guide (these folks could score big on "Jeopardy!"), check out the walking tours offered by the **92nd Street YMHA** (1395 Lexington Ave., tel 212/996–1100), which include such pleasures as Staten Island ferryboat rides, picnic hikes along the Old Croton Aqueduct Trailway, and brunch tours of Battery Park City. The **Urban Park Rangers** (tel 212/427–4040) know the city's parks like the backs of their hands, and take groups for jaunts absolutely free of charge. The **New York Audubon Society** (tel 212/691–7483) specializes in pointing out our feathered friends in Central Park's Ramble, and the **Central Park Bicycle Tour** (tel 212/541–8759) includes bike rental in the cost of a two–hour escorted cruise around the park.

A walk in the woods... It's hard to believe that green wilderness exists anyplace near Manhattan, but it's there to rejuvenate walkers whenever the concrete canyons of the city threaten to close in. Bring a pair of binoculars so you can watch the birds while trailblazing in Central Park's prime patch of forest, the **Ramble**, where the

Urban Park Rangers (tel 212/427–4040) lead nature walks on Sundays at 9am and 2pm, and the **Audubon Society** (tel 212/691–7483) organizes early-morning birdwatches in the spring and fall (believe it or not, Manhattan's located on a major North American migration flyway, and birders here make some spectacular sightings). If birding's your passion, take the upper promenade in **Riverside Park** between W. 114th and W. 120th streets for more bird sightings in the densely wooded sanctuary below. Nature and solitude await along the **Kazimiroff Nature Trail** at Pelham Bay Park (in the Bronx, accessible from the Hutchinson River Pkwy., tel 718/ 548–7070), or in the 14.5-square-mile birder's paradise of **Jamaica Bay Wildlife Preserve** in Queens (Exit 17, Belt Pkwy. or A train to Broad Channel, tel 718/ 474–0613).

Tour Time

"New Jersey is on the other side of the Hudson River." If this information is new to you, you might benefit from a stint aboard the bright red double-decker buses run by ***New York Apple Tour*** *(tel 800/876–9868). They stop at major sights every fifteen minutes, letting visitors disembark, look around, and then climb back on the next Apple bus that comes along. New York Apple tours offer three itineraries: Uptown and Harlem, downtown, or full–city, all conducted in Spanish, Japanese, German, English, Italian, and French.* ***Gray Line*** *(tel 212/ 397–2600) runs similar double–decker city tours; these two are the La-Z-Boy Recliners among NYC tours. You'll see and learn a lot more if you're willing to get off your duff and walk.* ***Citywalks*** *(tel 212/989–2456) offers weekend walking tours of historic districts like Greenwich Village, Chinatown, Soho, and Little Italy; call for a schedule. The* ***Municipal Art Society*** *(tel 212/439–1049) leads some fascinating tours, too, including one of Grand Central Station every Wednesday at 12:30, meeting at the east end of the main concourse (admission is free, but a hat is passed afterwards).*

Water, water everywhere... Watching the city glide by from the deck of a sightseeing tour boat (see Diversions) is a great way to feel the sun on your face and the breeze ripple through your hair. But for a more interactive experience, rent a rowboat from Central Park's **Loeb Boathouse** (near W. 74th St., tel 212/517–2233, spring through fall) or a pedalboat to churn across the Lullwater in Brooklyn's

Prospect Park from **Pelican Boat Rentals** (near Wollman Skating Rink, tel 718/287–9824). Liliputian-style boating takes over the **Conservatory Water** in Central Park (also called the Boat Pond, east side of the park near W. 74th St.) on weekends, when enthusiasts with transistor-operated model boats (some so fancy that they cost upwards of $3,000) hold their own regattas. You can launch a paper boat if you want, but remember: If you're racing, international yachting rules are staunchly upheld. The 20-boat **Sheepshead Bay fishing fleet** in Brooklyn takes old salts out sightseeing or fishing for flounder, fluke, and snapper in New York Harbor; half-day trips start at the Sheepshead Bay piers (D train to Sheepshead Bay) beginning at 8am, 10am, and 1pm; full-day trips leave at 6 and 7am, and nighttime excursions at 7pm; just show up at the dock (no reservations required). You can rent or bring your own bait and rods. City Island, which hugs the east coast of the Bronx, is the fishing and sailing capital of New York; it's just a mile and a half long, but about as close to Nantucket as you can get without leaving the five boroughs. If you have a car, you can reach it via the City Island drawbridge from Pelham Bay Park. Once there, you can watch a regatta or learn to sail at **Land's End Sailing School** (660 Minneford Ave., tel 718/885–2424), fish for porgies and flounder on the ***Apache*** (591 City Island Ave., tel 718/885–0843), rent a motorboat at **The Boat Livery** (663 City Island Ave., tel 718/885–1843), or become a certified scuba diver at **Capt. Mike's Diving Services** (634 City Island Ave., tel 718/885–1588).

The pick-up game... Central Park's well-worn 55-acre Great Lawn (mid-park from 81st to 85th streets) used to be the place to find yourself a pick-up game of softball or frisbee, but it's closed for renovation until 1997. And the big park's carefully maintained Heckscher Ballfields (near W. 64th St.) are often given over to established amateur leagues, who generally don't welcome ringers but can be fun to watch. (Between the Broadway show leagues, ad agency leagues, and publishing leagues, you may catch some semi-celebrities at play.) You should be able to find a game of softball at **Riverside Park**'s play area, which runs from West 101st to 111th streets, or in **Central Park**, mid-park at 98th Street. Basketball pros like Julius Erving and Chris Mullen started out in the wild, fast games played at the **W. 4th Street cages** (West 4th St. and Sixth Ave.). The **North Meadow Recreation Center** in Central Park (just above W. 97th St.) sees plenty of basketball action. And down at Piers 59-62, **The Chelsea Piers Sports and Entertainment Complex** (tel 212/336–6000, one-day membership $25) has basketball and volleyball courts (the latter with sand flooring). For further information on where to find softball, basketball, hockey, soccer, and volleyball pick-up games, keep your eyes open for a copy of the freebie newspaper ***Sports City***, distributed in health clubs and sports equipment stores around town.

Skating—straight up or on the rocks... Skating at the diamond-like rink at **Rockefeller Center** (E. 50th St. at Fifth Ave., lower plaza, tel 212/757–5730, open in winter) or Central Park's **Wollman Memorial Rink** (near W. 64th St., tel 212/517–4800, open winter) is like stepping into a picture postcard of New York, especially when the snow flies; there are always a few hot-doggers slicing patterns in the ice, but even if you forgot your fur muff and little pink skirt, you can stash your bags in a locker, rent skates, and give it a whirl. At the extreme uptown end of Central Park there's a more neighborhoody place to hit the ice, **Lasker Rink** (near W. 110th St. and the Harlem Meer, tel 212/534–7639, winter). **Sky Rink**, another element of the Chelsea Piers scene (tel 212/336–6100), is roomier and less show-offy, not to mention indoors and open year-round; lockers, equipment rental, skating instruction, and open ice-hockey frays are offered, too. But enough about ice skating (it's what Tonya Harding does, after all); let's talk about in-line skating, the sport of the moment in New York—you see Rollerbladers with briefcases stroking their way to Wall Street, sparks flying from grind plates everywhere, and if you still aren't convinced, in-line skating machines at the trendiest New York clubs. During the warm months, Central Park's **Wollman Rink** (see above) goes in-line, but the hot places to Rollerblade are the **Dead Road** in Central Park (mid-park from 66th to 69th streets, no boom boxes please), Central Park's **slalom course** (weekends, on the circular drive across from Tavern on the Green), alongside the dilapidated piers in the **West Village**, the 2.5-acre in-line center at **Chelsea Piers**, and the big loop in

Brooklyn's **Prospect Park**, for racers. Make sure to wear safety gear; it's a cool look, anyway. In-lines can be rented at **Blades East** (160 E. 86th St., tel 212/996–1644), **Blades West** (120 W. 72nd St., tel 212/787–3911), **Alex Sports** (128 Chambers St., tel 212/964–1944), and **Third Street Skate** (207 Seventh Ave. in Brooklyn, tel 718/768–9500). For skating instruction and two indoor rinks, try the **Chelsea Piers Roller Rinks** (at Pier 61, tel 212/336–6200); for roller hockey, head up to **Stanley M. Isaacs Park** (FDR Drive from 95th to 97th streets), where there's a brand-new roller rink.

Seesaws and sandboxes... Taking your children to a playground is a way to survey the more settled aspects of the New York City scene; go with a cup of java and the paper, then install yourself on a bench. Eavesdrop on discussions of whether Heather should go to the Dalton School or Brearley, scope out the different nannying styles of the various Jamaican, Guyanese, and Irish babysitters, and on weekends watch dads try hard to stand in as primary care-givers. The playgrounds at **Union Square Park** (E. 16th St. and Broadway), **Bleecker and Hudson streets, Washington Square Park** (W. 4th and MacDougal streets), **Pierrepont Park** in Brooklyn Heights (Furman St. and Columbia Heights), **Riverside Park** (at W. 91st St.—the "hippo park," nicknamed after its statues that kids clamber over—or the "dino park" at W. 97th St.), **Sutton Place** (E. 53rd St. and the FDR Drive), and at East 67th, West 85th, and East 96th streets in **Central Park** are top-of-the-line.

Courting... To swing a tennis racquet with the city skyline on the horizon, head to the **Central Park Tennis House** (mid-park, near W. 93rd St., tel 212/280–0205) where 26 courts are sprucely maintained thanks to a recent $1 million endowment from a private citizen. You must have a season permit to reserve a court, but if you stop by the tennis house in person, for $5 per person you can get a single-play ticket for an hour on any unreserved court. Weathered-faced tennis junkies of a certain age hang out there waiting for a free court, sometimes bringing a folding table to play bridge or pinochle while sitting on the park benches courtside—it's a scene. **Riverside Park** also has a set of clay courts near West 96th Street, which neighborhood volunteers maintain now that park budgets have been slashed; play is on a first-come-first-served basis. Tennis players can use the courts at a few indoor private clubs like **Crosstown Tennis** (114 W. 31st St., tel 212/947–5780), **The Tennis Club** (15 Vanderbilt Ave., over Grand Central Station, tel 212/687–3841), **Sutton East** (488 E. 60th St., tel 212/751–3452), and **Club La Racquette** (119 W. 56th St., tel 212/245–1144); call for fees and times. But this is New York, after all—do you think New Yorkers would be content with just a white-bread sport like tennis? No way. There are 12 handball courts in **Riverside Park** (at the W. 111th St. play area), and many more in **St. Vartan's Park** (35th St. between 1st and 2nd aves.); bocce courts at **DeWitt Clinton Park** (52nd St. between 11th and 12th aves.) and **Robert Moses Playground** (1st Ave. between 41st and 42nd sts.); regulation croquet/lawn bowling facilities in **Central Park** (west side near 69th St., tel 212/360–8133); and horseshoe pitching at **Battery Park** (State and South sts.) and **J.J. Murphy Park** (E. 17th St. and Avenue C).

Swimming holes in the concrete jungle... Among city pools, probably the best are the **Carmine Street Pool** (tel 212/242–5228, 7th Ave. S. and Clarkson St.) and the pool in **John Jay Park** (tel 212/794–6566, E. 77th St. and Cherokee Place), though they're crowded all summer long. A few hotels have swimming pools: the **Days Inn Hotel** (Eighth Ave. and W. 48th St., tel 212/581–7000), **Le Parker Meridien** (118 W. 57th St., tel 212/245–5000), **The Peninsula** (700 Fifth Ave., tel 212/247–2200), **Vista International** (3 World Trade Center, tel 212/938–9100), and the **U.N. Plaza** (1 United Nations Plaza, tel 212/355–3400). The centrally located **Vanderbilt YMCA** (224 E. 47th St., tel 212/756–9600) allows walk-ins as well as Vanderbilt YMCA Hotel guests (see Accommodations) to use the clean, though highly chlorinated, pool for $15 a day. A big indoor pool with a sundeck will be part of **The Sports Center** at Chelsea Piers (at Pier 60, tel 212/336–6000), which will allow day-use guests. What is more, a number of health clubs in the city have indoor and outdoor pools, like the **Atrium Club** (115 E. 57th St., tel 212/826–9640), **Manhattan Plaza** (482 W. 43rd St., tel 212/563–7001), **Printing House** (421 Hudson St., tel 212/243–7600), four branches of the

Vertical Club (tel 212/355–5100), six branches of **New York Health and Racquet Club** (tel 800/HRC–BEST), and two branches of the **New York Sports** clubs (tel 800/796–NYSC). These are particularly worth noting if you're a member of a health club back home that offers reciprocal club rights elsewhere, and I must confess, I occasionally pose as a prospective club member, take a tour of the facilities, and then talk my way into a free trial use of the pool.

Indoor fitness... You may be a pro at getting into places you're not supposed to go, but the truth is you've got to be a member to use the facilities in most New York health clubs. At some independent clubs, taking a tour with a guide from the membership department can win you a free fitness class (plus a sauna and/or steambath, if such amenities are available); if you have friends in the city, convince them to get you a guest pass (which usually costs $10 to $20) at their club; or check with your club at home to see if it has reciprocal privileges someplace in New York. The hot health clubs these days are the high tech **Reebok Sports Club/NY** (160 Columbus Ave., tel 212/362–6800) that has everything from a pool to a swimsuit spin dryer; **David Barton Gym** (552 Sixth Ave., tel 212/727–0004 and 30 E. 85th St., tel 212/517–7577), where the best male bodies are made; **Equinox** (344 Amsterdam Ave., tel 212/721–4200 and 897 Broadway, tel 212/780–9300), just a good all-around club ; and the westside **Printing House** (421 Hudson St., tel 212/243–7600), with its largely gay clientele, postage stamp-sized rooftop pool, and sweat sundeck. As for hotels, fitness freaks should book the **Doral Park Avenue** (70 Park Ave., tel 212/687–7050), which has a complete health facility in its Saturnalia Fitness Center (guests at the Doral Court, Doral Tuscany, and Doral Inn are welcome, as well). **The Sports Center** at Chelsea Piers (Pier 60, tel 212/336–6000) includes everything a workout requires, including cardiovascular weight training, aerobics, two tracks, and an indoor pool; day-use passes are available to out-of-towners for $25. And, joy of joys, **Crunch Fitness** (54 E. 13th St, tel 212/475–2018; 162 W. 82nd St., tel 212/875–1902; and 404 Lafayette St., tel 212/614–0120) admits one-time users for $15 a day. Exercise machines are available, but what sets Crunch apart is its fitness classes, with names like "Washboard Abs," "Brand New Butt," and "Uninhibited Funk." Crunch teachers are so top-notch that most of them develop loyal followers; but watch out, because the classes are hard. Walk-in yoga classes are available at the **Yoga Zone** (146 E. 56th St., tel 212/935-YOGA, and 138 Fifth Ave., tel 212/647–YOGA). For Chinese martial arts, try the **Northeastern Tai Chi Chuan Association** (10 W. 18th St., tel 212/741–1922) or the **New York Martial Arts Center** (598 Broadway, tel 212/431–1100).

Par for the course... Call me negative, but I don't think it makes a lot of sense to come to the city to play golf. Still, if you've just gotta get in 18 holes, no matter what, top courses in the tri-state area are: **Bethpage State Park** (in Bethpage, Long Island, tel 516/249–0701) with five 18-hole courses, including the impossibly difficult Black Course; **Tamarack Golf Course** (East Brunswick, NJ, tel 908/821–8881), ranked fourth-best in the state by *Golf Digest*; and **Split Rock** (Pelham Bay Park, the Bronx, tel 718/885–1258), one of the best public courses around, even if the cops have harvested 13 bodies from the woods adjacent to the fairways in the last 10 years.

Back in the saddle... You can go horseback riding at the **Claremont Riding Academy** (175 W. 89th St., tel 212/724–5100); experienced riders get to go out on the bridle paths in Central Park from here, cantering under arched trees and 19th-century bridges and along the reservoir.

You bowl me over... I have a friend who celebrates his birthday every year with a party at **Bowlmor Lanes** (110 University Place, tel 212/255–8188); maybe next year I can get him to try **Leisure Time** (625 Eighth Ave., tel 212/268–6909), an improbable, modern bowlatorium above the Port Authority Bus Station.

Climbing the walls... Just to prove that New York positively has it all—how about a little rock climbing at the **Central Park challenge wall** (tel 212/348–4867)?

shop

5

ping

A friend told me about a New York City woman who arrived for her first therapy session deeply distressed. "I need help—*I can't shop*," the woman said. "I've tried everything—Bloomingdale's, Charivari, the Lower East Side—nothing seems to work." An extreme case, of course, and possibly an apocryphal tale. But you get the idea: New Yorkers shop—over the phone, on their lunch breaks, after work, and especially on weekends, when street fairs, flea markets, and peddlers transform the city into one giant, never-ending, seductive bazaar. Visitors to the city can't help but catch the bug, especially those coming from countries with currencies more robust than the dollar. For them, deals on perennial New York draws like designer clothes, jewelry and watches, art and antiques, perfume, and toys can simply seem too good to pass up. These days you'll even find Italians and Argentines making special trips to New York to buy leather goods. The city has 10,000 shops and boutiques, including huge, new, value-driven superstores like **Barnes & Noble Bookstores**, **Bed, Bath & Beyond**, **Filene's Basement**, **Toys 'R' Us**, and **CompUSA**. So if you're wondering what to buy here, the answer is anything you want. Lawn mowers, bustiers, toucans, pastry marbles—don't worry, we got 'em.

Target zones

Fifth Avenue from 32nd to 57th streets is perhaps the world's most famous shopper's stroll—10,000 pass this way every day between the peak hours of 11am and 3pm. It has wide sidewalks assiduously cleaned in the morning, antique cast-iron clocks, a thrilling view up towards Central Park, and vendors selling nuts, pretzels, hot dogs, and hot watches. It also has some of the city's finest turn-of-the-century architecture, along with Rockefeller Center, the 68-story Trump Tower, and St. Patrick's Cathedral—where it might be wise to light a candle for your bank account before you start to shop. Perhaps you can afford a binge at **Fendi**, **Gianni Versace**, **Cartier**, **Christian Dior**, **Bergdorf Goodman**, or **Henri Bendel**; if not, head one long block west to Sixth Avenue, where the same 32nd-to-57th-street stretch offers plenty of bargain glad rags from stores like **Labels for Less**, clothier to temp workers, editorial assistants, and secretaries. Fifth Avenue has been changing, due to the advent of many mass-market, mall-type retailers who target shoppers under the age of 20: the **Coca-Cola** gift shop, the **Warner Brothers Studio Store**, **Tower Records**, the **Original Levi's Store**, and two newcomers not yet opened at press time, **Nike Town** and a **Disney Studio Store**. The intersection at 57th Street has come to be known as the "Four Carats" because its corners are occupied by high-end jewelers **Tiffany, Bulgari, Van Cleef & Arpels**—and carrot-chomping Bugs Bunny, who appears on T-shirts and mugs at the ever-packed **Warner Brothers** store.

Traditionalists rue the avenue's transmogrification, but young shoppers and foreign aficionados of American kitsch don't kvetch. The task of maintaining New York's high-class shopping standards has fallen to the **Upper East Side**, especially along Madison and Lexington avenues south of 76th Street. Classy **Bloomingdale's**, at 59th Street between Lexington and Third avenues, was for many years the last word in New York department stores, but then the ultra-chic uptown branch of **Barneys** came to Madison Avenue at 61st Street, making this intersection the city's top showplace for upscale stores, with **Ann Taylor**, **Calvin Klein**, and **Armani** in residence, as well. Small, posh specialty shops parade on up Madison, featuring clothing introduced on fashion show runways in Paris and Milan, elegant lingerie, and shoes that could turn any Cinderella into a princess. Farther downtown near Grand Central Station, **Madison Avenue** devotes itself to buttoned-up sorts of male attire, notably classic **Brooks Brothers** and **Paul Stuart**. The Upper West Side's **Columbus Avenue**, between 80th Street and Lincoln Center, came into the fore as a hip place to shop in the 1980s, when trendy retailers like **Charivari**, **Betsey Johnson**, and **Putumayo** moved in. The neighborhood has calmed down somewhat now, remaining a pleasant, not too pretentious place to shop.

Herald Square at the intersection of Broadway and Sixth Avenue was one of the city's busiest shopping districts in the 1930s and 1940s, starring (along with a heart-stoppingly young Natalie Wood) in the Christmastime classic *Miracle on 34th Street*. It remains at the nerve center of the city's bustling garment district; get in the way of someone wheeling a bulky clothing rack down the sidewalk and you'll need something nice to wear in your coffin. Alas, the only department store left is immense middle-class **Macy's**, where you can sometimes find great bargains on good-quality furnishings, accessories, clothing, and housewares, especially if you watch the newspaper ads for sales. But a rash of upscale national chain stores has lately colonized 34th Street, replacing the junky variety stores and cut-rate electronics emporiums that had clogged the arteries for the past couple of decades.

Shopping in the bohemian **East Village** (roughly everything east of Broadway between 14th and Houston streets) is almost always a wild ride. At Astor Place, street vendors hawk used jeans, tapes and records, books, and lamps that look utterly beyond reconditioning. From there, head east on St. Marks Place where the shops' wares spill out onto the sidewalk—punk regalia, sacrilegious jewelry, and cocktail dresses with more peek-a-boo holes than fabric. Broadway bisects the Village, growing ever darker and dirtier as it heads downtown; join the New York University students browsing among the jammed shelves at just-about-always-open **Tower Records** on 4th Street. Staid in comparison to the East, the **West Village** still has rewards for shoppers, like reasonably-priced shoes and hipster clothes on 8th Street between Fifth and Sixth avenues, vintage comic books arrayed on sidewalk tables along Sixth Avenue, Italian comestibles on Bleecker Street, and in the region around Sheridan Square, erotic leather goods, sex gear, condoms in all tastes and textures, and clothing stores catering to the gay male. Stroll across Houston Street to reach **SoHo**, with its turn-of-the-century cast-iron warehouses. Rediscovered by artists 20-odd years ago, SoHo has since become the display case for contemporary New York style. SoHo's art galleries (like **G.W. Einstein** for original photographs), hip designer showrooms (like **Comme des Garçons** and **J. Morgan Puett**), and remarkable furniture stores (like **Poltrona Frau**) are too good to miss. In many of the best SoHo stores the merchandise bears the stamp of the creator, not of an assembly line, so of course prices are astronomical. Or wend your way down Broadway below Spring Street, where you'll find discounters like Canal Jeans and the Soho Mill Outlet. **Downtown**, upscale Wall Streeters gravitate to the high-end shops inside the World Financial Center, and rank-and-file office workers shop the subway concourse mall below the World Trade Center or the discount stores around Nassau and Fulton streets; **Century 21** on Cortlandt Street is one of the city's best discount department stores. For exotic groceries, gaudy souvenirs, and a thick ethnic atmosphere, wander through **Little Italy** and **Chinatown**. Intrepid bargain hunters brave **Orchard Street** on the Lower East Side, where there are some incredible buys to be found on shoes and clothing (note that shops are closed for the Saturday sabbath, but open again on Sunday).

Bargain Hunting

Thrift stores and flea markets offer good buys in the open air, and of course, there are the devoted discounters like **Century 21**, **Loehmann's**, and **S&W**. Most clothing retailers and department stores hold big sales in August (sundresses and bathing suits), December (linens), and January (coats), and around major holidays like the Fourth of July, Columbus Day, and Presidents' Weekend (look for humongous newspaper ads with banner headlines touting "Blowout," "Midnight Madness," and "Spectacular Clearance"). The "Sales and Bargains" column in *New York* magazine offers excellent insider advice on sales at specialty stores and galleries.

Trading with the natives

Fleas and greenmarkets are fair territory for bargaining (for instance, ask how much the $8 peony bouquets would be if you bought two). Don't even think about haggling in upscale shops. Personal checks are rarely accepted unless the merchant knows you from the neighborhood; if you luck out and are allowed to pay by check, two forms of identification like a driver's license and credit card are generally required (occasionally you'll be asked for ID bearing your photo). Visa, Mastercard, and American Express have become virtually the coin of the realm, though credit card companies are currently warring over the city's merchants—a certain shop may turn up its nose at AmEx but happily accept your Mastercard (or vice versa). You're being gypped if someone tries to add a credit card service charge to the bill, and merchants aren't supposed to set a credit card minimum, though many do. High-end shops and grocery stores will deliver your purchases, often for an additional fee. Each store sets its own return policy, though it's fairly standard to get a store credit or a credit on your plastic rather than cash back. Most shops will allow you to return or exchange unwanted items within a specified time (often one week or 30 days), as long as you have your receipt.

Note that the numerous electronics shops on Fifth Avenue and in Times Square with large "Going Out of Business" signs have been going out of business for decades and will no doubt keep "closing out" through the next millennium. Take care when shopping here—you may wind up paying too much for very little. You may find sidewalk hawkers selling everything from used books to "designer" clothing and "gold" watches. The brand names are fake, of course, but if paying $30 to a street vendor is the only way you're ever going to own a (pseudo-) Patek Philippe wristwatch, go ahead. You know what you're getting.

Hours of business

As a rule, New York shops open at 10am and close at 5 or 6pm Monday to Saturday. Midtown and downtown is shut tight as a tomb on weekends, and the Lower East Side observes the Jewish sabbath on Friday afternoons and Saturdays. Saturdays are great for shopping during the day on the Upper East and West sides, but many stores take Sunday off. In the East and West Village and SoHo merchants are apparently nocturnal; some don't open up until noon, and take Monday rather than Sunday off. Remember, though, that New York is the city that never sleeps—in an emergency, you can almost always find what you need 24 hours a day by checking the Yellow Pages.

Sales Tax

The sales tax is 8.25% in New York City, unless the store ships your purchases out of state for you. It is non-refundable—foreign visitors will not be reimbursed at the airport.

The Lowdown

For aspiring Martha Stewarts... For serviceable, stylish, reasonably-priced interiors and entertaining storefront window displays, check out **Crate & Barrel** at the Madison and 59th crossroads. Or let yourself fantasize in SoHo at **Portico Bed & Bath** and **Portico Home**, where romantically-styled beds have names like "Soleil" and "Nathalie"; **Barton-Sharpe, Ltd.**, which specializes in handmade 18th-century American recreations; **Modern Age**, where the styles bespeak the 1950s; and **Scott Jordan Furniture** for handsome Mission-style beds, shelves, and tables. The **Manhattan Art & Antiques Center**, **Place des Antiquaires**, and the **Chelsea Antiques Building** are all excellent antiquers' target zones. But for something different, try **Old Japan, Inc.**, the art-deco **Wooster Gallery**, or **Jacques Carcanagues, Inc.** where that Korean step tansu you've been looking for can finally be found.

Incredible edibles... Among the city's gourmet grocery stores, **Zabar's** rules the Upper West Side, **Dean & Deluca** reigns in SoHo, and **Balducci's** is king of the West Village; but don't forget the neighborhoody **Jefferson Market** (in the West Village) and **Gourmet Garage** (in SoHo). **Florence Meat Market** makes no bones about selling the best veal in town; their chicken is just as tasty, and politically correct to boot. Up on the East Side, **Sherry-Lehmann** is a virtual wine museum (fancy a jeroboam of Château Lafite-Rothschild 1966 for $1,100?), with a staff of connoisseurs posing as clerks. The Village's **Astor Wines & Spirits** takes more of a bargain-basement approach to alcohol, but the selection alone could make you drunk. Coffee beans are available everywhere, but I make a steady diet of Peter's blend from my Village local, **Porto Rico Importing Company**. **Ferrara Foods and Confections** has been baking mini-sfogliatella and chocolate-dipped biscotti in Little Italy since 1892, and wrapping them up for carry-out in the loveliest little parcels. Fresh pasta comes in almost all the colors of the rainbow and tastes of the garden at **Raffetto's** in SoHo, nicely topped by gorgonzola or fontina from **Murray's Cheese Shop** in the West Village. And just to prove that the sun never sets on the British Empire, there's **Myer's of Keswick**, a Village village grocer late of the Lake District, where lovers of Milo Chocolate Food Drink find happiness at last.

Everything under one roof... There was a time, in the late 19th century, when almost all the city's department stores lined up in handsome, multi-storied buildings with exquisite cast-iron facades along the so-called Ladies Mile (Sixth Avenue from 8th Street to 23rd Street); B. Altman & Company was there, complete with a 500-horse stable for deliveries. In the early 1900s, most stores moved to what's now Midtown, and it's been downhill all the way since then. (Alas, poor Altman's closed its dowager store at 34th and Fifth in the late '80s.) **Bloomingdale's** and **Barneys** both have personal shopping departments for those who need help deciding what to buy, and both offer the very latest in clothing and furnishing styles; Barneys is postmodern-spare, Bloomie's so Upper-East-Side that it's become a cliché. **Saks Fifth Avenue** is quite simply a New York institution, especially for Christmas shopping and post-Christmas fancy dress sales. Frankly, though, big department stores make me woozy, which is why I was recently delighted to discover beguilingly chic **Felissimo**, in a fine old Midtown mansion with a grand curving staircase and tea room on the top floor; the stock is limited, but all worthy of a contessa with a palazzo. You could call the **Soho Emporium** a sort of a department store, and it too is manageably small, with stalls full of sweaters, toys, art, and jewelry sold by friendly entrepreneurs.

Finding the New You... If you're looking for scents, soaps, and unguents you won't find in malls all over the world, try the East Side's **Floris of London** or the Village's **Scents from Heaven**, where you can mix up your own fragrance from a wide array of natural oils. Or seek out **Kiehl's**, an ever-crowded little pharmacy that's been making its own natural beauty products behind the shop since 1851. The **Elizabeth Arden Red Door Salon** on Fifth Avenue has mainstream posh attractions (like Oribe, famed colorist from *Vogue*). Bergdorf Goodman has its beauty-world mecca, the **Frederick Fekkai Beauty Center**, the Waldorf-Astoria Hotel has the **Kenneth Salon**, and Bloomie's has the **Lancôme Institut de Beauté**. But if all you want are pots of paint try **M.A.C.** (Makeup and Cosmetics Limited), based in the West Village but with outposts at Saks and Henri Bendel. Get a haircut at SoHo's **Girl Loves Boy** or **Mud Honey**, where the prices are surprisingly reasonable and your locks get clipped in an art gallery atmosphere; the **Salon Dada** for trims in a gorgeous Chelsea space; or Midtown's industrial-chic **Bumble & Bumble**, where you and Broadway stars get revamped, with cuts starting at $44 and color at $86.

The vintage vantage point... New York's favorite flea market—where you might catch Barbra Streisand rummaging—is the **Annex Antiques Fair and Flea Market**, which takes over empty parking lots along Sixth Avenue between 24th and 27th streets on Saturdays and Sundays. About 425 vendors offer up costume jewelry, old bicycles, wigs, hats, bibelots—in short, oddities and treasures (you just have to be able to tell the difference). Two fine street markets seem to have settled in permanently, one just south of Tower Records on Broadway (in the Village) and the other at Wooster and Spring streets (in SoHo), where the goods tend toward thigh-high socks, strappy sundresses, tapes, and cast-off lots from The Gap; a newer one has turned up on Fifth Avenue at 42nd Street. The thrift shop at the **Church of St. Luke in the Fields** in the West Village sometimes has startlingly wonderful women's clothes, and special Saturday sales, as well. Prices are higher at SoHo's **Ina** and the East Village's **Screaming Mimi's**, but the buyers are hip and the clothes are so well reconditioned that they seem new. On the Upper East Side, **Encore** has been reselling "gently used" European and American designer fashions for 40 years, and anything you buy at **Repeat Performance**, near Gramercy Park, benefits the New York City Opera (watch for freshly donated batches of brand new clothes). And then—dare I mention it?—there's the **Ritz Thrift Shop**, where the lynx, raccoon, sable, and fox coats are second-hand but a far cry from ratty.

Kid stuff... If you didn't bring the kids to New York, take it back to them. You could brave the 57th Street crowds for a Daffy Duck cap from **The Warner Brothers Studio Store**, but you'll find a wider range of characters at SoHo's **Think Cartoons**. Funky kids' clothes like a tutu that plays *It's a Small World After All* or a pair of cool plastic sandals can be found in the West Village at **Peanut Butter and Jane**; for a pretty satin dress-up frock or perfect sailor suit, go to the Upper East Side's **Wicker Garden's Children**—then pick up a Japanese kite or toy plane from **Big City Kites**, or Italian building blocks and German jigsaw puzzles from **Penny Whistle Toys**. If the kids are along, **FAO Schwarz** is unavoidable—two stories of toys, including a whole department for Barbie dolls, the very latest in action figures, a whole zoo of immense stuffed animals, and a Lego department to die for.

Gadgets and gizmos... You've got to stay sharp when shopping for electronics in New York. Bargains are offered everywhere on computers, VCRs, and photography equipment, all with more bells and whistles than you ever dreamed of. Midtown west of Fifth Avenue is loaded with electronics stores, like the **Video Camera Palace** and old reliable **47th Street Photo**, where, like Monty Hall, they're always ready to make a deal. Downtown near City Hall is **J&R**, with computer, TV/VCR, video game, home and car stereo, small appliance, and tape and CD departments (in several buildings), and a whole army of helpful salespeople.

Exotica... Two East Village shops, **Enchantments** and **Lady and the Moon** cater to the witches among us, selling candles and personalized incense mixtures that come complete with a spell; stop in around Halloween or when there's a full moon. In the West Village, **Bird Jungle** has one of the city's most intriguing collections of exotic birds, many of which boast impressive vocabularies, and **Kate's Paperie** is a showplace for fine stationery, handmade cards, beautifully bound blank books, and marbleized wrapping paper too pretty to throw away. Up near the Museum of Natural History is a fitting location for **Maxilla and Mandible**, which stocks bones and fossils (weird but actually cool). At **Gotta Have It! Collectibles Inc.** on chic 57th Street, you'll find one-of-a-kind specialty items, like a signed Bob Dylan guitar.

For L.L. Bean types... Centrally located **Paragon Sporting Goods** is a great place to gear up for athletic endeavors from step aerobics to lacrosse, on three levels of a cavernous warehouse near Union Square; it offers reasonable prices and frequent sales. **Eastern Mountain Sports** can help you with sleeping bag pads, skis, rock-climbing equipment, and ice picks, though these days "gear heads" are making a beeline down to **Patagonia**, a link in the environmentally-conscious California sports-retailing chain; the store's fixtures were crafted from old railroad ties and planks from a vintage mill to give shoppers the feeling of being in the great outdoors. Nearby **Smith & Hawken** supplies stylish gardeners with seeds, bulbs, trowels, and mud boots, while classical music plays in the background.

Diamonds are a girl's best friend... If you can't find **Tiffany & Co.**, you're not trying hard enough. It's a Fifth Avenue lodestar, intimately bound up with the mythology of glamorous New York. Make a pilgrimage to the Tiffany Diamond, 287.42 carats cut in 1877, and then bag something slightly less pricy like a paper-thin Peretti brandy snifter for about $30. At the other end of the jewelry spectrum, there's the **Diamond District**, one discount jewelry store after another lined up along 47th Street between Fifth and Sixth avenues, where more than a few young grooms have purchased starter rings for their intendeds. **À La Vieille Russie** and **Ares Rare Jewelry** are pricy East Side purveyors of museum-quality antique glitter—Fabergé eggs, enameled snuff boxes, Egyptian scarabs, and the like. Gaudy costume gems can be found in the Village at **Out of Our Drawers, Inc.**, where ear piercing is painless and free for the cost of a pair of posts. All the major jewelry shops and department stores sell timepieces, but to get a Tourneau at the source, stop in at Midtown's **Tourneau**, where you'll also find the latest tony watch styles from Tag Heuer, Omega, Rolex, and

Longines. Or for something a little more whimsical for the wrist, check out **Swatch** at South Street Seaport.

100-percent leather... Well-heeled men get that way at **To Boot** (West Side) and **McCreedy & Schreiber** (East Side), both of which feature big American name brands like Bass, Rockport, and Timberland, plus too-cool Italian loafers and English ankle boots. **T.O. Dey** makes boots and shoes for hard-to-fit feet (male or female) in an unprepossessing Garment District warehouse; John Travolta's ostrich-skin boots and Liza Minelli's sequined pumps were custom made here. On the Madison Avenue boutique strip, **Cole Haan** shoes traditionalist male and female feet, and the first American location of **Patrick Cox**, otherwise of London, rivets high-end shoe fetishists of both sexes with such eye-poppers as fuchsia-toned jelly shoes; unaccountably, the shop also sells antiques from the 1950s. Down in SoHo there's a cluster of chic little shoe boîtes like **Jenny B.**, **Peter Fox**, and **Sacco**. Bargains on name brands like Stuart Weitzman and Charles Jourdan for men and women can be found at the Lower East Side's **The Lace Up**. Walking into any of the small leather stores in the West Village always makes me want to eat a good steak—the jackets, gloves, and handbags are that genuine. Try the **Village Tannery** or the **New York Leather Company**.

The printed page... **Gotham Book Mart** is an anomalous island in workaholic Midtown, perilously crammed with used, new, and rare finds under a little emblem that says "Wise men fish here"; **Three Lives**, a living-room-sized West Villager devoted to fiction, with a staff full of real readers; and **Coliseum Books** and **Shakespeare & Co.**, two richly-stocked independents on the West Side. In the Village, the **Strand** has 2.5 million used volumes, including half-price review copies. Then there are the wonderful little specialists—**The Drama Book Shop**, in the theater district, naturally, featuring play scripts and practical volumes for actors and directors; the Village's **Biography Book Shop**; **The Ballet Shop** near Lincoln Center; and **The Mysterious Book Shop** in Midtown, to name only a few.

The gallery scene... Every decade or so the New York art scene reassembles itself from the ground up; galleries open and close, artists come and go. But the **Leo Castelli**

Gallery, one of the early champions of the works of Jasper Johns, has endured, as has its SoHo neighbor **Mary Boone**, Julian Schnabel's champion. **Pace Wildenstein**, on E. 57th Street's gallery strip, and the **Gagosian Gallery**'s two branches are other extremely reliable showplaces for the latest trends in contemporary art.

To the highest bidder... The art and antiques auction game is played nowhere with more white-gloved aplomb than on Manhattan's Upper East Side at **Sotheby's** and **Christie's**, home of the multi-million-dollar collectible (a pair of Rudolph Nureyev's ballet slippers once fetched $9,000 at a Christie's auction). If you're serious about joining the oh-so-glamorous fray (night auctions are the real glitterati draws), attend the preview and study the catalogue before raising your hand. Both auction houses have somewhat less high-profile branches, **Sotheby's Arcade** and **Christie's East**, where one can swing excellent deals on porcelains, furniture, lamps, silver, and jewelry from family estates. The clothing auctions at **William Doyle Galleries** bring out the genteel blue-haired ladies of the Upper East Side; a more rambunctious gang finds furniture treasures at surprisingly low prices (which don't include often woefully needed reconditioning) at the **Tepper Galleries**.

Right out of GQ... Perhaps clothes don't make the man, but when they're from **Bergdorf Goodman for Men** (just across the street from the elegant main Fifth Avenue store) or the original downtown branch of **Barneys**, gentlemen can count on cutting fine figures. Stylish foreign and American sweaters, sportswear, and accessories are on hand, not to mention scads of perfectly tailored suits. (Watch for spring and fall warehouse sales at Barneys.) Drop-dead ties are the sole pursuit at the East Side's **Robert Talbott**. **Paul Stuart** is the current top contender among the traditional male outfitters clustered on Madison Avenue near Grand Central Station; the West Side's **Charivari for Men** attires cool guys who don't have to dress for the office, with radical designs by Gaultier, Cerutti, and Versace in wild colors and leather. Hip but tasteful downtown looks for men, with little retro touches, can be found at SoHo boutiques like **Agnès B.**, **New Republic Clothier**, and **Yohji Yamamoto**.

Women in *Vogue*... You know about the department stores, right? And that all the fancy designers (your **Valentino**s, **Yves Saint Laurent**s, **Norma Kamali**s, **Chanel**s, and **Nicole Miller**s) hang out on Madison Avenue and E. 57th Street? And that you can put together a fetching city look by shopping the hipper chains like **Street Life**, **Express Ltd.**, **Putumayo**, and **Urban Outfitters**? You've found the knock-off bargains at **Daffy's**? So now graduate to some of the special kinds of threads Manhattan weaves, all to be found below 14th Street in the wilds of SoHo and the Village. Start an affair with **Harriet Love**, a little closet of a shop with sweet, chic suits hinting at the 1940s, and little black dresses to die for. **Ibiza** makes an art of the gypsy look, Parisian **Stephane Kelian** has simple, subtly sexy styles for girls with tall-drink bodies, **J. Morgan Puett** could blow you away with its fantastical cottons and gauzes, **Kanae and Onyx** has bargains on urban teeny-bopper attire, and **Cynthia Rowley** does the sixties with all the vinyl and polka dots you could dream of, plus a little bit of whimsy. **Mark Montano** has cool but classic silks and chiffons; **Todd Oldham** does high-style women's shoes, accessories, and gowns; and **Odyssey** purveys tight stuff, rarely priced above $100.

Agnès B. Handsome, wearable styles for men, women, and kids.... *Tel 212/925–4649. 116 Prince St., N/R train to Prince St.; tel 212/570–9330. 1063 Madison Ave., 4/5/6 to 86th St.*

À La Vieille Russie. Art, antiques, and little bits of czarist Russia, complete with Fabergé eggs.... *Tel 212/752–1727. 781 5th Ave., N/R train to 5th Ave. Closed Sun, and Sat in summer.*

Ann Taylor. Updated classic clothes for women.... *Tel 212/832–2010. 645 Madison Ave., 4/5/6 to 59th St.; 25 Fulton St.(South Street Seaport), 2/3 to Fulton St.; and other locations.*

Ares Rare Jewelry. Exquisite antique jewels.... *Tel 212/988–0190. 961 Madison Ave., 6 train to 77th St. Closed Sun, and Sat in summer.*

Armani. Grand boutique that displays the couture line.... *Tel 212/988–9191. 815 Madison Ave., 6 train to 68th St. Closed Sun.*

Astor Wines & Spirits. The booze warehouse in the Village.... *Tel 212/674–7500. 12 Astor Place, 6 train to Astor Place or N/R to 8th St. Closed Sun.*

Balducci's. Gourmet comestibles, very fresh fish, and meat in the pink.... *Tel 212/673–2600. 424 6th Ave., F or L train to 14th St.*

The Ballet Shop. Books on la danse.... *Tel 212/581–7990. 1887 Broadway. 1/9, B/D, or A/C train to 59th St./Columbus Circle.*

Barneys. The New York department store of the moment. Uptown's good for women, downtown excels for men.... *Tel 212/929–9000, 106 7th Ave., 1/9 train to 18th St.; tel 212/826–8900, 660 Madison Ave., N/R to 5th Ave.*

Barton-Sharpe, Ltd. For handsome 18th-century hand-crafted furniture recreations.... *Tel 212/925–9562. 119 Spring St., 6 train to Spring St.*

Bed, Bath & Beyond. A huge array of reasonably priced home furnishings.... *Tel 212/255–3550. 620 6th Ave., F train to 23rd St.*

Bergdorf Goodman. High fashion for traditionalists mostly, in a landmark building.... *Tel 212/753–7300. 754 5th Ave., N/R train to 5th Ave.*

Bergdorf Goodman for Men. Mecca for male styles.... *Tel 212/753–7300. 745 5th Ave., N/R train to 5th Ave.*

Betsey Johnson. Glitter, glad rags, too-short tubes and minis—all for girls who just wanna have fun.... *Tel 212/362–3364. 248 Columbus Ave., 1/2/3/9 or B/C train to 72nd St.*

Big City Kites. Japanese and Chinese wind-worthy lovelies, plus toys.... *Tel 212/472–2623. 1201 Lexington Ave., 4/5/6 train to 86th St.*

Biography Book Shop. Small, very West Village, for the lives of the greats.... *Tel 212/807–8655. 400 Bleecker St., 1/9 train to Christopher St.*

Bird Jungle. Exotic birds.... *Tel 212/242–1757. 401 Bleecker St., 1/9 train to Christopher St.*

Bloomingdale's. The Upper East Side shops in this classy older department store.... *Tel 212/418–7100. 1000 3rd Ave., 4/5/6 train to 59th St. or N/R to Lexington Ave.*

Brooks Brothers. Ivy League clothes.... *Tel 212/682–8800. 346 Madison Ave., 4/5/6/7 train to Grand Central.*

Bulgari. Jewels and watches, in two words.... *Tel 212/315–9000. 730 5th Ave., B/Q train to 57th St. or N/R to 5th Ave. Closed Sat–Sun.*

Bumble & Bumble. Star-quality haircuts and color.... *Tel 212/371–4100. 146 E. 56th St., 4/5/6 to 59th St. or N/R to Lexington Ave.*

Calvin Klein. High-end styles from the king of fashion marketing.... *Tel 212/292–9000. 654 Madison Ave., N/R train to 5th Ave.*

Canal Jean Co. Sportswear and some vintage, discount prices.... *Tel 212/226–1130. 504 Broadway, B/D/Q/F train to Broadway/Lafayette or N/R to Prince St.*

Cartier. Another Fifth Avenue jewelry legend.... *Tel 212/446–3459. 2 E. 52nd St., E/F to 53rd St. Closed Sat–Sun in summer.*

Century 21. Department store bargains.... *Tel 212/227–9092. 22 Cortlandt St., 1/9 or N/R train to Cortlandt*

St., 2/3 to Park Place, or C/E to World Trade Center. Closed Sun.

Chanel. Classic French women's styles, especially suits and evening gowns.... *Tel 212/355–5050. 5 E. 57th St., N/R train to 5th Ave. Closed Sun.*

Charivari. Entertainingly radical clothing for man, woman, and child.... *Tel 212/333–4040, 18 W. 57th St., B/Q train to 57th St. or N/R to 5th Ave.; also at 1001 Madison Ave., N/R to 5th Ave.; 58 W. 72nd St., 1/2/3/9 or B/C to 72nd St.; 201 W. 79th St., 1/9 to 79th St.; 2315 Broadway, 1/9 to 86th St.*

Chelsea Antiques Building. Antiques emporium in a Chelsea warehouse.... *Tel 212/929–0909. 110 W. 25th St., 1/9 train to 23rd St.*

Christian Dior. Women's clothing, fresh from Paris.... *Tel 212/223–4646. 703 5th Ave., N/R train to 5th Ave. Closed Sun.*

Christie's. Art and antiques auctions, beloved of the blue-bloods.... *Tel 212/546–1000. 502 Park Ave; 4/5/6 train to 59th St. or N/R to Lexington Ave. Closed Sun in summer.*

Christie's East. Christie's less pricey spin-off, good for furniture.... *Tel 212/606–0400. 219 E. 67th St., 6 train to 68th St.*

Church of St. Luke in the Fields Thrift Shop. West Village cast-offs.... *Tel 212/924–9364. 487 Hudson St., 1/9 train to Christopher St. Closed Sun.*

Coca-Cola Fifth Avenue. Kitschy Coke collectibles.... *Tel 212/355–5475. 711 5th Ave., N/R train to 5th Ave.* Classy, conservative shoes and accessories for women and men.... ***Cole Haan***. *Tel 212/421–8440. 667 Madison Ave., N/R train to 5th Ave.*

Coliseum Books. Two floors of books, and an excellent magazine rack.... *Tel 212/757–8381. 1771 Broadway, 1/9/A/B/C/D train to Columbus Circle.*

Comme des Garçons. Japanese unisex cutting-edge styles.... *Tel 212/219–0660. 116 Wooster St., N/R train to Prince St.*

CompUSA. A computer superstore. Great prices, huge stock.... *Tel 212/782–7700. 420 5th Ave., B/D/Q/F or N/R train to 34th St.*

Crate & Barrel. Stylish baskets, glassware, lamps, rugs, and other accessories for the upwardly mobile home.... *Tel 212/308–0011. 650 Madison Ave., N/R train to 5th Ave.*

Cynthia Rowley. Women's styles from the high sixties, only slightly updated.... *Tel 212/334–1144. 112 Wooster St., N/R train to Prince St.*

Daffy's. Bargain threads for men, women, and children. Lotsa labels.... *Tel 212/529–4477, 111 5th Ave., 4/5/6 or N/R train to Union Square; tel 212/557–4422, 335 Madison Ave., 4/5/6 or 7 to Grand Central.*

Dean & Deluca. Specialty foods.... *Tel 212/431–1691. 560 Broadway, N/R train to Prince St.*

The Disney Studio Store. Opening in 1996, selling the expected memorabilia.... *5 E. 55th St., E/F train to 5th Ave.*

The Drama Book Shop. Essential for plays and theater books.... *Tel 212/944–0595. 723 7th Ave., 1/9 train to 50th St.*

Eastern Mountain Sports. Outfits backpackers, hikers, and other outdoor enthusiasts.... *Tel 212/397–4860, 20 W. 61st St., 1/9/A/B/C/D train to Columbus Circle; tel 212/505–9860, 611 Broadway, B/D/Q/F to Broadway/Lafayette.*

Elizabeth Arden Red Door Salon. Facials, manicure, makeup advice, and massages on two luxurious floors.... *Tel 212/546–0200. 691 5th Ave., E/F train to 5th Ave.*

Enchantments. Incense, spells, and candles for witches.... *Tel 212/228–4394. 341 E. 9th St., F train to 2nd Ave.*

Encore. The Upper East Side's most reliable clothing resale shop.... *Tel 212/879–2850. 1132 Madison Ave., 4/5/6 train to 86th St.*

Express Ltd. French clothing units for women.... *Tel 212/754–2721. 667 Madison Ave., N/R train to 5th Ave.; and other locations.*

FAO Schwarz. The first and last word in toys.... *Tel 212/644–9400. 767 5th Ave; N/R train to 5th Ave.*

Felissimo. A small department store with handsome women's clothes and home furnishings.... *Tel 212/247–5656. 10 W. 56th St., N/R train to 5th Ave. or B/Q to 57th St.*

Fendi. Designer clothing and accessories.... *Tel 212/767–0100. 720 5th Ave., N/R train to 5th Ave.*

Ferrara Foods and Confections. Italian cookies, pastries, and ices, to take out or eat in.... *Tel 212/226–6150. 195 Grand St., B/D/Q train to Grand St.*

Filene's Basement. A new branch of the discount clothing store from Boston.... *Tel 212/873–8000. 2220–2226 Broadway, 1/9 train to 79th St.*

Floris of London. The British perfumery.... *Tel 212/935–9100. 703 Madison Ave., N/R train to 5th Ave. Closed Sun.*

Florence Meat Market. The city's top restaurants get their meats here.... *Tel 212/242–6531. 5 Jones St., A/C or B/D/Q/F train to W. 4th St. Closed Sun.*

47th Street Photo. Electronics and good prices.... *Tel 212/398–1530. 115 W. 45th St., 1/2/3/9 train to Times Square. Closed Sat.*

Frederick Fekkai Beauty Center. For shampoos, scalp massages, and haircuts among the stars.... *Tel 212/753–9500. 754 5th Ave. (in Bergdorf Goodman), N/R train to 5th Ave.*

Gagosian Gallery. Perhaps the hottest contemporary art gallery on the scene.... *Tel 212/744–2313, 950 Madison Ave., 6 train to 77th St.; tel 212/228–2828, 136 Wooster St., N/R to Prince St. Closed Sat–Sun.*

Gianni Versace. Sexy, loud, fun styles from Italy.... *Tel 212/744–5572. 816 Madison Ave., 6 train to 68th St.*

Girl Loves Boy. A SoHo hair salon.... *Tel 212/226–2084. 63 Thompson St., N/R train to Prince St.*

Gotham Book Mart. Used and new volumes in a bibliophile's midtown oasis.... *Tel 212/719–4448. 41 W. 47th St., B/D/Q/F train to Rockefeller Center. Closed Sun.*

Gotta Have It! Collectibles Inc. For one-of-a-kind signed collectibles.... *Tel 212/750–7900. 153 E. 57th St., 4/5/6 train to 59th St. or N/R to Lexington Ave. Closed Sun.*

Gourmet Garage. Specialty foods, especially fruits and vegetables, at lower-than-Balducci's prices.... *Tel 212/941–5850. 47 Wooster St., N/R train to Prince St.*

G.W. Einstein. A SoHo photography showplace.... *Tel 212/226–1414. 591 Broadway, N/R train to Prince St.*

Harriet Love. Women's clothes with a 1940s cast.... *Tel 212/966–2280. 126 Prince St., N/R train to Prince St.*

Henri Bendel. Distinguished fashions.... *Tel 212/247–1100. 712 5th Ave., N/R train to 5th Ave.*

Ibiza. Flowy, costumey women's clothing and dramatic accessories.... *Tel 212/533–4614. 42 University Place, 4/5/6 or N/R train to Union Square.*

Ina. Glitz thrift, à la SoHo.... *Tel 212/941–4757. 101 Thompson St., 1/9 train to Houston St.*

Jacques Carcanagues. Antiques from all over the world.... *Tel 212/925–8110. 106 Spring St., 6 train to Spring St.*

Jefferson Market. Fine foods, virtually next door to Balducci's—but a lot less pretentious.... *Tel 212/675–2277. 450 6th Ave., F train to 14th St.*

Jenny B. Dashing, strappy shoes.... *Tel 212/343–9575. 118 Spring St., C/E train to Spring St.*

J. Morgan Puett. Fairy-tale styles for women, all gossamer and gauze.... *Tel 212/677–1200. 140 Wooster St., N/R train to Prince St.*

J & R. The downtown electronics hub.... *Tel 212/238–9000. 15, 23, 27, and 31 Park Row, N/R or 4/5/6 to Brooklyn Bridge/City Hall or J/M/Z to Chambers St.*

Kanae and Onyx. East Village hip youth.... *Tel 212/254–7703. 75 E. 7th St., 6 train to Astor Place or N/R to 8th St.*

Kate's Paperie. Pretty stationery, desk accessories, and wrappings.... *Tel 212/633–0570, 8 W. 13th St., 1/2/3/9 train to 14th St.; tel 212/941–9816, 561 Broadway, N/R to Prince St.*

Kenneth Salon. Spa treatments at the Waldorf.... *Tel 212/752–1800. 301 Park Ave.; 6 train to 51st St. Closed Sun.*

Kiehl's. Natural beauty aids, since 1851.... *Tel 212/475–3400. 109 Third Ave., L/N/R/4/5/6 train to Union Square. Closed Sun.*

Labels for Less. Discount styles for women.... *Tel 212/956–2450. 1345 6th Ave., B/Q train to 57th St.; and other branches.*

Lady and the Moon. Equipment for witchery.... *Tel 212/473–8486. 115 St. Mark's Place, 6 train to Astor Place.*

Lancôme Institut de Beauté. Facial specialists.... *Tel 212/473–8486. 1000 3rd Ave. (in Bloomingdale's), 4/5/6 train to 59th St. or N/R to Lexington Ave.*

Leo Castelli Gallery. Long-time leader in contemporary painting.... *Tel 212/431–5160. 420 W. Broadway, N/R train to Prince St.*

Loehmann's. Bargain-basement women's clothes.... *Tel 718/543–6420. 5749 Broadway, Riverdale; 1/9/A/B/C/D train to Columbus Circle, take shuttle from 62nd and Columbus (call for more information).*

Macy's. The Herald Square department store standard.... *Tel 212/695–4400. 151 W. 34th St., 1/2/3/9 train to Penn Station or B/D/Q/F/N/R to 34th St.*

M.A.C. Cosmetics. *Tel 212/243–4150. 14 Christopher St., 1/9 train to Christopher St. Also at Henri Bendel and Saks Fifth Avenue.*

Manhattan Art & Antiques Center. One hundred dealers on three floors, somewhat less pricey than Madison Avenue....

Tel 212/355–4400. 1050 2nd Ave., 4/5/6 train to 59th St. or N/R to Lexington Ave.

Mark Montano. Whimsical women's wear.... *Tel 212/505–0325. 434 E. 9th St., 6 train to Astor Place.*

Mary Boone Gallery. Major contemporary art gallery.... *Tel 212/431–1818. 417 W. Broadway, N/R train to Prince St. By appointment in summer.*

Maxilla and Mandible. Collectible bones, fossils, and all the skeletons in your closet.... *Tel 212/724–6173. 451 Columbus Ave., B/C train to 81st St.*

McCreedy & Schreiber. Men's shoes, especially boots.... *Tel 212/759–9241. 213 E. 59th St., 4/5/6 train to 59th St. or N/R to Lexington Ave.*

Modern Age. Trend-setting interior design.... *Tel 212/966–0669. 102 Wooster St., 6 train to Spring St. Closed Sun.*

Mud Honey. Haircuts in a SoHo gallery.... *Tel 212/533–1160. 148 Sullivan St., N/R train to Prince St.*

Murray's Cheese Shop. A small crowded shop where they're happy to give samples.... *Tel 212/243–3289. 257 Bleecker St., 1/9 train to Christopher St.*

Myer's of Keswick. For those craving British food staples, like PG Tips and Cornish pasties.... *Tel 212/691–4194. 634 Hudson St., A/C/E/L to 14th St.*

Mysterious Book Store. Murder and mayhem in Midtown.... *Tel 212/765–0900. 129 W. 56th St., N/R train to 57th St.*

New Republic Clothier. Handsome men's clothes.... *Tel 212/219–3005. 93 Spring St., N/R train to Prince St.*

New York Leather Company. Jackets, bags, etc.... *Tel 212/243–2710. 33 Christopher St., 1/9 train to Christopher St.*

Nicole Miller. Tastefully cool women's apparel.... *Tel 212/288–9779, 780 Madison Ave., 4/5/6 train to 59th St. or N/R to Lexington Ave.; tel 212/343–1362, 134 Prince St., N/R to Prince St.*

Nike Town. A glitzy temple to sports and sneakers, opening in 1996.... *4–10 E. 57th St., N/R train to 5th Ave.*

Norma Kamali. Stark, stylish women's designs.... *Tel 212/957–9797. 11 W. 56th St., N/R train to 5th Ave. Closed Sun.*

Odyssey. Cool, close-to-the-skin clothes.... *Tel 212/254–5492. 659 Broadway, B/D/Q/F train to Broadway/Lafayette.*

Old Japan, Inc. Antique kimonos and furniture.... *Tel 212/633–0922. 382 Bleecker St., 6 train to Bleecker St. Closed Mon–Tue.*

The Original Levi's Store. Flagship store for name denims.... *Tel 212/838—2125. 3 E. 57th St., N/R to 5th Ave.*

Out of Our Drawers, Inc. Earrings sold singly and in pairs, plus free ear piercing.... *Tel 212/929–4473. 184 7th Ave. S., 1/2/3/9 train to 14th St.*

Pace Wildenstein Gallery. Much-touted modern art.... *Tel 212/421–3292. 32 E. 57th St., N/R train to 5th Ave. Closed Sun–Mon.*

Paragon Sporting Goods. Equips every sport on the field, plus exercise togs.... *Tel 212/255–8036. 867 Broadway, 4/5/6/L/N/R train to Union Square.*

Patagonia. Eco-conscious sports gear, and totally trendy.... *Tel 212/343–1776. 101 Wooster St., N/R train to Prince St.*

Patrick Cox. High-style shoes from London.... *Tel 212/759–3910. 702 Madison Ave., 4/5/6 train to 59th St. or N/R to Lexington Ave.*

Paul Stuart. Smart men's clothiers.... *Tel 212/682–0320. Madison Ave. & 45th St., 4/5/6 or 7 train to Grand Central.*

Peanut Butter and Jane. Children's clothes and toys.... *Tel 212/620–7952. 617 Hudson St, 1/2/3/9 train to 14th St. Closed Sun.*

Penny Whistle Toys. Small but smartly-stocked toy store.... *Tel 212/873–9090, 483 Columbus Ave., B/C train to 81st St.; tel 212/369–3868, 1283 Madison Ave., 6 to 96th St.*

Peter Fox. Attractive women's shoes.... *Tel 212/431–6359. 105 Thompson St., N/R train to Prince St.*

Place des Antiquaires. High-end antiques, astronomically priced.... *Tel 212/758–2900. 125 E. 57th St., 4/5/6 train to 59th St. or N/R to Lexington Ave.*

Poltrona Frau. For leather-upholstered furniture in knock-out contemporary styles.... *Tel 212/777–7592. 141 Wooster St., N/R train to Prince St. Closed Sun.*

Portico Bed & Bath. Lovely bedroom and bathroom furnishings.... *Tel 212/941–7722. 139 Spring St., 6 train to Spring St.*

Portico Home. Eclectic furnishings.... *Tel 212/941–7800. 379 West Broadway, 1/9 train to Canal St.*

Porto Rico Importing Company. Great coffee, amazingly low prices, long lines.... *Tel 212/477–5421, 201 Bleecker St., 6 train to Bleecker St.; tel 212/533–1982, 40 1/2 St. Mark's Place, 6 to Astor Place or N/R to 8th St.*

Putumayo. Women's styles inspired by the Third World.... *Tel 212/595–3441. 341 Columbus Ave., 1/2/3/9 or B/C train to 72nd St.*

Raffetto's. Homemade pastry cut to size or shape right before your eyes.... *Tel 212/777–1261. 144 W. Houston St., N/R train to Prince St.*

Repeat Performance. A thrift that supports the New York City Opera.... *Tel 212/684–5344. 220 E. 23rd St., 6 train to 23rd St. Closed Sat–Sun in summer.*

Ritz Thrift Shop. Recycled furs.... *Tel 212/265–4559. 107 W. 57th St., B/Q to 57th St. Closed Sat–Sun in summer.*

Robert Talbott. Wide selection of exquisite ties.... *Tel 212/751–1200. 680 Madison Ave., 4/5/6 train to 59th St. or N/R to Lexington Ave.*

Sacco. SoHo shoes.... *Tel 212/925–8010. 111 Thompson St., N/R train to Prince St.; and other locations.*

Saks Fifth Avenue. Sleek, traditional department store goods.... *Tel 212/753–4000. 611 5th Ave; E/F train to 5th Ave.*

Salon Dada. Beautiful Chelsea architecture and chopped locks.... *Tel 212/741–3232. 4 W. 16th St., L/N/R/4/5/6 train to Union Square.*

Scents from Heaven. Mix-your-own natural oils.... *Tel 212/741–2595. 333 Bleecker St., 1/9 train to Christopher St.*

Scott Jordan. Mission-style furniture.... *Tel 212/620–4682. 137 Varick St., 1/9 train to Canal St.*

Screaming Mimi. Wild old styles, recycled largely from the sixties.... *Tel 212/677–6464. 382 Lafayette St., 6 train to Astor Place or N/R to 8th St.*

Shakespeare & Co. For book lovers on the Upper West Side.... *Tel 212/580–7800. 2259 Broadway, 1/9 train to 79th St.*

Sherry-Lehmann. An extraordinary selection of wine.... *Tel 212/838–7500. 679 Madison Ave., 4/5/6 train to 59th St. or N/R to Lexington Ave. Closed Sun.*

Smith & Hawken. Gardening goods, for stylish green thumbs.... *Tel 212/925–0687. 394 W. Broadway, C/E train to Spring St.*

Soho Emporium. Several dozen stalls under one roof, selling clothes and jewelry above all.... *Tel 212/966–6091. 375 W. Broadway, 1/9 train to Houston St.*

Soho Mill Outlet. Discount linens.... *Tel 212/226–8040. 490 Broadway, 1/9 train to Houston St.*

Sotheby's/Sotheby's Arcade. Auctioneers of note.... *Tel 212/606–7000. 1334 York Ave., 6 train to 72nd St.*

Stephane Kelian. Cover-girl-quality frocks.... *Tel 212/980–1919, 717 Madison Ave., 4/5/6 train to 59th St. or N/R to Lexington Ave.; tel 212/925–3077, 120 Wooster St., N/R to Prince St. or B/D/Q/F to Broadway/Lafayette.*

Strand Book Store. A browser's paradise for used books.... *Tel 212/473–1452. 828 Broadway, L/N/R/4/5/6 to Union Square.*

Street Life. Clothes for city girls.... *Tel 212/255–6411. 140 5th Ave., N/R train to 23rd St.; and other locations.*

S&W. Bargain women's clothes and accessories.... *Tel 212/924–6656. 165 W. 26th St., 1/9 train to 28th St. Closed Sat.*

Swatch. Plastic timepieces, of course.... *Tel 212/571–6400. Pier 17, South Street Seaport, 2/3/4/5/J/M/Z train to Fulton St. or A/C to Broadway/Nassau.*

Tepper Galleries. Better bargains in auctions.... *Tel 212/677–5300. 110 E. 25th St., 6 train to 28th St. Call for schedule.*

The Lace Up. Discount designer shoes on the Lower East Side.... *Tel 212/475–8040. 110 Orchard St., F train to Delancey St.*

Think Cartoons. T-shirts, mugs, caps—all bearing your favorite cartoon characters.... *Tel 212/431–5540. 505 Broome St., C/E train to Spring St. or 1/9 to Canal St.*

Three Lives. West Village fiction specialists.... *Tel 212/741–2069. 154 W. 10th St., F train to 14th St.*

Tiffany & Co. Gold, silver, gems, and crystal.... *Tel 212/755–8000. 757 5th Ave., N/R train to 5th Ave. Closed Sun.*

To Boot. Shoes and boots.... *Tel 212/724–8249. 256 Columbus Ave., 1/2/3/9 train to 72nd St.*

Todd Oldham Store. Well-cut gowns and goofy pop designs.... *Tel 212/219–3531. 123 Wooster St., N/R train to Prince St.*

T.O. Dey. Custom-made shoes.... *Tel 212/683–6300. 9 E. 38th St., B/D/Q/F train to 42nd St. or 7 to 5th Ave. Closed Sun.*

Tourneau. For high-end watches.... *Tel 212/758–6098. 500 Madison Ave., E/F train to 5th Ave.; and other locations.*

Tower Records/Tower Books/Tower Video. Grist for the CD player and VCR.... *Tel 212/505–1500, 692 Broadway, 6 train to Astor Place or N/R to 8th St.; tel 212/799–2500, 2107 Broadway, 1/2/3/9 train to 72nd St.; tel 212/838–8110, 57 5th Ave., E/F to 5th Ave.*

Toys 'R' Us. The big toy chain.... *Tel 212/594–8697, 1293 Broadway, N/R or B/D/Q/F train to 34th St.; tel 212/674–8697, 24–32 Union Square E., 4/5/6, N/R, or L to Union Square.*

Urban Outfitters. Mass-market hip, Timberland boots, for youths.... *Tel 212/475–0009, 628 Broadway, 1/9 train to Houston St.; tel 212/677–9350, 360 6th Ave., A/C/E/F train to W. 4th St.*

Valentino. The stylish designer showroom, sophisticated prêt à porter.... *Tel 212/744–0200. 825 Madison Ave., 6 train to 68th St.*

Van Cleef & Arpels. Fifth Avenue jewels.... *Tel 212/644–9500. 744 5th Ave., N/R train to 5th Ave. Closed Sat–Sun.*

Video Camera Palace. All kinds of electronics.... *Tel 212/629–8977. 885 6th Ave., B/D/Q/F or N/R train to 34th St.*

Village Tannery. West Village leather goods.... *Tel 212/673–5444. 173 Bleecker St., A/C/E or B/D/Q/F to W. 4th St.; and other locations.*

Warner Brothers Studio Store. Cartoon and movie memorabilia.... *Tel 212/754–0300. 1 E. 57th St., N/R train to 5th Ave.*

Wicker Garden's Children. Infant wear and clothing for well-clad kids.... *Tel 212/410–7001. 1327 Madison Ave., 6 train to 96th St. Closed Sat–Sun.*

William Doyle Galleries. Classic furniture auction house, very East Side.... *Tel 212/427–2730. 175 E. 87th St., 4/5/6 train to 86th St.*

Wooster Gallery. Art-deco furniture and fixtures, in SoHo.... *Tel 212/219–2190. 86 Wooster St., 6 train to Spring St.*

Yohji Yamamoto. Hip, slightly Edwardian men's and women's clothes.... *Tel 212/966–9066. 103 Grand St., N/R train to Prince St.*

Yves Saint Laurent. The classic French designer's Manhattan branch.... *Tel 212/246–9494. 855 Madison Ave., 6 train to 68th St.*

Zabar's. All the food that's fit to eat, plus great housewares upstairs.... *Tel 212/787–2000. 2245 Broadway, 1/9 train to 79th St.*

nigh

6

tlife

If you can't find something to do at night in New York, you should have stayed home. Though the city's vaunted nightlife doesn't shimmy at quite the same speed it did in the Jazz Age of the '20s, when Uptown sophistication and lowlife excess freely mingled, it does rip along at a pretty relentless pace. Sex, drugs, and androgyny were standard operating procedure in the '70s at clubs like Max's Kansas City, while during the '80s new money mixed it up with art-world all-stars and downtown hipsters at the Mudd Club, Nell's, Limelight, and the Palladium. Much has changed since the bottom fell out of the "Decade of Greed", but the yuppified high times of the '80s have been replaced in the '90s by a vastly more appealing, and certainly more democratic, moveable feast of eclectic club offerings matched with venerable cosmopolitan customs.

A few tips: New Yorkers do everything later than the rest of the country, so take a nap before undertaking the club crawl. And eat something; it's a rare NYC nighttime bacchanal that includes much more than sparse finger-food and pricey booze. A few weeks before visiting the Big Apple, try to get a vibe for what to wear out, but keep it simple—New York at night can be a dispiriting experience if you look stupid. Dressing right isn't all that hard if you stick to the basics. (Black always works.) Weeknights are the slicker evenings to negotiate the club circuit—the kids who make the scene regard weekends contemptuously as a time for unsuited stiffs to intrude on their dominion. The velvet ropes have mostly disappeared, so getting in isn't the humiliating trial it used to be. And if the desired scene isn't at one club, move on. Club-hopping is a way of life for most of the city's devoted nightlife denizens, so get in the swing by tasting a bit of several places during a single evening.

In the '90s, clubs in New York have taken a much more thematic approach to their weekly schedules: What was clearly a straight scene on Monday night can be transformed into a queer extravaganza for Tuesday, from a relatively sedate evening of jazz-meets-rap on Thursday to a hard-core house-mix frenzy on Friday. Some clubs even shift locations from night to night, with the site a privileged secret among a select few hipsters—at least until the word spreads, which it inevitably does. Make a couple of new friends on the dance floor and your chances of being swept along for the ride increase. If the club gets too intense, there's Manhattan's burgeoning lounge scene to explore, where clubland intrigues can be pursued in vastly more subdued digs. Wind down the night at one of Manhattan's several notable after-hours eateries (see Dining); omelettes and coffee at 4am are as much a part of a quality clubbing experience as any dance hall pyrotechnics.

Sources

Paper magazine, while not the clubgoers' bible it once was, is still the definitive guidebook to what's hot for many, not in the least because of its voracious appetite for ferreting out the newest, gaudiest scenes. If your tastes run to drag queens and teenage urchins done up like extras in "Speed Racer: The Musical," then the pages of *Paper* are where you'll want to turn for tips. The ever-reliable ***Village Voice*** does a better job of chronicling the music scene than the club world, but the weekly alternative tabloid still devotes a sizable chunk of its back pages to nightlife advertising, and scenester-diva Michael Musto's dishy gossip column "La Dolce Musto" often catches the club-trotting fabulous with their pants down. ***Time Out*** magazine, which comes out weekly, provides exhaustive weekly listings of nightlife options. ***Outweek***, ***The Advocate***, and a stack of lesser weekly newsletters chronicle the city's vibrant queer scene. Depending on one's predilections, it's usually a good idea to stick to the first two, which are more professional and established, but for the anything-goes set, the personals in ***H/X*** (Homo-Extra) are always a treat. This slim, usually free (though you might be charged $2.50 in NYC, $1.50 out of town) gay weekly covers the queer club scene (which has become increasingly indistinguishable from the club scene at large) in roughly the same manner that *Playbill* reports on theater: succinctly and in a easy-to-carry size. ***Sound Views***, a free-in-New-York, $2-elsewhere fanzine has been

The Naked City

Girls! Girls! Girls!... Live Nude Acts... *They used to call Forty-Second Street between Seventh and Ninth Avenues "The Deuce"; Eighth Avenue from 40th Street to Central Park West was "Minnesota Strip," because many of the hookers who patrolled here even in the dead of winter had toughened up back on Midwestern farms, where they grew up. The hinterlands of Times Square remain the domain of pimps, prostitutes, peep shows, and adult entertainment video stores. Forty-Second Street, though, is in the midst of a massive redevelopment project, spearheaded by the Disney Corporation. But as jaded New Yorkers know, this will only push the sleaze factor elsewhere. The sleaze has already crept south to the environs of the Port Authority Bus Terminal and Javits Convention Center, west of Eleventh Avenue between 34th and 38th streets. X-rated shows and video porn shops are scattered in the east Fifties between Third and Second avenues, catering specifically to well-heeled businessmen with exceedingly malleable expense allowances. And transvestite hookers stroll the West Side Highway and Washington Street in the Village.*

reporting on the extremes of the subterranean music scene for more than 30 issues. If your interests run to bands with names like "Kurt Cobain Haiku," this is the rag for you. ***aRUDE***, a new quarterly, follows the adventures of the neo-Warholian crowd, combining beefy interviews with cultural figures like Bill T. Jones with dishy and opinionated ruminations on downtown's endlessly percolating cafe society. If nightlife reports that combine dandified dramatics with some IQ are what you crave, then this style journal of Nigerian artist Iké Udé's is your cup of tea. On occasion, The "Style" section of the Sunday ***New York Times*** (it's tucked into the "Metro" section) glosses over a club event in the course of chasing another trend or tracking a mainstream celebrity. If you have any interest at all in where Madonna was last seen, this would be a good place to start. ***New York Press*** includes a Dance Clubs listing in its weekly summary of events—clipped and generally reliable, but not exactly fabulous. It's good for a very quick take on a place you've never been.

Liquor Laws

Despite rumors that the legal drinking age in New York City is 10, one *can* get busted for proffering fake ID. Of course, if the clubs locked out all the underagers, their business would quickly evaporate, as would their cachet of youth chic. If you're not yet 21, New York State's legal drinking age, don't expect to get served once you get in. If you can't get in, go someplace else; chances are at least one benevolent doorman or bouncer somewhere will take a shine to the way you've worked your look. Some clubs offer special drinks, called "smart drinks," for patrons who've depleted themselves on the dance floor: these nutrient-addled beverages offer a quick fix for dehydration and decreased electrolytes, all without alcohol.

Drugs

"Just say no" is not the New York club tramp's motto. Cocaine is no longer the narcotic of choice, and crackheads are usually too busy getting toasted to think about dancing, but speed and ecstasy help many a clubgoer keep up with a hammering techno beat. It's part of the scene, so look the other way.

The Lowdown

Hot spots below 14th Street... Most New Yorkers will tell you that the only geographic point worth knowing is 14th Street—everything above 14th is square, everything below potentially cool. There are longtime downtown residents who can count on the fingers of one hand the number of times they've crossed this cultural divide. These days, the slickest sub-14th neighborhood is the Lower East Side around Ludlow Street, where there are several lounges/clubs/bars, including the white hot **Sapphire**, late night home to a slickly-fashionable crowd, and **bOb**, a laid-back scene on weeknights, but so crowded on the weekend that body armor is in order. For the less trendy, a wonderful spot for a few gently drawn stouts is **288**, a bar whose loftlike, breezy architecture redefines the whole idea of a beer joint. Farther west, the truly raving downtown society victim will not fail to put in an appearance at **Bowery Bar**, the new epicenter of Manhattan chic, or **Odeon** (see Dining), a TriBeCa '80s go-go landmark that has recently undergone a renaissance.

Hot spots above 14th Street... Union Square's **Coffee Shop** (see Dining) is technically north of 14th Street, although 14th Street's fiat actually extends to the northern edge of Union Square; this fashion-model hangout set the standard for posing and gawking. **Flowers**, a cafe in the French style, gives models another casual environment in which to drink water, smoke cigarettes, and gaze longingly at the menu. Midtown's Bryant Park, home to the chic-at-lunchtime **Bryant Park Grill** (see Dining), takes Manhattan to the drive-in with a series of free summer film screenings that start at dusk. Arrive early and bring booze and a blanket.

Gotta dance... The newest thing to hit town, after rampant success in London, is jungle vibe, which has found a Monday-night home at **Wetlands**, Manhattan's most prominent neo-hippie joint. The scene is vibrantly multicult and the vibe deeply positive when an assortment of DJs and spoken-word poets brings Koncrete Jungle into the house. **Nell's** can no longer claim the central status it once held in New York's clubland zeitgeist of the 1980s, but its plush Victorian decor now plays host on Monday nights to Funky Buddha, a classy scene that attracts a lower-key clientele than the city's trendier boogie shacks. And forget not **The Roxy**, whose venerable dance-hall walls in Chelsea shelter Rollerballs on Monday nights, a carnival of classic-disco-meets-in-line-skating-tricksterism—just don't call it a rink! On Tuesday nights, **The Bar Room**, far west on 14th Street, belongs to Jackie 60, ribald brainchild of DJ Johnny Dynell and MC Chi Chi Valenti, who preside over a decadent fall-of-Rome scenario where drag queens rub elbows with trashy club strumpets outfitted in T-shirts so tiny and tight that you'll never be in doubt over their body temperature. The club has set up a hotline to provide newcomers with the dope, but even if you know what to wear and how to wear it, Jackie 60's enactment of life's zanier fantasies is not for the faint of heart. The scene at **Sound Factory Bar** is supremely down and has been for years: On Wednesday nights, Underground Network holds sway, jamming through sweaty evenings of Manhattan's hottest, most popular house mix. A must stop if high-impact aerobic clubbing is why you came to town. Hip-hop rules at Saturday night's Honeycomb Hideout, which rollicks into **Astor's** on Lafayette Street. Veterans of '80s clubbing remember the **Tunnel** as a splendid goth cavern where everyone looked scrumptiously pallid in the calculated gloom; well, Tunnel is back, featuring a Sunday night hip-hop fest called Mecca.

Live and loud... Ever since punk broke and grunge hit (and dithered out), New York has seen its once-proud dominance of the pop music scene shift to cities like Seattle, Austin, Chapel Hill, and—perish the thought—San Francisco. But New York can still boast of the clubs where the "New York Sound" got started in the late '60s and early '70s with bands like The Velvet Underground, the Patti Smith Group, Television, the Talking Heads, and The Ramones. Don't forget, either, that rap and hip-hop cut their teeth in New York, an urban groove typified by Public Enemy and The Beastie Boys. No survey of the Downtown club scene is complete without a visit to **CBGB/OMFUG**, a dingy Bowery rathole with a sound system known throughout the tri-state area for its Homeric volume; to echo a line from *This Is Spinal Tap*, the noise at CBGB doesn't go to eleven; it goes to twelve. Drop a few bucks on a bottle of Rolling Rock and settle in for an evening of eardrum torture—there might be a name act, might be just some Jersey kids who've just learned how to play in tune, sort of. For a more acoustic, folksy vibe, slip next door to **CB's 313 Gallery**, virtually a clean, well-lighted place in comparison to its older brother. **Sin-é**

(pronounced shin-AY), a tiny street-level space in the East Village, shelters Irish expats; expect an unannounced set from whichever Irish songster happens to have washed up on Manhattan's shores. Waiting for Sinead O'Connor to breeze in and wail through a set of Van Morrison covers is half the fun, but don't get your hopes up. **Webster Hall**, a huge space near an NYU dorm, diversifies its offerings; some evenings, the scene is DJs and the merciless pulsing of the rhythm nation, but on others the audience turns out to catch a rising band of rude boys last glimpsed on MTV's "Buzz Cuts." The booking habits of **Wetlands**, that free-spirited West Village club, have exhibited a more adventurous edge in the past few years: Hear bands like Rise Robots Rise, a curious collective of rappers drunk on Frank Zappa. Down the street from frightfully genteel Gramercy Park dwells **Irving Plaza**, a flat-out great place to see a show—there's enough open space here to dampen the roar issuing from turbo-amped Fender Stratocasters and Rickenbacker Hollow Bodies. The management regularly books up-and-comers on their first swing through the Apple. Last coup: P. J. Harvey, a wan British heir to Patti Smith's jagged laurels. A welcome beacon in a scary neighborhood (the Lower East Side, for all its newfound boho credentials), **Ludlow Street Cafe** has been home for countless Monday nights to Beat Rodeo, a butt-kicking, no-BS area band that steadfastly refuses to compromise its loyalties by getting as famous as it should. Over on East Houston Street, **Mercury Lounge** opens its doors to the disaffected detritus that slinks nightly out of Lucky Cheng's or Babyland, the pick-up palaces a beer-can's throw away; whether rejected or accepted, here they can settle into a steady diet of fresh, cool sounds. The truly intrepid wait beside the West Side Highway for the show to start at **Marquee**, one of the few New York clubs that seems willing to book in refugees from bands you haven't heard of since 1982. If fierce ole thumpin' base riffs and growling vocals are what you seek, **Tramps** might have your blues (or zydeco) medicine. Mighty loud on some nights, but almost always good as gold. **SOB**'s (Sounds of Brazil) is bossa nova's and world beat's residence this side of the equator; if Tito Puente or Astrud Gilberto is what you crave, this is where you should turn. Two outer-borough joints set the cadence for the cutting edge: **Maxwell's** in Hoboken, NJ, and **Lauterbach's** in Brooklyn. Maxwell's may make it into *The New Yorker* more often, but it's hard to argue with Lauterbach's ambience: it's like a double-wide trailer home crossed with the basement set of *Wayne's World.*

For neo-lounge lizards and nightcrawlers... Ever since rappers figured out that their music owed a debt to New York's glorious jazz masters of the 1950s and '60s, hip-hop meets be-bop (known locally as acid jazz or jazzmatazz) nights have fueled Giant Step, a supercool Thursday-night festival. Itinerant during its early years, Giant Step now hangs its porkpie hat at E. Houston Street's **The Bank**. A pack of Phillies Blunts and some casually slick threads, plus $10, gets you in the door. On Wednesday nights, duck into **Buddha Bar** for Opium Den—an earful of Isaac Hayes, Otis Redding, and others (and an eyeful of that special someone at the next table). Then head for Second Avenue, draw aside the chain-mail curtain, and enter **Flamingo East**, one of the East Village's first neo-lounges. It's dark, it's fashionable, it's full of skinny boys with unwashed hair. Posture is the first thing that gets checked when you walk in the door, so slouch like a true lounge lizard.

See-and-be-scenes... **Bar d'O**, in a charming nook of the West Village, has picked an unlikely neighborhood for its version of lounge meets drag. On Saturdays and Tuesdays, Joey Arias and several other high-heeled divas put on a torchy, intimate show. Not an unpleasant alternative to the dance-till-you-drop frenzy encountered elsewhere in clubland. It's dark as a whale's belly, but the gloom helps everyone look sexier in the flickering candlelight. **Tenth Street Lounge**, with massive metal doors, mission furnishings, lambent ambience, and God-awful expensive booze, is where the East-Village-chic set convenes nightly for stylish posing, though lately the joint has been colonized by some bold out-of-towners toting Macy's bags. The desperately fashionable staff, however, continues to snub on an equal-opportunity basis. For the fearless, there's the frequently odious but always sexy **Bowery Bar**, where the velvet rope has actually made a comeback and reservations are de rigueur for *drinks*. If supermodel Veronica Webb, art dealer Larry Gagosian, or *Rolling Stone* publisher Jann Wenner are on your list of celebs to spot, the search begins here. A much more accessible, and sometimes even literary, crowd gathers around the corner at **Marion's**, a kitschy hole-in-the-wall bar drenched in '50s lounge karma. The martini is what everyone eventually orders here, just because the decor demands it. (Reasonably good food, too.) The beautifully designed **M&R**, just off Houston Street, is transporting: Its imagined destination is Europe in the 1950s. Tenderly catered to by its conscientious staff, M&R also features a bar that sports some of the largest ashtrays in town. It opens at 5pm, just in time for a Campari and soda after a day of parched East Village thrifting or SoHo gallery hopping. Up in Midtown, the **Paramount** hotel and the **Royalton** hotel each have lobbies designed by architect Philipe Starck, whose aesthetic dictates softly curving furniture in deep, soothing colors, dramatic glass banisters, antique Bakelite telephones, and severe bathrooms shingled with chrome and mirrors (the urinals in the Royalton's men's room showcase Manhattan's best-known waterfall). The Royalton is where the Condé Nast crowd and the editors of *The New Yorker* assemble for power lunches; at night, a stylish crowd gathers to fortify themselves for a evening of socializing. The Paramount's Whiskey Bar hops with a more down-to-earth after-work drinks scene.

If Sinatra's your style... Though the city's nightlife scene is geared toward the youthquake's latest rumblings, you can rage in your own way with some very urbane sophisticates. **The Rainbow Room**, perhaps Gotham's most famous bar, possesses one of the city's grandest views, taking in the whole sweep of the island in four directions from its windowed home atop Midtown's Rockefeller Center. Revolving dance floor, big-band music, the works; top cabaret acts perform at the attached **Rainbow & Stars**. **Tavern on the Green**, Central Park's twinkle-lit restaurant, attracts jazz luminaries like Margaret Whiting and Lionel Hampton to its Chestnut Room; in summer, you can dance cheek-to-cheek outside in the garden, under glowing chintz-covered lanterns. The legendary **Algonquin** hotel, once home to the scabrous wit of Dorothy Parker and the Round Table's clutch of literary regulars (among them humorist Robert Benchley and *New Yorker* founder Harold Ross), still offers clubby charm, and its Oak Room books superb pop- and jazz-standard vocalists on the order of Andrea Marcovicci and Michael Feinstein. But for the quintessential New York crooner, you'll have to work your way north and east to the **Carlyle Hotel**, where Bobby Short holds court at Cafe Carlyle when he's in town. Bemelman's Bar, also in the Carlyle, is rumored to pour the city's finest martini.

Painting the town pink... Some of New York's gay and lesbian hangouts have become as widely known as Stonewall itself, the climactic event that set the whole homo-liberation movement in motion. The scenes vary, however, so know your tastes before stepping out. A great neighborhood to get started in (for men) is Chelsea—between the leather-boys and gym-bunnies, this is fag heaven (lesbians will have better luck in the West Village). **David Barton Gym** on Sixth Avenue is a good place to gawk at the sculpted; some nights it seems like everyone who enters or leaves the establishment has less than one-percent body fat and abs to die for. A few blocks away is **Splash**, a genial happytime cruising facility—the name suggests a pool party, and water metaphors abound, but the scene is so friendly you'll forget about all the queer-cruising cliches. **Rawhide**, on Eighth Avenue, serves cheap drinks from 8am, for those just spilling out of the clubs. Don't knock over any of the custom Harleys parked out front; this is a leather-and-Levis scene that lives up to its name. Way the hell over on the West Side is **The Spike**, a serious leather scene that, with the recent surge in S/M interest, now draws a more eclectic crowd. Monday is movie night, Tuesday club night, Wednesday bikers and blue jeans. It's advisable to wear something waterproof. Everyone eventually swings through **The Bar**, an East Village institution with a bohemian roadhouse/pool-hall persona. It's an excellent choice for beer and cruising after a performance at La Mama (see Entertainment), the nearby alternative-theater mecca. The cruising is both splendid and silly at **Wonder Bar**, a very friendly East Villager crammed with goofy erotica and colorful fixtures. **The Monster** screams West Village—shimmery, slightly garish, and full of attractive gay men—fulfilling every cruiser's dream while remaining devoted to cabaret and dancing. Though some have knocked it for appealing mainly to lesbian professional types, **Julie's**, a romantic piano lounge in Midtown, is really one of the most sophisticated rooms around, regardless of one's sexuality. For the most part, however, men are not particularly welcome, unless they come with company. **Crazy Nanny's** (just "Nanny's" to most regulars) and **Henrietta Hudson** are two of the most popular dyke bars in town, providing all the basics (pool table, jukebox, cheap drinks) plus dancing and (occasionally) comedy; along with the more upscale **Orbit**, they form a sort of downtown pink triangle of cruising possibilities.

Bars where you can hear yourself think... Bloomsbury junkies will fall in love immediately with **Book Friends Cafe** in the Flatiron district; the decor is straight out of the twenties, all green baize and dark wood and piles of musty old books, and tea paraphernalia abounds. Frequent readings share space with summertime ballroom-style dancing. Or try two other charming cafes in the West Village—**Cafe de Bruxelles** (see Dining), with its long bar and a dozen varieties of Belgian beer, and the **Cornelia Street Cafe**, easily the best first-date restaurant in the city. There's a white-tableclothed sidewalk set-up out front, a just-the-right-size bar, a back room with a fireplace, and lots of readings and live music downstairs, all with a delightful staff and extremely professional barkeeps.

C'mon get happy... For the poverty-stricken and terminally out-of-work, **Sidewalk Cafe**, an East Village bastion, gets started at 2pm and doesn't end its two-for-one offer until 8. That's six uninterrupted hours, kids. No one in town has the chutzpah to beat that. **Man Ray**, however, does offer a pretty similar deal to its generally more well-heeled Chelsea patrons: from 4 to 6, any drink is two-for-one, and the kitchen serves up some of the tastiest pizza in the city for free. You can actually think of this as an early dinner if you're in the right frame of mind.

Getting lucky... When it opened in 1994, everyone thought it was going to be SoHo's contribution to the city's exploding lounge scene. But contrary to expectations, **The Cub Room** became a Wall Street–singles outpost, constantly shrouded in a testosterone and estrogen fog, where straight white girls in pumps ogle and get ogled by straight white boys in pinstripes and loosened ties. That notwithstanding, it remains a killer room, jammed with gorgeous chintz sofas lit by tastefully small lamps. There's a superb restaurant attached. **America**, a vast space in the Flatiron district, owns not only the longest menu in Manhattan, but also a thriving pick-up scene after business hours, rivaled only by **Zip City**, a microbrewery one block east. Both places are usually packed with predatory ad execs and wolfen market-jocks, so ladies should keep their legs crossed. **The Old Town Bar**, one of Manhattan's oldest and best-loved watering holes, shouldn't have a singles scene, but it does. After five, the place fills up remarkably fast with Flatiron-district office drones on the prowl. A curiosity: With the passage of New York's anti-smoking ordinance, lighting up is prohibited at the booths but permitted five feet farther west, at the long bar. For a slightly more open-minded and decidedly sexier scene, try **Cafe Tabac**, a small East Village bar and restaurant decorated with a French Moroccan flavor. It's every man and woman for him- or herself at **Live Bait**, a sometimes terrifying Flatiron joint decorated like a beachcomber bar, where fashion and photographers' models get endlessly hit on by jobless guys who tool around on Harleys. On SoHo's main drag, the place to get cruised is **I Tre Merli**, an enormous bar and restaurant that can open its entire front facade to the parade of hunks and lovelies that stalk West Broadway after dark. **Lucky Strike**, a little farther south, reminds everyone of that bar they used to go to in college; the aesthetic is barnyard bric-a-brac, but the crowd is hip and youthful. For a fabulous pastiche of different types, from multi-pierced men to women tottering on platform Adidas, **Stingy Lulu's** in the East Village is where the tattooed set goes.

Kink... For those whose pleasures lean toward far left field, **The Vault** offers a heavily gothic S/M dungeon scene right out of Anne Rice: manslaves locked in cages, strapped to bondage crosses, or trussed from harnesses moan eagerly in response to insults from their mistresses. Women can play, too, or just watch, which is what a fair portion of the crowd does. Frankly, though, The Vault can be quite a turn off if the sight of a dozen men engaged in group masturbation makes you uncomfortable. For more conventional kinkiness, there's **Billy's Topless**, one of Manhattan's most beloved strip joints, where you can blow 50 bucks on lap dances. Or else just cruise Times Square's good old-fashioned American porn palaces (found mainly on 42nd Street and Eighth Avenue), many of which feature films and live sex shows—it offers something prurient for everyone, gay or straight.

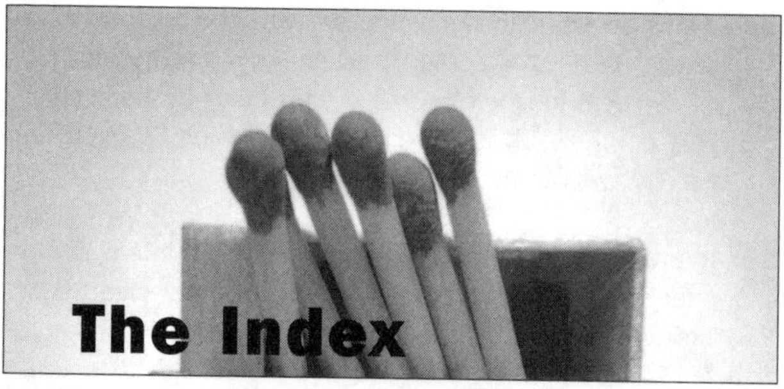

The Index

Algonquin. An elegant lounge-cum-lobby in front and The Oak Room in back make this Manhattan literary landmark one of the city's most celebrated places to meet before stepping out. Some of the jazz world's finest crooners play here.... *Tel 212/840–6800. 59 W. 44th St., B/D/Q/F train to 42nd St. or 7 to Fifth Ave.*

America. Vast. Simply furnished. Scads of tables and a bar that's an event in itself. The crowd is eclectic and sometimes cruisy after five, but the bloom of youth is not a prerequisite. An easy place to land in the newly chic Flatiron district.... *Tel 212/505–2110. 9 E. 18th St., N/R, 4/5/6, or L train to Union Square.*

Astor's. A hard-core hip-hop club stop, and therefore a young scene (the median age probably hovers around 19). Attire is baggy street wear, baggy skateboard gear, or exposed skin.... *Tel 212/473–1698. 428 Lafayette St., N/R train to Prince St. or B/D/Q/F to Broadway/Lafayette.*

The Bank. Loud, loud, loud music—and often throbbing techno—fill this high-ceilinged space, which also features a light-system borrowed from an arena-rock act. Thursday nights belong to Giant Step.... *Tel 212/505–5033; hotline 212/414–8001. 225 E. Houston St., B/D/Q/F train to Broadway/Lafayette. Cover charge.*

The Bar. Laid-back queer scene for leather, Levis, boho shagginess, and khakis (everybody's welcome!). Not much inside beyond cheap drinks, benches, and a minimally lit pool table, but the cruising is solid. Beer is $2 and drinks $2.50 during the 4–8 happy hour Mon–Fri.... *Tel 212/674–9714. 68 Second Ave. (at 4th St.), F train to Second Ave.*

Bar d'O. A comfortable lounge tucked away in the almost loungeless West Village. The neighborhood's well-heeled residents seem to ignore it—the nights belong to the lethargically hip.... *Tel 212/627-1580. 34 Downing St., A/C/E/ or B/D/Q/F train to W. 4th St.*

Bar Room. DJ Toni C provides an irresistable mix in a club that offers a weekly feast of divine display–from Jackie 60 on Tuesday to the Clit Club lesbian dance frenzy on Friday.... *Tel 212/505-5033; theme and dress-code hotline 212/677-6060. 432 W. 14th St., A/C/E train to 14th St.*

Billy's Topless. Yes, the ladies take their blouses off. Predictable and sleazy, with the sort of ambience that only a lecher could love. Still, not an outlandish alternative to peep shows.... *729 Sixth Ave., F Train to 23rd St.*

bOb. The lounge as weekend shimmy shack. Not a half-bad place on the Lower East Side for subdued drinks during the weeks, but on Friday and Saturday, the breathing room disappears.... *245 Eldridge St., F train to Broadway/Lafayette.*

Book Friends Cafe. Is that a tea dance? And what about that guy in the tweeds digging through old copies of *Eminent Victorians*? If shameless Victorian, but with a fair dash of tasty food in an endlessly inviting book shop setting, is your cup, then get on over to the emerald of West 18th Street's used-book row.... *Tel 212/255-7407. 16 W. 18th St., F train to 14th St.*

Bowery Bar. An enormous walled garden encloses New York's trendy and fabulous as they steal drags from each other's Marlboro Lights and try to steal peeks at the designer labels. If fashion divas, fashion victims, and scenesters with limited verbal skills are what you crave, look no further. Reservations a must.... *Tel 212/475-2220. 358 Bowery, B/D/Q/F train to Broadway/Lafayette. Reservations required.*

Buddha Bar. A hot-buttered, low-key love habitat that plays host to one of the city's most consistently sexy crowds. Most are content to sit, drink, and quietly study each other. No live music, but who needs it when you can make your own?.... *Tel 212/255-4433. 150 Varick St., 1/9 train to Houston St.*

Cafe Tabac. A romantic gem for some, a place to spot Madonna for others, it all depends on your attitude. Come here for something tall and cool, either to drink or to go home with.... *Tel 212/674–7072. 232 E. 9th St., 6 train to Astor Place or N/R to 8th St.*

Carlyle Hotel. An older, intelligent, stylish mafia with a taste for jazz standards and well-mixed drinks call the Cafe Carlyle home, especially when Bobby Short takes up residence and the ivories.... *Tel 212/744–1600. 983 Madison Ave., 6 train to 77th St. $45 cover. Reservations required.*

CBGB/OMFUG and CB's 313 Gallery. The aesthetic: untrammeled filth. The decor: layers of wheat-pasted posters and decades of graffiti. Suggested attire: something torn. So much music got going at this club, though, that playing the joint has become a necessary rite of passage. Next door's 313 Gallery showcases quieter acts.... *Tel 212/982–4052. 315–313 Bowery, B/D/Q/F train to Broadway/Lafayette.*

Cornelia Street Cafe. Something of a tightly guarded West Village secret, the perfect spot for a quiet first date or a few unemcumbered hours at barside. Plus the only legitimate sidewalk cafe west of Sixth Avenue. Absolutely dependable, a beacon on any night.... *Tel 212/989–9319. 29 Cornelia St., F train to West 4th St.*

Crazy Nanny's. One of the Village's lesbian standbys, a friendly room where girls will be girls. If you walk in lonely and depressed, the relaxed atmosphere will most likely perk you up and maybe even connect you with someone special.... *Tel 212/366–6312. 21 Seventh Ave. S., A/C/E or B/D/Q/F train to W. 4th St.*

The Cub Room. A scalding singles scene for both the sleazy and the button-down sets. The food is also pretty fair (chef Henry Meer formerly called Lutèce home), as are the surroundings, which feature comfy sofas and tables large enough to hold more than a gimlet.... *Tel 212/677–4100. 131 Sullivan St., C/E train to Spring St.*

David Barton Gym. They're buff and they're proud. The clientele at this Chelsea sweat den isn't exclusively gay, but the guys that are have bodies that command attention.... *Tel 212/727–0004. 552 Sixth Ave., F train to 14th St.*

Flamingo East. No, it's not just you; everyone in this lounge looks as if a few days at the beach would do them a world of good. But why leave town when you can beat the heat with other members of your downtown boho brood?.... *Tel 212/533–2860. 219 Second Ave., 4/5/6, N/R, or L train to Union Square.*

Flowers. Models, models, models. They may not eat, but they gotta drink someplace, and this perfectly lovely bistro is one of the photo district's main venues for scoping out the starved and the leggy. Good food, polite service, and very discreet.... *Tel 212/691–8888. 21 W. 17th St., F train to 14th St.*

Henrietta Hudson. Another of the Village's perfectly delightful dyke bars, where k.d. lang's singles have been retired from the jukebox.... *Tel 212/924–3347. 438 Hudson St., 1/9 train to Christopher St.*

Irving Plaza. Big old place to see alternative acts; the management has shown some redoubtable booking talent, as well as prescience about the next hot thing.... *Tel 212/249–8870. 17 Irving Place, 4/5/6, N/R, or L train to Union Square. Tickets range $8 to $30.*

I Tre Merli. A cavernous SoHo emporium for cruising the very beautiful.... *Tel 212/254-8699. 463 W. Broadway, C/E train to Spring St. or N/R to Prince St.*

Julie's. Not just the mellowest and most dignified lesbian hangout in Midtown, but a jewel in the crown of the city's whole queer piano-bar scene. You can always come as you are and invite envious glares from the power-suited crowd.... *Tel 212/688–1294. 204 E. 58th St., 4/5/6 train to 59th St. or N/R to Lexington Ave.*

Lauterbach's. A rec room with a pool table in front and a stage in the back. Brooklyn's beautiful losers as well as legit talent blow in to shake the house.... *Tel 718/788–9140. 335 Prospect Ave., Brooklyn; F train to 15th St./Prospect Park.*

Live Bait. If you leave this Flatiron dive lacking company, you just haven't been working hard enough on your mojo. Heaven for guys with a hundred lines and leggy models who've heard them all.... *Tel 212/353–2400. 14 E. 23rd St., N/R train to 23rd St.*

Lucky Strike. You're liable to get pushed out the door and onto the street if you don't snag a table early at this SoHo bar. The young and attractive crowd sometimes seems as if it's never heard the word trousers, but that's okay—most of them look too good in jeans to care.... *Tel 212/941–0479. 59 Grand St., B/D/Q/F to Grand St.*

Ludlow Street Cafe. Anchor of the Lower East Side's neo-bohemia. Somebody plays here almost every night of the week.... *Tel 212/353–0536. 165 Ludlow St., B/D/Q/F train to Broadway/Lafayette.*

M&R. Disappear here to a vanished version of Continental charm and style. An admirably stocked bar gives way to an inviting dining room decorated with nudes that only just border on kitsch. Don't miss the Lower East Side's largest collection of truly gigantic liquor bottles.... *Tel 212/226–0559. 264 Elizabeth St., B/D/Q/F train to Broadway/Lafayette.*

Man Ray. The space is manicured to an almost ridiculous degree, as are most of the people hanging out and killing time before the next dance performance at the nearby Joyce Theater. Park yourself in the glow of a votive candle at one of the bar's small-ish tables and wait for something interesting to amble in.... *Tel 212/627–4220. 169 Eighth Ave., C/E train to 23rd St.*

Marion's. Hep, man. One of the only bars in town to find even 22-year-olds huddled over silky, arid martinis. (It probably has something to do with the neon sign out front, a tilted Martini glass.) Well, you can't swill Bud forever.... *Tel 212/475–7621. 354 Bowery, B/D/Q/F train to Broadway/Lafayette.*

Marquee. The far, far West Side's warehouse/loading dock is home to a succession of pop and alternative acts, many with a distinctly British accent.... *Tel 212/929–3257. 547 W. 21st St., C/E train to 23rd St. $20 cover.*

Maxwell's. New Jersey's main claim to the alternative music scene. Scads of bands with contracts played here when they were getting by on Spaghetti-O's and comp beer.... *Tel 201/798–4064. Washington and 11th St., Hoboken, NJ; NJ Transit or PATH train to Hoboken.*

Mercury Lounge. On it's way to becoming an East Village legend, with an eclectic schedule of bands offering something for every alternative taste.... *Tel 212/260–4700. 217 E. Houston St., F train to Second Ave.*

The Monster. Find a gay man in New York who hasn't passed an evening at Sheridan Square's best-known fag bar and you'll have found yourself a legitimate recluse.... *Tel 212/924–3558. 80 Grove St., 1/9 train to Christopher St.*

Nell's. Still crazy after all these years, continuing to appeal to the shifting appetites of the '90s style tribes.... *Tel 212/675–1567. 246 W. 14th St., A/C/E train to 14th St.*

The Old Town Bar. Nobody messes with The Old Town, and four-person booths the size of gazebos along with a slightly yupped-out but still polite crowd make sure no one wants to.... *Tel 212/529–6732. 45 E. 18th St., 4/5/6, N/R, or L train to Union Square.*

Orbit. Chicks! But boys shouldn't get their hopes up: Most of the female regulars only have eyes for the other female regulars. A cozy place for an early evening rendezvous, though several of the bartenders have an odd habit of putting scotch in a wine glass.... *Tel 212/463–8717. 46 Bedford St., A/C/E or B/D/Q/F train to W. 4th St.*

Paramount. A temple of design, from the film-noir house phones to the elegant curve of the lucite banister that guides hipsters up to The Whiskey Bar, where the house specialty is a gigantic martini with a gigantic olive.... *Tel 212/819–0404. 235 W. 46th St., 1/2/3/9 train to Times Square.*

The Rainbow Room/Rainbow & Stars. Two words for you: The View. You'll never think of the Empire State building as anything other than magical after you see it loom in the south windows here.... *Tel 212/632–5100. 30 Rockefeller Plaza, B/D/Q/F train to Rockefeller Center.*

Rawhide. Yeee-hah! For unbearably sexy leather-and-Levis scenes, not to mention all those hogs (as in Harleys) lined up on the sidewalk outside. This Chelsea gay bar is Shangri-La. A litter of nightly offerings, from porn flicks to special dance nights.... *Tel 212/242–9332. 212 Eighth Ave., C/E train to 23rd St.*

The Roxy. Strap on those skates and takes a turn around the immense dance floor at this longtime favorite among locals and tourists alike. Not a cutting-edge scene.... *Tel 212/645–5156. 515 W. 18th St., A/C/E train to 14th St. Cover charge.*

Royalton. Was that Alec Baldwin in the chic lobby lounge? Kim Basinger? Nah, just another Condé Nast editor trying to woo some superhip writer into contributing an article to *Details*. If you're a fella, don't be intimidated by the Versailles-like bathrooms (that is, if you can find them).... *Tel 212/944–8844. 44 W. 44th St., 1/2/3/9 train to Times Square.*

Sapphire Lounge. A nightly hotspot for the fashionably bohemian Lower East Side set, heir apparent to Cafe Tabac. More subdued and loungey than some of its more boisterous neighbors, like bOb.... *Tel 212/777–5153. 249 Eldridge St., F train to Broadway/Lafayette.*

Sidewalk Cafe. Slacker paradise, from the deep cheap booze to the substantial portions of food. The Fort, a small performance space in back, features live music several nights each week. No cover, but the tip jar usually goes around.... *Tel 212/473–7373. 94 Avenue A, F train to Second Ave.*

Sin-é. A little Irish dive in the East Village. Atmosphere is everything.... *Tel 212/982–0370; band hotline 212/475–3991. 122 St. Mark's Place, 6 train to Astor Place or F to Second Ave.*

SOB's (Sounds of Brazil). Got a taste for salsa? SOB's serves up a rich mixture.... *Tel 212/243–4940. 204 Varick St., 1/9 train to Houston St. $15 cover.*

Sound Factory Bar. The definitive home to customized house mix, with some of the city's most sought-after DJs. Hyper-youthful.... *Tel 212/206–7770. 12 W. 21st St., F train to 23rd St. Cover charge.*

The Spike. If the clean-cut gay pickup scene begins to bore, consider a radically different flavor—lots of big moustaches and crotch-contorting Levis—at this recently democratized S/M and leather paradise.... *Tel 212/243–9688. 120 Eleventh Ave., A/C/E train to 14th St.*

Splash. A friendly gay bar scene; tasty musical offerings, too. If Chelsea pretty boys and professional types are objects of your desire, come on down.... *Tel 212/691–0073. 50 W. 17th St., F train to 14th St.*

Stingy Lulu's. Patrons parked at the sidewalk tables here during the summer run a lively gamut from immaculately coiffed to downright stringy—but hey, this is the East Village. Order the cheapest screwdriver in town and gawk at the freaks spilling out of Tompkins Square Park across the way.... *Tel 212/674–3545. 129 St. Mark's Place, 6 train to Astor Place or F to Second Ave.*

Tavern on the Green. Central Park's landmark restaurant has been rescued from tourist-trap hell with a new executive chef, jazz artists booked into the Chestnut Room, and summertime dancing in the garden. A big, glitzy restaurant where every table seems to be celebrating some special event.... *Tel 212/873–3200. Central Park W. at 67th St., B/C train to 72nd St. Cover charge; no music or dancing Mon.*

Tenth Street Lounge. So cool you might not be able to stand yourself after three or four $7 cognacs. It could take the bartender a few minutes to adjust her form-fitting black minidress and take your drink order, but dress like a booking agent and you'll surely get prompter service. Very comfortable if you can evade the attitude.... *Tel 212/473–5252. 212 E. 10th St., 4/5/6, N/R, or L train to Union Square.*

288. The Lower East Side's idea of an alehouse. Beautiful, vaulted decor with a nod to loft living. Lots of wood, but also the world's most impressive collection of monogrammed punch bowls. Check all stereotypes at the door.... *288 Elizabeth St., F train to Broadway/Lafayette.*

Tramps. In its new location, this blues club now stands as one of Manhattan's true musical treasures.... *Tel 212/727–7788. 54 W. 21st St., F train to 23rd St. $15 cover.*

Tunnel. A subterranean club—literally and figuratively what its name says. Dance below the street in a place that D. H. Lawrence would have taken a shine to. Not the cheapest option around.... *Tel 212/695–7292. 220 Twelfth Ave., A/C/E train to 14th St. Cover charge.*

The Vault. Harsh, harsh, harsh, but always chock-full of consenting adults and the men who love to watch them (women, too, sometimes). Worth a stop for kicks and kink, but only the experienced should, as regulars put it, "play".... *Tel 212/255–6758. 28 Tenth Ave., 1/9 train to Christopher St.*

Webster Hall. Five spacious floors, each offering a different style of music to mostly college-aged crowds.... *Tel 212/353–1600. 125 E. 11th St., 4/5/6 train to Union Square. Cover charge.*

Wetlands. New York's hippie trippy love shack, where earnest young'uns gather for live music and poetry readings. Gobble some granola and polish up your tie-dye.... *Tel 212/966–4225. 161 Hudson St., 1/9 train to Christopher St. Cover charge.*

Wonder Bar. A festival of silliness for gay men on the make. It might make you feel like you're trapped in an interior design time warp that can't make up its mind. The East Village location makes access to plenty of cheap Italian and Indian restaurants a simple matter of falling out the door with a buddy in tow. Not for older cruisers.... *Tel 212/777–9105. 505 E. 6th St., 6 train to Astor Place or F to Second Ave.*

Zip City. Microbreweries are the newest thing to hit town. This enormous room hardly suggests anything "micro," however; from the huge vats behind the bar to the mobbed singles scene after 5pm, the owners have colonized the Flatiron district in a major way. They also have an impressive selection of single-malt scotches.... *Tel 212/366–6333. 3 W. 18th St., 4/5/6, N/R, or L train to Union Square.*

enterta

7

inment

It's a big country, but no one guzzles culture quite like New Yorkers. And there are so many entertainment options here, sometimes you can feel it's hopeless even to try to keep up. Frankly, it *is* hopeless. On a given day, a dozen must-see acts will pass through town, twice as many during the height of the spring and fall seasons, when all the opera companies and orchestras are in residence and every dance troupe in town is premiering new work. And these aren't just performances; they are world-class performances, in everything from acid jazz to chamber music to grand opera to cabaret to basketball.

Simple advice: spend some time planning your entertainment itinerary before the plane lands. *The New Yorker* and the *Village Voice* are superb resources, with tidy weekly listings of what's going on, and both publications are widely available outside Manhattan. To get advance tickets to most mainstream events, all you need is a credit card and a telephone. Keep it flexible, though; the show you'd planned for weeks to catch might have sold out, the club might not have any tables free, and even the scalpers you expected to be selling tickets outside Lincoln Center might have stayed home on a rainy evening. There are a lot of people in New York, and if an event is hot, that just means a lot of other people will have heard about it too. But for every failed plan in Gotham, an unexplored opportunity lurks in the wings. It's simply a matter of digging a little deeper.

Sources

The New York ***Times*** Sunday "Arts and Leisure" section contains a thorough list of the upcoming week's entertainment options, delivered in an even tone that makes few discernible attempts to help readers figure out what's worth their trouble. A helpful source, but not much fun. The unflaggingly comprehensive ***Time Out***, a weekly newcomer to the New York scene, lists anything and everything you could want.

The New Yorker's "Goings On About Town" section provides a swift, disputatious rundown of the upcoming week's events, delivered in the magazine's arch, vaguely bemused style. The film reviews are particularly useful, although not always extensive or exhaustive. Priceless bon mots from retired film critic Pauline Kael (the grande dame of American film criticism, actually) often adorn the revival-house listings, and witty hatchet jobs are frequently tucked away in the section's columns of tiny print. The magazine hits the stands each Monday.

The ***Village Voice***, available bright and early every Wednesday morning, performs for the Downtown scene the service that *The New Yorker* supplies to the Uptown crowd. Though its once impeccable alternative credentials are increasingly tarnished these days, the paper's "Choices" listing remains top-drawer, if at times awfully predictable. And the *Voice* features the opinions of two of the best critics in the world on a weekly basis: art writer Peter Schjeldahl and film god J. Hoberman.

The ***New York Press*** combines a poverty-stricken slacker sensibility with a larder of gallivanting sarcasm, particularly in J. R. Taylor's frequently flippant, often nasty, and usually accurate rundown of the week's most anticipated entertainment options. The "Movie Clock" section supplies compressed versions of Godfrey Cheshire's dandy film critiques, and the paper features a very reliable cluster of neighborhood-by-neighborhood restaurant reviews. There's also a calendar of the week's hottest (as determined by the staff) events, plus very extensive listings of everything from clubs to readings. Best of all, the paper is free, dispensed from green street-corner boxes and distributed from numerous Downtown venues.

New York magazine covers more ground than *The New Yorker*, but culture-scarred Gothamites tend to view the publication as a very expensively produced newsletter for inhabitants of the Upper East and West Sides. New editor Kurt Anderson, however, of *Spy* fame, has done yeoman duty to expand the magazine's attention span, turning its gaze toward hipper venues. The back-of-the-book rundown of weekly events is not only *The New Yorker*'s main competition, but may have surpassed it as the most colorful and *au courant* available.

The New York ***Observer*** runs a weekly calendar of stuff worth seeing ("The Eight-Day Week"), but be careful: the rag

Occult NYC

Fortune telling is a misdemeanor in New York, but thousands of psychics, palm readers, astrologers, and tarot card readers squeeze through a loophole in the law allowing storefront mystics to operate for the purpose of entertainment. A 15-minute palm reading or tarot session can cost as little as $10; if you want a glimpse into a crystal ball or a multi-session "regression" into your past lives, it could set you back quite a bit more. Venture in wherever you see the psychic or clairvoyant sign. ***Zena*** *(tel 212/807–0498) in the West Village advertises with a dramatically lit crucifix in a corner building on Seventh Avenue and Bleecker Street; the reading room fittings are stylishly Second Empire (after all, Zena has a branch in Cannes). The* ***Gypsy Tea Kettle*** *(tel 212/752–5890) on Lexington Avenue and 56th Street looks like a luncheonette; at the counter you pay first and are assigned to a booth where a psychic is stationed.* ***Lisa's Psychic Hotline*** *(tel 212/714–8202) offers occult guidance in the comfort of your own home or hotel room.*

is wry and snooty, which makes for great reading but doesn't always transmit the most straightforward summary of what's hot and what's not. "The Transom" gossip column, however, rarely fails to catch at least a few of the rich and fabulous at this or that current trendoid paradise. ***Paper*** used to be the club-scene bible in its lower-rent days, but the magazine's recent switch to a glossy, four-color format has taken some of the edge off. A good place to scan for trends, however, even if they're starting to get a bit dated.

Getting Tickets

The swiftest means of garnering tickets to major theatrical events is by hitting the **TKTS** booth in Duffy Square (at 47th and Broadway) or the one in the World Trade Center, where discounted tickets go on sale the day of performances. Lines can be long, so your best bet is to show up early. Wednesday and Saturday matinees are on sale from 10am to 2; tickets to evening performances sell from 3 to 8; and Sunday performances, both matinee and evening, are offered from noon to 8. What's available is posted on a digital bulletin board that's updated as ticket supplies dwindle. Remember, TKTS accepts only cash or traveler's checks, no credit cards.

To secure seats in advance, the surest plan of attack is to phone the theater's **box office**. It's sensible to call several weeks in advance for big-time Broadway musicals, but off- and off-off-Broadway theaters and performance venues often have tickets right up till show time. A lot of box offices will first steer you toward **Ticketmaster** (tel 307–7171), **Telecharge** (tel 239–6200), or **Centercharge** (tel 721–6500).

For eleventh-hour enthusiasts, the concierge at your hotel is a better bet than any overpriced ticket agency. Ticket **scalpers** are always an option, too. Look for forlorn types hanging around in front of the theater or concert hall with their tickets raised. Expect to cough up some serious cash for this last-resort technique, though at lesser-known shows the price of scalped tickets drops depending on the amount of time left before the curtain rises. It doesn't hurt to visit the box office first, either, particularly at Lincoln Center, to ask if there are any last-minute **returns**. Don't bet on obtaining anything if Yo-Yo Ma is playing Carnegie Hall, but for a spontaneous night out, this is often a way to luck into an interesting evening. And who knows who you'll meet in line?

The Lowdown

All that jazz... All roads lead to the **Village Vanguard**, which cannot really be trumped by any other of the city's plentiful jazz meccas. This underground former speakeasy oozes credibility from every nicotated pore. Listeners really listen, with an intensity that often verges on the pathological. For catching the next Wynton Marsalis or Joshua Redman, the Vanguard can't be beat. **Iridium**, with its Dr. Seuss-meets-Gaudi decor, somehow simultaneously gloomy and iridescent, looked like it was going to suffer the usual Uptown-seeks-Downtown audience identity crisis, but the deeply weird downstairs space has established an admirable record for booking the best of the best and the sharpest of the up-and-coming. The **Blue Note** sports a history that most other clubs would give up a year's worth of door receipts to borrow, and it shows both in the gargantuan ticket prices and the gift shop. The place is a shrine, and no one's going to knock it—everyone who still is anyone, from Dave Brubeck to the Modern Jazz Quartet, has the Blue Note slotted as their venue of choice in Gotham. The club's rampant traditionalism can be a drawback, however, as few jazz maniacs turn their attentions here for the next cool thing. The **Café Carlyle** in the Carlyle Hotel books in other performers, but the one who keeps well-heeled connoisseurs of American pop standards coming back is Bobby Short, an Uptown institution at the hotel's grand piano. Short plays and sings his songbook like it was meant to be, with unparalleled urbanity and sophistication (he looks devilishly comfortable in a tux). **Fat Tuesday's**, tucked off the beaten path in a residential neighborhood better known for Old New York history, is where electric-guitar mavens congregate on Monday nights to hear Les Paul lead his trio. Other jazz and blues legends also frequent the very small club; with this downstairs space's low ceilings, and tables nearly surrounding the musicians, this is the place for fans who like their heroes *really* up close and personal. **Sweet Basil**, which outwardly resembles a glorified coffee shop, has a split personality: By night, the talent that takes to its stage is often of such a high caliber that the appropriate response is to fawn; by day (on weekends, at any rate) it's home to 90-year-old Doc Cheatham, who performs a jazz brunch loaded with peerlessly performed Dixieland chestnuts and episodes of somewhat windy storytelling.

If old-style jazz is getting you down, the **Knitting Factory** puts on occasional off-the-wall jazz festivals that feature the likes of Cecil Taylor and John Zorn. If loud is what you're after, then **Fez** supplies an awesome wall of sound: every Thursday night (when it's not on tour), The Mingus Big Band, a smoking large ensemble, draws an eclectic crowd hungry for the group's take on the output of their late master, the relentlessly experimental bandleader Charlie Mingus. **Visiones**—a club that features young, less expensive players—possesses limited chic but rarely fails to draw in the knowledgeable jazz buffs who understand that money isn't everything.

Cheap jazz and cabaret... There's always room for cheap jazz and cabaret, most of which is clustered around Sheridan Square in a neighborhood famous for its large gay population. Anchoring the scene if **The Duplex,** a glittery, garish, gloriously tasteless club that plays home to a piano bar downstairs and to various camp, comedy, and performance acts upstairs in the Game Room. Out of favor in recent years, but lately staging a comeback thanks to several critically-acclaimed young talents. On nearby Grove Street, **Arthur's Tavern** books in less-than-serious jazz from semi-vanished musicians—which doesn't mean that the blowing isn't good; it's just cheaper than at the haughtier joints. Next door, **Marie's Crisis Cafe** could be rightly accused of suffering from a crisis of decor (the color scheme is wood and red), but it's a genial and casual place to hang out by the piano for a few hours. **Smalls,** on West 10th Street, has reintroduced the jazz marathon to budget-conscious afficianado. For $10 you get ten hours of music, from 10 pm to 8 am every night, plus free food and drinks.

Men in tights... In the past decade, New York has conceded some of its dominance of the dance world to Seattle and San Francisco, but Gotham still has more venues where the absolute best and brightest perform regularly than any other city on earth. The perfect place to start is at Lincoln Center, where the **New York City Ballet** holds two seasons a year at the New York State Theater. This is classical dance with a strong modernist edge, the product of ballet master George Balanchine's longtime creative influence and Lincoln Kirstein's intellectual enthusiasm for the art form. Nowadays, Peter Martins runs the show, but Balanchine's chosen successor is not without his troubles: several prominent dance critics have been calling for his head. Despite the politics and critical opinions about the corruption of the Balanchine legacy, the company soldiers on; it has traditionally shunned the star system, but that hasn't quieted the ovations for Darci Kistler, Wendy Whelan, Damien Woetzel (perhaps the finest classical male dancer in the world), Jock Soto, and Ethan Stiefel. December belongs to *The Nutcracker*, a New York holiday institution. During the summer, when NYCB retires to its off-season home in Saratoga, the State Theater's stage is turned over to the likes of the Mark Morris Dance Company and Barishnikov's White Oaks Project.

American Ballet Theater (ABT) also holds court at Lincoln Center, but in the Metropolitan Opera House, for two short seasons at the beginning of summer and fall. What City Ballet is to modernist severity and innovation, ABT is to reliable, melodramatic gush like *Giselle* and *Swan Lake:* a romantic museum for *la danse classique.* Mikhail Barishnikov presided over the company for a while, but since his departure ABT has been struggling to build an identity, recently reanimated by several promising young dancers.

City Center, a gloomy Spanish baroque pile (fast by Carnegie Hall) that was City Ballet's home long ago, now most often plays host to New York's great post-Balanchine experimental companies, such as Merce Cunningham, Paul Taylor, and Alvin Ailey.

Downtown, the **Joyce Theater**, with its unpretentious architecture, intimate scale, and unobstructed views, may be the best place in town to catch a performance. A constant stream of local, regional, and international talent crosses the Joyce's stage, everyone from Garth Fagen and Bill T. Jones to Eliot Feld and a gaggle of Native American and European companies. On a clear, cool night, during intermission, the contemporary dance junkies on the sidewalk out front are the city's most beautiful loiterers. (If you have time to kill before a show, take advantage of Man Ray's happy hour next door, which features scrumptious free pizza.) Right around the corner is **Dance Theater Workshop** (DTW), the liveliest of the city's alternative dance spaces, where the critics go to check the pulse of postmodern choreography and performance. Farther downtown, **St. Mark's Church-in-the-Bowery**, a converted church, opens its iron gates to a variety of innovative young companies, as does Soho's **Ohio Theater. P.S. 122**, a central venue for the alternative East Village theater and arts scene, often features performances that involve dance, though that could as easily mean someone writhing on the floor as something more upstanding.

The **Brooklyn Academy of Music** (BAM) plays host each year to the vaunted Next Wave Festival, a smorgasbord of avant-garde performances that never fails to include the work of some inventive new choreographer; Mark Morris first began to capture critical attention here. Next Wave is also the only look at Brooklyn that some Manhattanites ever get.

What's opera, doc?... Scratch a New Yorker and you'll find an opera lover. The problem is that most of them are too intimidated by the hopelessly garish Metropolitan Opera House to be properly Italian in their passions toward the city's largest opera company, the **Metropolitan Opera**. The Big House, as some have less-than-affectionately dubbed it, instead seems like a high-art cathedral for corporate sponsors and wealthy expatriate Eurotrash, a sorry state of affairs borne out by bloated ticket prices and overblown staging. Still, this is grand opera on a vast scale, the only house in America with the wherewithal to stage Wagner's compete Ring Cycle on consecutive nights and provide a home for conductor James Levine, who directs one of the world's finest opera orchestras. The ultra-cheap seats are miles from the action, but if you have $30 and a powerful set of binoculars, you can hang out with the opera queens and longtime devotees, some of whom whip themselves into a scary lather of "bravos" for curtain calls. All operas are sung in the original language, but in the 1995-96 season the Met is premiering a system of supertitles projected on the backs of each row of seats; it remains to be seen how that will fly with the cognoscenti. You can always buy a libretto at the gift shop a few days before the performance and bone up.

A pleasant alternative is provided by the perennially strapped **New York City Opera**, where supertitles accompany a more dynamic series of seasonal offerings at Lincoln

Center's New York State Theater. Culture-watchers have been hailing City Opera as the more interesting option for years, but the institution-in-waiting has yet to catch on with the public. The quality of the performances is high, however, and radically eclectic, recently showcasing classic Broadway musicals and new work such as an opera about slain San Francisco gay activist Harvey Milk.

The truly intrepid will board the subway or cross the Brooklyn Bridge and visit the **Brooklyn Academy of Music** (BAM), whose lushly renovated opera house combines starkly experimental offerings and an occasional tidbit from the canon. The building itself is a jewel, a remnant from the days when Brooklyn competed with Manhattan in a interborough contest to rule the city's cultural roost.

Miscellaneous operatic treats are available on a catch-as-catch-can basis at **Carnegie Hall**, where opera's living legends sometimes sing solo gigs, and at several smaller venues around town, including the Bowery's tiny **Amato Opera Company**.

Comedy tonight... Comedy in New York is hit-or-miss: amateur nights are as common as headliner-thick extravaganzas (although the former are usually much cheaper). As a rule, it's not one of the less-expensive entertainment options in town, but clubs like **ReBar** and **Stand-up New York** have begun to reverse the upwardly-mobile trend established by glossy venues such as **Caroline's**, where many popular current comics got their big breaks. A number of bars and clubs, attempting to capitalize on the comedy boom, have added stand-up nights to their weekly schedules of live music.

The theatah... Theater courses through the veins of New York. No other city in the world, save perhaps London, can match Manhattan for sheer volume of nightly offerings, and Wednesdays and Sundays add matinees as well. The scene separates into three groups, with ticket prices falling accordingly. Broadway means large-scale musical productions, à la Andrew Lloyd Weber's *Sunset Boulevard* and the recent revival hits *Showboat* and *How to Succeed in Business...*, as well as beloved dramas featuring big Hollywood names, like Kathleen Turner in Tennessee Williams' *Cat on a Hot Tin Roof* or Ralph Fiennes in a touring British production of *Hamlet*. Most Broadway theaters are clustered around Times Square. Off-Broadway is quirkier and more artistically aloof, though not immune to booking goofy acts like magicians Penn & Teller. You're more likely to find plays here rather than musicals. Off-off Broadway is anything-goes territory, with theaters scattered all over town, largely in Greenwich Village, the East Village, SoHo, and Tribeca. For alternative performances and the avant-garde, this is where you'll want to focus your energies. On Broadway, *Cats* has been at the **Winter Garden** forever, playing to unsophisticated outsiders who don't realize what a local joke it has become. Theaters like the Schubert and the Martin Beck continue to host full-scale events even though their physical spaces are somewhat cramped (most common comment from first-time New York theatergoers: "I had no idea they'd be so small..."). Bigger theaters like the cavernous Gershwin Theater present just the opposite problem: if you sit in back you can't see anything without binoculars, or hear anything except the reverberations of over-amplified dialogue. (Hardly a show on Broadway these days isn't miked—actors have practically forgotten how to project.) The St. James recently mounted what many consider to be the loudest show ever on the Great White Way—Who guitarist Pete Townshend and choreographer Tommy Tune's Tony-winning *Tommy*. Broadway has absorbed plenty of criticism over the past fifteen years for sacrificing the great American musical (*Oklahoma!*, *Guys and Dolls*) for overblown production extravaganzas imported from London, but a recent resurgence of native talent, notably from legendary director Hal Prince, has raised local temperatures. The 1993–94 season was heralded by many as the greatest Broadway had seen since the glory days of the '50s and '60s. Good thing, too, with orchestra seats now going at $75 for the big shows. At Lincoln Center, tucked behind the Metropolitan Opera House, discriminating theatergoes will find the Vivian Beaumont Theatre, where recent years have seen formidable plays on the order of *Arcadia* and *Six Degrees of Separation*.

Off-Broadway begins on Ninth Avenue and stretches to Tenth along 42nd Street's Theater Row, a neighborhood of houses that can't seat the large audiences drawn to the Broadway houses. Hailing a cab Downtown will extend your off-Broadway excursion; theaters that specialize in the serious work of sustaining American drama down here include **Circle Rep**, **Circle in the Square**, the **Provincetown Playhouse**, the **Orpheum**, and the **Roundabout**. Farther uptown and off Broadway's beaten path reside the **Manhattan Theater Club**, **Playwright's Horizons**, and the **Promenade/Second Stage**. For the denizens of Downtown, Joe Papp's legendary **Public Theatre**, now under new direction, presents some of the finest contemporary drama available to New Yorkers, including the likes of Sam Shepard.

Off-off Broadway experiments can be found far from the Theater District's madding throngs; catching satirist David Sedaris' latest zany ensemble exercise or the debut by a previously unheard-of playwright at a Downtown venue can add up to ample hipster cachet. **P.S. 122** and the fabled **LaMama** fall into this camp. In another category, performance art (ridiculed by some stodgy critics as being neither) and camp excess, along with some pretty respectable satires of contemporary mores, regularly take over spaces (not theaters, kiddo, performance spaces) like The **Kitchen**, **Franklin Furnace**, **P.S. 122**, and the **Brooklyn Academy of Music** (BAM).

Classical sounds... Lincoln Center's **Avery Fisher Hall** boasts the New York Philharmonic, considered by many in the know as the best band in America. Unfortunately, the hall has never provided acoustics to match the Philharmonic's world-class reputation, but new maestro Kurt Masur has assured the public that something is being done. Watch carefully from week to week as those weird-looking hunks of dampening material hanging from the ceiling are shifted around. In recent years, programming at the Philharmonic has fallen into a bit of a rut, at the expense of forays into dense and complicated 20th–century music. Still a great place to hear Beethoven and Mahler, however. During the summer, be sure to catch the Mostly Mozart Festival, during which an impressive roster of classical-music greats most certainly do not limit themselves to the output of Austria's boy genius.

Adjoining Avery Fisher is the more intimate (and acoustically satisfying) **Alice Tully Hall**, a cube into which are squeezed devotees of the Chamber Society of Lincoln Center and the assorted groups affiliated with the **Juilliard School**.

Ten or so blocks from Lincoln Center is the forever glorious **Carnegie Hall**, which to out-of-towners remains synonymous with American music and the tradition of classical performances in New York. The interior is sturdy and patriotic, the sound extraordinary and irreplaceable, even after its successful 1986 renovation. Upstairs, its Weill Recital Hall hosts smaller recitals and chamber groups.

The cerebral modern-music crowd hangs out at **Merkin Concert Hall**, just north of Lincoln Center, where they discuss music matters in hushed and reverent whispers. Make no mistake: this stuff is not for everybody, and the likelihood is slim that you'll meet someone at intermission whose specialty is light banter. But the chance that you'll find yourself sitting next to the composer is pretty good, and even if you know nothing of 12-tone architectures or sound-poems, eavesdropping on post-performance conversations can be entertaining as well as instructional.

BargeMusic, on the East River, on a barge, is a hopeless name for a great idea: a strictly classical musical menu played on a barge tethered to its Brooklyn mooring. Way Uptown, at City College's **Aaron Davis Hall**, the World Music Institute lures string-and-reed junkies from around Manhattan to listen to the unusual performances that regularly crop up on its schedule. Downtown, **Grace Church** puts together occasional performances of classical and sacred music. Church-concert enthusiasts will want to make the long subway trek Uptown to the **Cathedral of St. John the Divine**, a vast superterranean cavern—still unfinished—where the fare runs from New Age acts, such as the Paul Winter Consort, to performances of Native American music and dance, to AIDS benefit concerts. Back in Midtown, the **Museum of Modern Art**'s sculpture garden plays host to a variety of free "Summergarden" concerts that often feature dense, cerebral 20th-century music. At **Lincoln Center**, any of a number of the groups associated with the Julliard School also give frequent free recitals.

In concert... The really happening music happens in the clubs—see the Nightlife chapter for the dirt on that scene. Larger venues such as the **Bottom Line**, the **Beacon Theater**, and **Roseland** can be depended upon to bring in somebody you've heard of before, probably someone with piles of CDs on the racks at Tower Records, probably someone slogging through a multi-record deal. Of these, the Beacon has the healthiest attitude toward juicy live performances. Not a hopeless option if you'd prefer to catch an act in a venue where your feet won't stick to the floor and where mosh pits are as rare as robust sales for Brian Eno's latest release.

Major-label bands explore their arena potential at New York's larger locations, including **Giants Stadium** in East Rutherford, NJ. The big acts also put in appearances at **Madison Square Garden** and the **Brendan Byrne Arena** at the Meadowlands, in the same complex as Giants Stadium. The **Paramount**, which is within the Madison Square Garden building, also offers plenty of room to stretch out and rock, but if the likes of Bette Midler are more your taste, make tracks for **Radio City Music Hall** at Rockefeller Center, still home to the fabulous, leggy Rockettes.

Spoken word... A neo-Beatnik revival of "spoke word" or "performance" poetry has been invigorating New York's literary life. Used to be that almost none of the poets who took the stage at the **Nuyorican Poet's Café** had published anything with anyone, but that's all changing now with limber-lyricked wordsmiths like Paul Beatty, Reg E. Gaines, Sapphire, and Carl Hancock Rux. The scene is much, much less white-bread than it was in the good old Beat days. Ribald, often hilarious, frequently affecting rhymes are laid down by spoken word poets, performance artists who incorporate poetic texts into their acts, and rappers out to check their heads with a little of that freestyle vibe. Not to be missed are the Nuyorican's Friday night Poetry Slams, where a group of readers compete for the favor of judges (as well as a highly participatory audience) who rate performances on a 1–10 scale. A welter of other spaces have followed its lead. **Fez** sometimes hosts rap-meets-poetry nights, and several independent bookstores have taken to letting scenesters organize spoken-word evenings. The whole scene is hit-or-miss, however, with some dreadful stuff joining the cooler versifications.

For traditional poetry, there are the Academy of American Poets' seasonal readings at **The New School** and the **92nd St. Y**'s continuing series of readings. This is the place to hear old white male poets. The **Dia Center for the Arts**, on Mercer Street, also offers a reading series that features noted poets on the order of Richard Howard and Thom Gunn. Check out the monthly Poetry Calendar, available at B.Dalton in the Village and at St.Mark's Book Shop, to scan all of the poetic offerings.

The big game... With everything else there is to do in New York, watching sports could be confined to sports bars, where one can also watch sports fans who've gone to seed swill beer and cheer one of the city's numerous teams as it fails to win a championship. Good spots for sports bar potatoes are: **Boomer's** (349 Amsterdam Ave., tel 212/362–5400), **Mickey Mantle's** 42 Central Park S., tel 212/688–7777), **Rusty Staub's** (575 Fifth Ave., tel 212/682–1000), and the **Sporting Club** (99 Hudson St., tel 212/219–0900), and in a post-season where a local club is still in the running, virtually any neighborhood bar with a television.

Of course, if that strikes you as a pale substitute for the real thing, you can mosey up to **Yankee Stadium** in the Bronx or **Shea Stadium** in Queens to watch, respectively, the storied Yankees and the upstart Mets. Tickets are easy to come by right now for both. For football fans, the Giants and Jets knock heads with their NFL rivals at **Giants Stadium** in the Meadowlands; tickets are hard to find for Jets games and impossible for the Giants. The hockey puck flies at **Madison Square Garden**, where the 1994 Stanley Cup champion Rangers slap it around. The 1995 champs, the New Jersey Devils, play at the **Brendan Byrne Arena** across the Hudson, while the New York Islanders can be found at the **Nassau Coliseum** in Uniondale, Long Island. The Rangers are the toughest ticket out of the three. During basketball season the New York Knicks share the Garden with the Rangers, and their Jersey counterparts, the Nets, alternate with the Devils at Byrne Arena. Knicks' tickets have been hard to come by the last few years, but the departure of Pat Riley may change that. The **U.S.T.A. National Tennis Center** in Flushing, Queens, plays host each year to the US Open Tennis Championships (tickets cost a mint and must be secured a year in advance), a grueling two-week affair around Labor Day that showcases the best the sport has to offer. Later each fall, the New York City Marathon is run in November on a 26-mile course that winds through each of Manhattan's five boroughs. There's thoroughbred horseracing at **Aqueduct Racetrack** and at **Belmont Park**, home to the hotly followed last race in the Triple Crown, the Belmont Stakes. But for the truly urbane, the spectator sport of choice is billiards; rack 'em up for a languid game of eight-ball or a swift game of nine-ball at **Julian's Famous Poolroom**, the city's best-known pool hall.

The silver screen... At $8 a seat, it's expensive by some standards, but film in New York is also thorough, with major Hollywood flicks premiering at the same time as cerebral art-house releases. The **Film Forum** maintains an untrammeled reputation for uncovering independent gems as well as for scheduling festivals and revivals of classics, often in series spotlighting a particular director or genre. **Anthology Film Archives** monitors the avant-garde, presenting documentary shorts and experimental celluloid from indy legends such as Stan Brackidge. The **Angelika Film Center** brings in an endless supply of minor European films and small-budget American stuff, all as lively and eclectic as possible; enjoy a muffin and espresso prior to the show at their inviting upstairs cafe. The **Public Theater** puts together well-curated festivals, as well as short-run re-releases and experimental gallery projects, such as video artist Matthew Barney's *Cremaster 4*. Uptown and for the more retrospectively inclined, there's the **Museum of Modern Art**, which screens stuff from its enormous archives; it doesn't shy away from the controversial—half the audience once walked out on a screening of Werner Herzog's *Even Dwarfs Started Small.* The **Whitney Museum of American Art** has a respectable interest in films by gay, lesbian, ethnic, and African-American movie- and videomakers (PixleVision maven Sadie Benning first achieved notice at the Whitney's Biennial show, which features a film and video program alongside more traditional artworks). Lincoln Center's **Walter Reade Theater** gives film buffs the New York Film Festival, and during the rest of the year puts together ambitious surveys of whole directorial careers. An excellent place, by the way, to spot Susan Sontag with a huge tub of popcorn, if that strikes your fancy. In Queens, the **American Museum of the Moving Image** attempts to do for film what the Metropolitan Museum has done for oil and canvas. A strong foreign-film diet can be cultivated at **Lincoln Plaza**, where the Muzak between showings is as lovely and sophisticated as the well-heeled crowd. If what you desire is a maximum-large, good old-fashioned cinematic experience, the giant screen at the **Ziegfield** provides a grand alternative to the suburban-mall multiplex.

The Index

Aaron Davis Hall (at City College). Venture far uptown for a varied tasting of concert offerings.... *Tel 212/650–7100. W. 134th St. at Convent Ave., 1/9 train to 137th St.*

Alice Tully Hall. Avery Fisher's younger sister, a smaller venue that comfortably contains the Chamber Music Society of Lincoln Center.... *Tel 212/875–5050. 65 W. 65th St., 1/9 train to 66th St./Lincoln Center.*

Amato Opera Company. A diminutive space in the heart of the Grunge District where young opera talent cut their chops. Notable neighbor: seminal punk-rock club CBGB.... *Tel 212/228–8200. 319 Bowery, B/D/Q/F train to Broadway/ Lafayette or F to Second Ave.*

American Ballet Theater (ABT). Where the classics thrive, performed by some outstanding younger dancers. Legitimate competition for the recently lethargic New York City Ballet for the first time ever.... *Tel 212/477–3030. Lincoln Center, 1/9 train to 66th St./Lincoln Center.*

American Museum of the Moving Image. Intrepid souls will not wilt at the prospect of schlepping all the way out to Queens (it's not that far) to catch a rare film offering here. The museum is located hard by the venerable and still busy Kaufman Astoria Film Studios where everyone from the Marx Brothers *(Cocoanuts)* to Harrison Ford (the recent remake of *Sabrina*) have put in time.... *Tel 718/784–0077. 3601 36th St. (entrance on 35th Ave.), Queens, N train to Queensborough Plaza.*

Angelika Film Center. One critic once commented that the crowd on line here, with their spiky haircuts, thick-soled work shoes, and outré fashion sense, looked like an assembly of "French heroin addicts." Not a uniformly true observation, but sometimes. As the hippest multiplex in this hipper-than-thou neighborhood, it can be offputtingly crowded on weekends.... *Tel 212/995–2000. 18 W. Houston St., B/D/Q/F train to Broadway/Lafayette.*

Anthology Film Archives. Even if you're a dyed-in-the-wool film whore who can count Roman Polanski's student flicks among the celluloid you've sat through, this small East Village theater will show something you've never heard of. Bet on it.... *Tel 212/505–5181. 32–34 Second Ave., B/D/Q/F train to Broadway/Lafayette.*

Aqueduct Racetrack. Thoroughbred racing here runs from late October or early November to early May.... *Tel 718/641–4700. Rockaway Beach, Queens; A train to North Conduit. Closed Mon and Tue.*

Arthur's Tavern. Low-rent jazz for fans with flexible standards. Not for the Marsalis-phile, but dandy for a little music with your drinks. Cover varies....*Tel 212/675–6879. 57 Grove St., 1/9 train to Christopher St.*

Avery Fisher Hall. Always less democratic than it should be, given the promises of former director Leonard Bernstein, but the posh crowd shouldn't ruin an evening with the generally fabulous, if rarely provocative, New York Philharmonic.... *Tel 212/875–5030. Lincoln Center, 1/9 train to 66th St./Lincoln Center.*

BargeMusic. Sounds like a stupid idea, but on a nice cool night with a bottle of wine and someone to hold close, a cultured way to get an earful of splendid music.... *Tel 718/624–4061. Fulton Ferry Landing, Brooklyn, 2/3 train to Fulton St.*

Beacon Theater. A decent-sized house that books in a wide variety of mainstream and semi-mainstream acts.... *Tel 212/496–7070. 2124 Broadway, 1/9 or 2/3 train to 72nd St.*

Belmont Park. Whenever the horses don't run at Aqueduct (see above), except for a hiatus in July and August, they're racing here. Season May to mid-July and late August or early September to October.... *Tel 718/641–4700. Hempstead Ave., Elmont, Long Island, LIRR Belmont Express from Penn Station or Flatbush Ave.—$8 round trip includes admission to park. Closed Mon and Tue.*

Blue Note. Expensive tickets and too damn much merchandise on the way out, but also the place for live performances by jazz's living giants... *Tel 212/475–8592. 131 W. 3rd St., A/C/E or B/D/Q/F train to W. 4th St.*

Bottom Line. No surprises, ever, at this club, which is more likely to bring in an easy-listening heartthrob than a guitar-slashing punkster. Still, a solid, appealing standby.... *Tel 212/228–6300. 15 W. 4th St., A/C/E or B/D/Q/F train to W. 4th St.*

Brendan Byrne Arena. The recent emergence of the Devils as an NHL power, culminating in the 1995 Stanley Cup, has made this cavernous arena across the Hudson in New Jersey an exciting place to visit. Don't expect the same energy or talent on a night the woeful NBA Nets are playing, though. *Tel 201/935–3900. The Meadowlands, East Rutherford, NJ, Buses from Port Authority (42nd St. and Eighth Ave.).*

Brooklyn Academy of Music (BAM). Where the avant-garde hangs its beret. The Next Wave Festival is famed for giving the likes of Robert Wilson and Laurie Anderson grand exposure and for pulling hard-core Manhattanites off the island for an evening or two. One of the most intimidating-looking theater mobs in New York, however.... *Tel 718/636–4100. 30 Lafayette Ave., Brooklyn; D/Q, 2/3, or 4/5 train to Atlantic Ave. or B, M, or N/R to Pacific St.*

Café Carlyle. Two words: Bobby Short. If American pop standards rendered with sophisticated reverence and witty songsterism are your bag, then Mr. Short is your man. Whe he is elsewhere, look for the likes of Julie Wilson. Reservations are essential, as is cash (and lots of it).... *Tel 212/744–1600. 981 Madison Ave., 6 train to 77th St.*

Carnegie Hall. The most celebrated performance space for live music in New York. The air is thick with the ghosts of greats.... *Tel 212/247–7800. 156 W. 57th St., N/R train to 57th St.*

Caroline's. An essential space for stand-up in Manhattan. The room is huge, but surprisingly intimate. Covers run about $15, with two-drink minimums.... *Tel 212/757–4100. 1626 Broadway, 1/9 train to 50th St. or N/R to 49th St.*

Cathedral of St. John the Divine. So vast you wouldn't think it would be much fun, but it's actually one of the city's most free-spirited concert spaces... *Tel 212/316–7400. 1047 Amsterdam Ave., 1/9 train to 110th St./Cathedral Parkway.*

Cherry Lane Theater. This small off-Broadway theater in a hidden-away corner of the West Village near Sheridan Square, so picturesque it looks like some back-lot fantasy version of New York. Usually books lower-key, more artistically substantial shows... *Tel 212/989–2020. 38 Commerce St., 1/9 train to Christopher St.*

Circle in the Square. A home to intense dramaturgy in the vein of O'Neill and Miller.... *Tel 212/239–6200. 1633 Broadway, 1/9 train to 50th St. or N/R to 49th St.*

Circle Rep. Low-key Downtown theater that maintains an experimental program without going off the deep end. Playwright Lanford Wilson, William Hurt and many other notables got some early attention here, and remain company members.... *Tel 212/254–6330. 159 Bleecker St., A/C/E or B/D/Q/F train to W. 4th St.*

City Center. Before Lincoln Center took over its sprawling expanse, this was one of New York's main mansions of performance. Nowadays, it hosts an eclectic mix of dance, music, and miscellany.... *Tel 212/581–7907. 131 W. 55th St., N/R or B/Q to 57th St.*

Dance Theater Workshop (DTW). Chelsea's crucible for developing and spotting new choreographic and dance talent. A nice space, but a bit cramped.... *Tel 212/924–0077. 219 W. 19th St., C/E train to 23rd St.*

Dia Center fot the Arts. A Chelsea Gallery that provides an excellent space for a variety of artistic media... *Tel 212/989–5566. 548 W. 22nd St., E/C train to 23rd St.*

The Duplex. First stop for a variety of cabaret and comedy acts, along with the obligatory piano bars. Covers range from $3 to $12, usually with a two-drink minimum....*Tel 212/255–5438. Corner of Christopher St. and Seventh Ave., 1/9 train to Christopher St.*

Fat Tuesday's. A premier blues and jazz joint, tucked off the beaten track a few blocks east of Union Square.... *Tel 212/533–7902. 190 Third Ave., 4/5/6 or N/R train to Union Square.*

Fez. If you have an itch for spoken word performance, fresh pop, or smoking jazz, this is an excellent room to drop in on.... *Tel 212/533–2680. 380 Lafayette St., B/D/Q/F train to Broadway/Lafayette, 6 to Astor Place, or N/R to 8th St.*

Film Forum. The jewel in New York's cinema crown. With the disappearance of all the old revival houses, Film Forum has been almost single-handedly feeding the Big Apple's voracious appetite for avant-garde cinema. Discount memberships are available.... *Tel 212/727–8110. 209 W. Houston St., 1/9 train to Houston St.*

Franklin Furnace. Some of the best and most extreme, not to mention unwatchable, performance artists have passed through this Tribeca space.... *Tel 212/925–4671. 112 Franklin St., 1/9 to Franklin St.*

Giants Stadium. Arena rock acts, football's Jets and Giants. A long way to go to spend a lot of money for a crummy view of the Stones, but it's a great place to watch football.... *Tel 201/935–3900. The Meadowlands, East Rutherford, NJ; buses from Port Authority (42nd St. and Eighth Ave.).*

Grace Church. Beloved old gothic church, complete with an elegant spire, that sits on the border between the West and East Villages. Frequent classical music concerts... *Tel 212/254–2000. 802 Broadway, 6 train to Astor Place.*

Iridium. Upstairs, a tired new-money crowd sucks down exotic libation in an effort to get prepped for Lincoln Center; downstairs, knowledgeable jazz junkies gather to score a glimpse at this or that giant. The surreal decor might prompt an acid flashback.... *Tel 212/582–2121. 44 W. 63rd St., 1/9 train to 66th St./Lincoln Center.*

Joyce Theater. The best theater in New York for contemporary dance, it's also home to Eliot Feld's company, The Feld Ballet.... *Tel 212/242–0800. 175 Eighth Ave., C/E train to 23rd St. or 1/9 to 18th St.*

Juilliard School. The famous school for the performing arts schedules numerous concerts by its students. Price is usually low to nil.... *Tel 212/799–5000, ext. 235. Lincoln Center, 1/9 train to 66th St./Lincoln Center.*

Julian's Famous Poolroom. Used to have better green-felt credentials before the yuppifying makeover, but this E. 14th Street landmark remains the place to rack 'em up.... *Tel 212/598–9884. 138 E. 14th St., 4/5/6 or N/R to Union Square.*

Kitchen. Performance art space extraordinaire, recently relocated to roomier digs in Chelsea.... *Tel 212/255–5793. 512 W. 19th St., A/C/E train to 14th St.*

Knitting Factory. Ensconced in fancier environs, this former celebrant of the rock-bottom cover charge and the college-rock playlist has gotten posher and more expensive, but maturity hasn't much softened its attitude.... *Tel 212/219–3055. 74 Leonard St., 1/9 train to Franklin St.*

LaMama. Venerable East Village performance space with years of showcasing new talent under its belt.... *Tel 212/475–7710. 74 E. 4th St., B/D/Q/F train to Broadway/Lafayette or 6 to Astor Place.*

Lincoln Plaza. If it's up for "Best Foreign Film" at the Oscars, it probably played here... *Tel 212/757–2280. Broadway and 62nd St.; 1/9 to 59th St./Columbus Circle.*

Madison Square Garden. Home to the Rangers and the Knicks, this hideous arena built in the '60s on the site of the razed Pennsylvania Station also occasionally presents big music acts—U2 when they're in town, or Elvis Costello when he wants to suck down some big money. Costello comments that it's "not even round, not square, either." It's oval.... *Tel 212/465–6741. 4 Pennsylvania Plaza, 1/9 or 2/3 train to Penn Station.*

Manhattan Theater Club. Seminal new theater is offered a first chance here... *Tel 212/645–5590. 453 W. 16th St., F train to 14th St.*

Marie's Crisis Cafe. Nowhere near the height of style, but plenty friendly. Piano bar opens at 8....*Tel 212/243–9323. 59 Grove St., 1/9 train to Christopher St.*

Merkin Concert Hall. Contemporary classical's NYC home, so brush up on those obscure composers and fire up your intellectual mojo.... *Tel 212/362–8719. 129 W. 67th St. (Abraham Goodman House), 1/9 train to 66th St./Lincoln Center.*

Metropolitan Opera. Where fur-bearing dames of the culture circuit drag their investment-banker husbands to hear the fat lady sing. Far from the action, in the nosebleed seats, a dedicated passel of opera queens roars its approval.... *Tel 212/362–6000. Lincoln Center, 1/9 train to 66th St./Lincoln Center.*

Museum of Modern Art. New York's temple to modernism also supports an ambitious film program, as well as the free Summergarden concert series.... *Tel 212/708–9480. 11 W. 53rd St., E/F train to Fifth Ave.*

Nassau Coliseum. The glory days of the Islanders are long past and this stadium could probably use some serious sprucing up, but if you're looking for a chance to watch NHL hockey amidst relaxed, family-oriented surroundings, this is your place.... *Tel 800/888-9000. Uniondale, NY; LIRR to Hempstead Station, then N70, N71 or N72 bus.*

New School. If reedy poets in carefully chosen tweeds floats your versifying boat, then the Academy of American Poets seasonal readings here are just what Dr. Johnson ordered. Sometimes host David Lehman is a master of the wry, obscure one-liner. $10 at the door.... *Tel 212/229–5600. 66 W. 12th St., F train to 14th St.*

New York City Ballet. Unabashed beauty, with a trust of ballets so good that you'll want to see most of them over and over. Eccentric cartoonist Edward Gorey joined the likes of poet Frank O'Hara for almost every performance back in the early days, but left town on ballet master Balanchine's death.... *Tel 212/870–5570. Lincoln Center, 1/9 train to 66th St./Lincoln Center.*

New York City Opera. The little opera that could—maybe. Much cheaper and much more fun, in many respects, than the Met's grander offerings across the plaza.... *Tel 212/870–5570. Lincoln Center, 1/9 train to 66th St./Lincoln Center.*

92nd St. Y. Uptown home to the Ecco Press and *Paris Review* crowd, where poetry is read mainly by white guys who still wear khakis.... *Tel 212/415–5440. 1395 Lexington Ave., 4/5/6 train to 96th St.*

Nuyorican Poet's Cafe. Polar opposite of its academic brethren, this East Village haunt practically invented the notorious Poetry Slam and continues to be the vanguard of the spoken word scene.... *Tel 212/505–8183. 236 E. 3rd St.; F train to Second Ave.*

Ohio Theater. Small SoHo theater that frequently presents experimental choreography.... *Tel 212/966–4844. 66 Wooster St., C/E train to Spring St. or N/R to Prince St.*

Orpheum. This off-Broadway space has recently hosted long-run *Stomp*, a frenzy of Brits with nearly shaved heads banging on all sorts of industrial detritus.... *Tel 212/307–4100. 126 Second Ave., 6 train to Astor Place or N/R to 8th St.*

Playwright's Horizons. If you're feeling bold, this is an excellent venue for freshly minted drama... *Tel 212/279–4200. 416 W. 42nd St., A/C/E train to Times Square.*

Promenade/Second Stage. A home to second runs of quality shows. The theater's artistic directorship is first-rate. *Tel 212/580–1313. 2162 Broadway, 1/9 train to 79th St.*

Provincetown Playhouse. Genial, smallish Downtown venue for sometimes serious, never stodgy, and often madcap thespian forays.... *Tel 212/674–8043. 133 MacDougal St., A/C/E or B/D/Q/F Train to W. 4th St.*

P.S. 122. Mabou Mines in the back, as well as whatever/whoever's in the main space, consistently push the extremes of Downtown performance.... *Tel 212/477–5288. 150 First Ave., 6 train to Astor Place.*

Public Theater. Joe Papp, the übermensch of New York theater, ran the show here for years, transforming a limited Downtown operation into a world leader in theatrical experimentation. Was its success due sheerly to Papp's genius, or can new director George C. Wolfe turn the trick, too? The Public's best-known program, summertime Shakespeare in the Park, is still running strong, starring big names at Central Park's Delacorte Theater.... *Tel 212/260–2400. 425 Lafayette St., 6 train to Astor Place or N/R to 8th St.*

Radio City Music Hall. An Art-Deco cathedral with erratic booking and always the high-kicking Rockettes.... *Tel 212/247–4777. 1260 Sixth Ave., B/D/F/Q train to Rockefeller Center.*

ReBar. A new haven for young comics. Quite a scene in the last year or so, but almost tragically twentysomething.... *Tel 212/627–1680. 127 Eighth Ave., A/C/E train to 14th St.*

Roseland. A relic from the days of swing and lindy, this remains an actual ballroom on Tuesdays and Sundays, complete with rumbas, mambos and foxtrots; on other nights the vibe inside is informed by pop and rock rhythms.... *Tel 212/247–0200. 239 W. 52nd St., A/C, B/D or 1/9 train to Columbus Circle.*

Roundabout. Broadway theater that insists on resisting the big-production currents that rule Broadway.... *Tel 212/869–8400. 1520 Broadway, 1/9, 2/3, or N/R train to Times Square.*

St. Mark's Church-in-the-Bowery. Wonderful performance space on the edge of the East Village.... *Tel 212/674–8194 (Danspace Project); 212/533–4650 (Ontological Theater); 212/674–0910 (Poetry Project). 131 E. 10th St., 6 train to Astor Place.*

Shea Stadium. Fairly generic, early Sixties-style ballyard at the end of the number 7 subway line, complete with views of the rusting Unisphere (The World's Fair was out here), is home to the Mets, once underdog champs but hoping to emerge from half a decade of haplessness.... *Tel 718/507–8499. 126th St. at Roosevelt Ave., Queens; 7 train to Willets Point/Shea Stadium.*

Smalls. Great programming, great price, open practically all hours. The ten-hour $10 jazz marathon gets going, of course, at 10.... *Tel 212/929–7565. 183 W. 10th St. at Seventh Ave., 1/9 train to Christopher St.*

Stand-up New York. The Upper West Side's answer to the comedy craze mixes amateur nights with more established acts. Cover runs from $5 to $15, with the usual two-drink minimum.... *Tel 212/595–0850. 236 W. 78th St., 1/9 train to 79th St.*

Sweet Basil. Nighttime gigs usually start at 9 and 11, with a $15 minimum charge; Dixieland trumpet legend and world-class nonlinear raconteur Doc Cheetham holds a jazz brunch here on weekends.... *Tel 212/242–1785. 88 Seventh Ave. S., 1/9 train to Christopher St.*

U.S.T.A. National Tennis Center. Tennis' finest do battle on the hard courts here each year at the U.S. Open championships.... *Tel 718/760–6200. Flushing Meadows, Queens; 7 train to Willets Point/Shea Stadium.*

Village Vanguard. The Downtown jazz joint for the truly devoted. Always an intense, 'round-midnight scene. Music charge around $15.... *Tel 212/255–4037. 178 Seventh Ave. S., 1/9 train to Christopher St.*

Vivian Beaumont. Lincoln Center's main theater space... *Tel 212/362–6000. Lincoln Center, 1/9 train to 68th St./ Lincoln Center.*

Walter Reade Theater. Home to the annual New York Film Festival. At other times, a merely great program of art-house revivals and essential cinema, presented under the aegis of the Film Society of Lincoln Center.... *Tel 212/875–5600. 65 W. 65th St., above Alice Tully Hall, 1/9 train to 66th St./Lincoln Center.*

Whitney Museum of American Art. One of the few film facilities in New York that's not shy of experiments like Andy Warhol's marathon studies of sleep and the Empire State Building.... *Tel 212/570–3676. 945 Madison Ave., 6 train to 77th St.*

Winter Garden Theatre. Home to many great Broadway shows over the years, now home to *Cats* for the foreseeable future.... *Tel 212/239–6200. 1634 Broadway, 1/9 train to 50th St.*

Yankee Stadium. The House that Ruth Built, itself still splendid, sits in a crummy neighborhood that freaks out the baseball crowds. The spirits of DiMaggio and Gehrig continue to hover, however much the current patrons complain. Owner George Steinbrenner gets as many headlines as his players.... *Tel 718/293–6000. 161st St. and River Ave., Bronx, 4 train to 161st St.*

The Ziegfield. The biggest of New York's big screens. Gotham's antidote to the postage-stamps at the multiplex. Sit close.... *Tel 212/765-7600. Sixth Ave. and 54th St., F train to 53rd and Third.*

25
10
5
1
ABC 2
DEF 3
GHI 4
JKL 5
MNO 6
PRS 7
TUV 8
WXY 9
*
0
#
PUSH
(401)555-1212
COIN RETURN
PULL

hotlines & other basics

Airports... New York City is served by three major airports—**La Guardia Airport** (tel 718/533–3400), **John F. Kennedy (JFK) International Airport** (tel 718/244–4444), and **Newark International Airport** (tel 201/961–6000) in New Jersey. JFK, in southeastern Queens, is the major international airport for the entire East Coast, and serves both international and domestic travelers. Domestic passengers usually prefer LaGuardia Airport, also in Queens, but a shorter ride and cheaper cab or bus fare to Manhattan. More attractive airfares or available seats may lure you to Newark Airport, but be aware that cab drivers sometimes get lost on the way back from here. **Carey Airport Express Buses** (tel 718/632–0500 or 800/284–0909) connect LaGuardia and JFK, and **Mark One Bus Services** (tel 800/309–7070) link LaGuardia with Newark—so if you miss a flight at one airport you may be able to catch a plane at another.

Airport transportation to the city... The cheapest way to get into the city **from JFK** is via the free **Port Authority Shuttle Bus** to the Howard Beach **subway** station, where you can catch an "A" train into Manhattan (subway fare $1.50). Subway transport is possible **from LaGuardia** by taking a **Q33 bus** (fare $1.50, exact change or token) to the subway's Roosevelt Avenue station, where for another $1.50 token you can ride the number 7 train to Midtown. Either trip takes well over an hour. It's less of a hassle to catch a **Carey Airport Express Bus** from either JFK or LaGuardia to Manhattan (tel 718/632–0500 or 800/284–0909). Buses leave every 20 to 30 minutes: the trip in from JFK costs $13 and takes about an hour; from La Guardia it's $10 and takes 45 minutes. Carey buses stop at the Port Authority Bus Terminal (42nd St. and 8th Ave.) and Grand Central train terminal (42nd St. and Park Ave.); Carey then provides a free shuttle service between Grand Central and most Midtown hotels. Leaving **Newark Airport**, catch the **Olympia Trails Airport Express** (tel 212/964–6233) for a $7, 30-minute ride to Penn Station (34th St. and 8th Ave.), Grand Central, or the World Trade Center downtown. Buses leave every 20 to 30 minutes. **Gray Line Air Shuttle** (tel 212/315–3006) operates a minibus service between all three airports and a number of Manhattan hotels for $16 from JFK, $13 from LaGuardia, and $18 from Newark. Those who prefer a **cab** ride into the city should ignore the tempting offers of freelance limousine drivers and march straight to the taxi stand, where a uniformed dispatcher ushers passengers into licensed cabs. Cab fares from JFK and Newark run about $40, including tolls and tip; $25 from LaGuardia. Legitimate limousine pickup is available at all three airports from such private companies as **Olympia Limousines, Inc.** (tel 212/995–1200). The cost is about $20 from LaGuardia, $30 from JFK or Newark, based on a round-trip purchase and not counting tips and tolls. If you arrive on Delta Airline's Boston or Washington shuttles, the **Delta Water Shuttle** (tel 800/54–FERRY) between LaGuardia's Marine Air Terminal and Manhattan's 34th Street (a 25-minute ride) and Wall Street's Pier 11 (40 minutes) is a pleasant alternative to ground traffic, though it operates weekdays only. It costs $20 one way, $30 round-trip. Or fly into Manhattan instead, via **New York Helicopter** (tel 800/645–3494)—chartered helicopters carry up to five passengers between the three airports and Manhattan's heliport at 34th Street and the East Side Highway for only $299 a person.

All-night pharmacies... A must in the city that never sleeps, 24-hour drug stores include **Duane Reade Drugs** at Broadway and 57th Street (tel 212/541–9708),

Broadway and 91st Street (tel 212/799–3172), Third Avenue and 74th Street (tel 212/744–2668), and Lexington Avenue and 47th Street (tel 212/682–5338); and the absurdly overpriced **Kaufman Pharmacy** (tel 212/755–2266) at Lexington Avenue and 50th Street.

Buses... **MTA-New York City Transit** (tel 718/330–1234) operates the world's largest fleet of public buses, running round the clock. The fare is a subway token (sold in all subway stations, where bus route maps are also available) or $1.50 in exact change (no pennies). To transfer to a second bus, request a transfer slip from the driver of the first bus when you pay your fare. Each bus's destination appears above its front windshield; routes are posted at most bus stops. Children under 3 feet 8 inches tall ride free—and if you disagree over size, there's a line near the driver's seat against which to measure your child. The **Port Authority Bus Terminal** (tel 212/564–8484, 8th Ave. at 42nd St.) serves **Greyhound**, **Trailways**, and other long-distance bus lines.

Car rentals... Cars are the least efficient way to get around town, but if you must drive, keep in mind that car rental rates at the airports are often lower (**Budget Rent-A-Car**'s $70-per-day rate for an economy car with unlimited mileage, for example) than those in Midtown ($99 per day for the same car, with only 100 free miles). Banish all fantasies of whipping a Ferrari around New York City streets—modest economy- or mid-sized cars are more likely to survive parallel parking, taxicab-bumping, and other everyday urban experiences. Try **Budget** (tel 212/807–8700, JFK, plus seven NYC locations); **Avis** (tel 800/831–2847, all three airports plus 10 NYC locations); **Hertz** (tel 800/654–3131, all airports plus 9 Manhattan locations); or **Village Rent A Car** (tel 212/243–9200, 19 E. 12th St.), which rents nearly new compacts for $40 per day, mid-sized cars for $50—both with 100 free miles. Since the least attractive car is the least likely to be vandalized or stolen, your best bet for city driving might actually be **Rent-A-Wreck** (tel 718/784–3302), which charges an average of $80 for two days, though this involves a subway ride to Queens, where someone from the office will pick you up. On the other hand, if you feel a sudden urge to take off for the Hamptons for the weekend, consider a Mercedes 500 SL convertible from **Vogel's Eurocars, Inc.** (tel 914/968–8200), for only $495 per day plus pick-up and delivery charges.

Child care services... Many New York hotels provide baby-sitting services, or keep a list of reliable sitters. If your hotel isn't among them, call **The Baby Sitters Guild** (tel 212/682–0227) or the **Frances Stewart Agency** (tel 212/439–9222). Both services provide in-room child care as well as on-request trips to the playground, the Central Park Zoo, etc., for children of all ages, with licensed, bonded, insured sitters (baby nurses are trained in CPR). Parents who want to keep their young children with them can lighten their child care load at **WonderCamp Entertainment** (tel 212/243–1111), a souped-up, indoor playground at 27 W. 23rd Street between 5th and 6th Avenues. Admission is $4.95 per person Mon–Fri and $5.49 on weekends. **Hackers, Hitters and Hoops** (tel 212/929–7482, 123 W. 28th St.) will appeal to older children, with its minature golf course, basketball courts, and video games.

Convention center... I.M. Pei designed the spectacular glass **Jacob Javitz Convention Center** (tel 212/216–2000, 655 W. 34th St.), a multifaceted "glass house" on the Hudson River that provides a sense of space and light equalled only by the Winter Garden downtown. It has established itself as a national venue despite grim surroundings (frequented by some of New York's most flamboyant ladies of the night) and the reputedly extortionate practices of local workmen's unions.

Cultural-events hotlines... New York's free, 24-hour **Interactive Cultural Hotline** (tel 212/765–ARTS) lists music, theater, museum, and other events in more than 750 New York City venues. For more information on theater, music and dance performances, call **NYC On Stage** (tel 212/768–1818). The **City Parks Special Events Hotline** (tel 212/360–3456) provides news of outdoor concerts and performances and New York Roadrunner Club events, while **Mediabridge Infosystems** (tel 212/932–8509, e-mail nyc@mediabridge.com) offers online business and leisure information for all of New York.

Dentists... You can get a list of dentists near you by calling **Dental Emergency Service** (tel 212/679–3966). Emergency dental service is also available from **ABC Dental Care** (tel 212/888–0015).

Disability services... The **Admiral Ambulance Service, Inc.** (tel 718/994–8800) provides ambulette service for the disabled. Note that the subway system remains largely inaccessible to the disabled, but 95% of the city's buses are equipped to carry wheelchairs.

Doctors... **Dial-A-Doctor** (tel 212/971–9692) sends physicians on house- or hotel calls 24 hours a day, as does **Doctors On Call** (tel 718/238–2100).

Driving around... In Midtown, and other spots where the police feel it's vital to keep traffic flowing, your illegally parked car will be towed in minutes, so don't even think of violating parking laws there. Elsewhere, officers are required to complete any parking ticket they've begun filling out, so begging or threatening will do no good. To find out where your car has been towed, call the **Borough Tow Pound** (tel 212/971–0770). For information on parking regulations currently in effect, call the **New York City Department of Transportation** (tel 212/442–7080). (See also Parking, below.)

Emergencies... The number to know is **911**, for police, fire, and ambulance service. Other emergency numbers include **Animal Bites** (tel 212/334–2618), **Deaf Emergency** (tel 800/342–4357), **Park Emergencies** (tel 800/834–3832), **Poison Control** (tel 212/340–4494), **Rape Hotline** (tel 800/551–0008), **Suicide Prevention** (tel 212/532–2400), and **Traveler's Aid** (tel 212/944–0013).

Ferries... At 50¢, the **Staten Island Ferry** (tel 718/727–2508) at Battery Park remains the best way to enjoy views of the Manhattan skyline, New York Harbor, and the Statue of Liberty. Still, other ferries work the harbor as well: the **Ellis Island and Statue of Liberty Ferry** (tel 212/269–5755) leaves Battery Park every 15–30 minutes for two of the city's most popular tourist destinations, for $7 round-trip. The **New York Waterway Ferry and Bus System** (tel 201/902–8700) has instituted a spiffy new service between New Jersey and Manhattan for $5 each way.

Festivals and special events... New York thrives on festivals, and the best way to find out about them is to pick up a copy of ***The Big Apple Visitors Guide*** at your hotel, or call the **The New York Convention & Visitors Bureau** (tel 800/NYC–VISIT, 59th St. and Broadway). The guide lists a year's worth of art exhibits, walking tours, children's entertainment, ethnic festivals, and performances. Some events draw such a crowd that you'll want to reserve your hotel room, plane tickets, and events tickets well in advance. These include: **New Year's Eve** In Times Square; the **St. Patrick's Day Parade** down Fifth

Avenue in March; the **Gay Pride March** on the last Sunday in June; **Macy's July 4th Fireworks Extravaganza**; the **U.S. Open Tennis Championships** in Flushing Meadows, Queens, in September; the **New York Film Festival** in late September/early October; the **Macy's Thanksgiving Day Parade**; and the **Christmas Tree Lighting** at Rockefeller Center on December 5.

Foreign currency exchange... **American Express Travel Agencies** (tel 212/640–4885) will exchange currency at offices in the World Financial Center, at Bloomingdale's and Macy's department stores, Seaport Plaza, JFK Airport, and half a dozen other locations. The offices of **Thomas Cook Currency Services** (212/757–6915) are open from about 9:30–5 in Times Square, Grand Central Station, Herald Square, Wall Street, Greenwich Village, and on Madison Avenue at 53rd Street. **Chemical Bank Foreign Currency Exchanges** (tel 212/935–9935) are set up at 2 World Trade Center, 1 U.N. Plaza, Wall Street, and elsewhere.

Friends... A number of city residents are so eager to dispel negative "New Yorker" stereotypes that they volunteer as companions and guides to visitors through the **Big Apple Greeter's Program** (tel 212/669–2896). The service is free.

Gay and lesbian resources... New York boasts a gay and lesbian population large enough to support such organizations as **Act Up** (tel 212/564–2437) and the **Gay Men's Health Crisis** (tel 212/807–6664), and institutions including **A Different Light Bookstore and Cafe** (tel 212/989–4850, 151 W. 19th St.) and **Three Lives Bookstore** (tel 212/741–2069, Waverly Place and W. 10th St.). ***The Village Voice*** remains a dependable source of gay-related news and entertainment listings.

Jazz hotline... Sponsored by the Jazz Foundation of America, **Jazzline** (tel 212/479–7888) will clue you in on all such performances currently happening in the jazz capital of the world.

Limousine and car services... **Gotham Limousine, Inc.** (tel 718/361–2401) rates range from $35 per hour for a chauffeured four-passenger sedan to $85 per hour for a 10-passenger stretch limousine; Rates for **Capricorn Limousine Service** at the Regency Hotel (tel 212/688–5530) run from $45 to $60 per hour; and **Promenade Car Service** (tel 718/858–6666) offers non-luxury cars with a driver for $25 per hour, and individual pick-ups and deliveries for slightly lower than yellow cab rates.

Movie hotline... Listings of commercial films are available through **Moviefone** (tel 212/777–FILM), which also allows you to pre-purchase movie tickets via credit card.

Newspapers... Manhattan newsstands offer a blizzard of political, professional, academic, alternative, business, and foreign language periodicals. Where to begin? Perhaps with the three major English-language dailies: ***The New York Times***, ***The Daily News***, and ***The New York Post***. Briefly, the *Times* is the "official" paper, the *News* is the boroughs' favorite, and the *Post* is a tabloid owned by Mr. Murdoch. ***The New York Observer***, a brash weekly printed on salmon-colored newsprint, focuses on fads, fashion, and gossip, particularly within the media. ***The Wall Street Journal***, is also edited here, and is still all about money. ***The Village Voice*** offers liberal politics, entertainment listings, and the biggest personal ad section in New York.

Parking... Space is so tight in New York that some residents are willing to pay $30,000 for parking-garage "condos" for their cars—so who can blame garage owners for charging a fortune to watch your wheels for a few hours? Garages dot Manhattan streets every two blocks or so, with rates averaging about $5 for less than two hours, $12 for half a day, and $30 overnight. Prices are sometimes lower at night in business districts and during the day in residential areas; outdoor lots are less expensive, when you can find them. Our advice: find a hotel that offers free parking, such as the **Franklin** or the **Algonquin** (see Accommodations). Most Midtown hotels provide valet parking at about $35 per night. A partial list of garages: **Kinney System, Inc.** (tel 800/KNY–PARK), with over 150 garages; **Rapid Park** (tel 212/865–8656), with over 30 locations; **GMC** (tel 212/888–7400), with 55 locations.

Personal services... **The Intrepid New Yorker** (tel 212/534–5071) is available 24 hours a day to help visitors find personal shoppers, get around town, and otherwise cope with New York. Their fee is $25 per request. Cash, checks, or money orders are accepted.

Phone facts... The area code for Manhattan is 212. To call Brooklyn, Queens, Staten Island, or the Bronx (at no charge), dial 1, then area code 718, then the phone number. For directory assistance, dial 411. There are public phones on every other street corner in Manhattan, though not all of them are in what you'd call working order; a local call costs 25 cents. For fax service, a private booth, or TDDs, try the **AT&T Public Calling Center** (tel 800/CALL–ATT) at Grand Central Terminal at 42nd Street and Lexington Avenue.

Post offices... The **Main Post Office** at 8th Avenue and 33rd Street (tel 212/967–8585) is open 8:30-5:30, Mon–Fri. Some express-mail stations remain open until midnight. Call the **Postal Answer Line** (tel 212/330–4000) for information.

Radio stations... On the FM dial, **WPLJ (95.5)** concentrates on Top 40 hits, **WBLS (107.5)** plays soul and R&B, **WFMU (91.1)** offers alternative, eclectic fare, **HOT 97** does urban contemporary, **WRKS (KISS-FM, 98.7)** has soul classics, **Z100** specializes in rock, and **WKCR (89.9)** offers jazz. Tune in to **WNYC (93.9)** for classical music, and **WXRK (92.3)** for Howard Stern. AM stations include **WNYC (820)**, the National Public Radio affiliate, **WFAN (660)** for sports, and **WCBS (880)** and **WINS (1010)** for continual news.

Restrooms... Freud himself was reputedly scandalized by New York's lack of public restrooms, and the situation has not changed much since then. Restrooms do exist in **Central Park** across from the Delacorte Theater, mid-park at 79th Street; **Bryant Park**, at 42nd Street and 6th Avenue behind the New York Public Library, now offers clean, guarded restrooms free of charge. The library itself has nice, large bathrooms that are easy to duck into, as do most of the branch libraries throughout the city. If you can't find a public facility, do what the natives do: stride into the nearest hotel lobby or cafe and back to the ladies' or gents' like you own the place. No one is likely to stop you.

Smoking... New York's stringent new smoking regulations forbid smoking in all but the smallest restaurants (though you can light up at bars) and in many workplaces—you'll see office workers madly puffing just outside lobby entrances at buildings all over town. Forget smoking on buses and subway trains, or in taxis (unless your driver is sympathetic). Taxi drivers are not allowed to smoke themselves, unless you the passenger say it's okay.

Subways... Operated by the New York City Metropolitan Transit Authority (tel 718/330–1234), the subway transports three-and-a-half-million people per day from 469 stations in Manhattan, Brooklyn, Queens, and the Bronx—so give the MTA a break if some stations are a tad grimy or the trains a little noisy. Even mildly adventurous visitors should feel comfortable underground from 7am–10pm. Tokens, sold at booths in each station, are $1.50 each. For your token you can ride the rails as long as and as far as you like, changing lines at any of more than 50 free transfer points—as long as you don't exit the system. Children under 44 inches ride free. Maps are posted inside stations and in most cars.

Taxes... Sales tax is 8.25%, charged on everything except groceries and take-out food. Hotels add a 13.25% hotel tax to room rates.

Taxis... The only taxis authorized to pick up passengers hailing them on the street are **yellow cabs**, which have an official taxi medallion screwed onto the hood. So-called "gypsy cabs," working for car services, sometimes stop illegally for passengers on the street, but since they have no meter, you'll have to negotiate your own fare with the driver, and you'll have no legal recourse if there's a problem (besides, some gypsy cabs are filthy rattletraps). To know whether a yellow taxi is free, look for the lit-up sign on the roof of the cab; off-duty cabs (side sections of the roof sign lit) may pick up passengers at their own discretion. Taxi meters calculate the fare: $1.50 when you get in, plus 25 cents for each 1/6th of a mile or 60 seconds of waiting time in traffic. There's an extra 50-cent charge 8pm–6am. Passengers pay

Taxi Fair

Despite the enduring re-run success of the TV series Taxi, *New York cabbies these days are more like the Andy Kaufman character, Latka, than like Judd Hirsch's Alex. Gone is the colorful, colloquial, salty, and shrewd cabbie of legend, replaced by recent immigrants who speak little English and don't care how the Yankees are playing. Drivers are required to take you anywhere within the five boroughs, Westchester and Nassau Counties, and should ask you to specify the route. They're supposed to be pros, so I often leave it up to them; but don't be shy about telling the driver to change his course if he (or she) gets caught in traffic or road construction. From Newark Airport and LaGuardia the routes to Midtown are fairly straightforward (though trips from LaGuardia to midtown or downtown shouldn't have anything to do with the Triborough Bridge). JFK is another story—I suggest telling the driver to take the Long Island Expressway and Midtown Tunnel. Cab fares to Midtown from JFK and Newark should run about $40, including tolls and tip; $25 from LaGuardia.*

any bridge or tunnel tolls. A 15–20% tip is expected. Complaints concerning limousines, car services, or cabs should be directed to the **NYC Taxi and Limousine Commission** (tel 212/221–8294).

Ticket charge lines... Telecharge (tel 212/239–6200); **Ticketmaster** (tel 212/307–7171).

Tipping... When calculating a restaurant tip, many New Yorkers simply double the tax amount on their check (2 x 8.25% = 16.5%, a reasonable tip). But New York waitpeople work hard for their money, so round it up to 20% if you can. At top restaurants, give the waiter 15% and the captain 5%. Taxi drivers get 15–20 % with a 25¢ minimum. Tip hotel doormen $1 per taxi, and bellhops and airport porters $1 per bag.

Trains... There are two major railway terminals in Manhattan: **Grand Central Terminal** at 42nd Street and Lexington Avenue, and **Pennsylvania (Penn) Station** at 33rd Street and 7th Avenue. **Amtrak** trains (tel 800/872–7245) depart Penn Station for points across the country. Among them are Amtrak's Metroliner, an hourly express train to Washington, D.C. Also operating out of Penn Station are the **New Jersey Transit** (tel 201/762–5100) and **Long Island Railroad** (tel 718/217–5477) commuter lines. The **Metro-North Commuter Railroad** (212/532–4900) serves Connecticut and New York State from Grand Central.

TV stations... CBS plays on Channel 2; **NBC** is Channel 4; the **Fox** network is Channel 5; **ABC** plays on Channel 7; Channel 13 is reserved for **PBS** (two other PBS stations are at 21 and 31 on the dial). The other channels reel with foreign-language, public access, sports, news, and additional networks—Manhattan has been divided up among a couple of different cable franchises, so the channel numbers differ depending on what part of town you're in. Get out the remote and start surfing.

Visitor information... The New York Convention & Visitors Bureau's Visitors Information Center (2 Columbus Circle, 59th St. and Broadway, southwest corner of Central Park) is open seven days a week, providing maps, advice, and sightseeing suggestions, along with "two-fers" for savings on Broadway and Off-Broadway plays. The Visitors Bureau's toll-free, 24-hour **information hotline** (tel 800-NYC–VISIT or 212/397–8222 outside the U.S.) offers similar information by phone.

FROMMER'S COMPLETE TRAVEL GUIDES

(Comprehensive guides to sightseeing, dining and accommodations, with selections in all price ranges—from deluxe to budget)

Acapulco/Ixtapa/Taxco, 2nd Ed.	C157
Alaska '94-'95	C131
Arizona '95	C166
Australia '94-'95	C147
Austria, 6th Ed.	C162
Bahamas '96 (avail. 8/95)	C172
Belgium/Holland/Luxembourg, 4th Ed.	C170
Bermuda '96 (avail. 8/95)	C174
California '95	C164
Canada '94-'95	C145
Caribbean '96 (avail. 9/95)	C173
Carolinas/Georgia, 2nd Ed.	C128
Colorado '96 (avail. 11/95)	C179
Costa Rica, 1st Ed.	C161
Cruises '95-'96	C150
Delaware/Maryland '94-'95	C136
England '96 (avail. 10/95)	C180
Florida '96 (avail. 9/95)	C181
France '96 (avail. 11/95)	C182
Germany '96 (avail. 9/95)	C176
Honolulu/Waikiki/Oahu, 4th Ed. (avail. 10/95)	C178
Ireland, 1st Ed.	C168
Italy '96 (avail. 11/95)	C183
Jamaica/Barbados, 2nd Ed.	C149
Japan '94-'95	C144
Maui, 1st Ed.	C153
Nepal, 3rd Ed. (avail. 11/95)	C184
New England '95	C165
New Mexico, 3rd Ed.	C167
New York State, 4th Ed.	C133
Northwest, 5th Ed.	C140
Portugal '94-'95	C141
Puerto Rico '95-'96	C151
Puerto Vallarta/Manzanillo/ Guadalajara, 2nd Ed.	C135
Scandinavia, 16th Ed.	C169
Scotland '94-'95	C146
South Pacific '94-'95	C138
Spain, 16th Ed.	C163
Switzerland, 7th Ed. (avail. 9/95)	C177
Thailand, 2nd Ed.	C154
U.S.A., 4th Ed.	C156
Virgin Islands, 3rd Ed. (avail. 8/95)	C175
Virginia '94-'95	C142
Yucatán '95-'96	C155

FROMMER'S $-A-DAY GUIDES

(Dream Vacations at Down-to-Earth Prices)

Australia on $45 '95-'96	D122
Berlin from $50, 3rd Ed. (avail. 10/95)	D137
Caribbean from $60, 1st Ed. (avail. 9/95)	D133
Costa Rica/Guatemala/Belize on $35, 3rd Ed.	D126
Eastern Europe on $30, 5th Ed.	D129
England from $50 '96 (avail. 11/95)	D138
Europe from $50 '96 (avail. 10/95)	D139
Greece from $45, 6th Ed.	D131
Hawaii from $60 '96 (avail. 9/95)	D134
Ireland on $45 '94-'95	D118
Israel on $45, 15th Ed.	D130
London from $55 '96 (avail. 11/95)	D136
Madrid on $50 '94-'95	D119
Mexico from $35 '96 (avail. 10/95)	D135
New York on $70 '94-'95	D121
New Zealand from $45, 6th Ed.	D132
Paris on $45 '94-'95	D117
South America on $40, 16th Ed.	D123
Washington, D.C. on $50 '94-'95	D120

FROMMER'S COMPLETE CITY GUIDES

(Comprehensive guides to sightseeing, dining, and accommodations in all price ranges)

Amsterdam, 8th Ed.	S176	Miami '95-'96	S149
Athens, 10th Ed.	S174	Minneapolis/St. Paul, 4th Ed.	S159
Atlanta & the Summer Olympic Games '96 (avail. 11/95)	S181	Montréal/Québec City '95	S166
Atlantic City/Cape May, 5th Ed.	S130	Nashville/Memphis, 1st Ed.	S141
Bangkok, 2nd Ed.	S147	New Orleans '96 (avail. 10/95)	S182
Barcelona '93-'94	S115	New York City '96 (avail. 11/95)	S183
Berlin, 3rd Ed.	S162	Paris '96 (avail. 9/95)	S180
Boston '95	S160	Philadelphia, 8th Ed.	S167
Budapest, 1st Ed.	S139	Prague, 1st Ed.	S143
Chicago '95	S169	Rome, 10th Ed.	S168
Denver/Boulder/Colorado Springs, 3rd Ed.	S154	St. Louis/Kansas City, 2nd Ed.	S127
Disney World/Orlando '96 (avail. 9/95)	S178	San Antonio/Austin, 1st Ed.	S177
Dublin, 2nd Ed.	S157	San Diego '95	S158
Hong Kong '94-'95	S140	San Francisco '96 (avail. 10/95)	S184
Las Vegas '95	S163	Santa Fe/Taos/Albuquerque '95	S172
London '96 (avail. 9/95)	S179	Seattle/Portland '94-'95	S137
Los Angeles '95	S164	Sydney, 4th Ed.	S171
Madrid/Costa del Sol, 2nd Ed.	S165	Tampa/St. Petersburg, 3rd Ed.	S146
Mexico City, 1st Ed.	S175	Tokyo '94-'95	S144
		Toronto, 3rd Ed.	S173
		Vancouver/Victoria '94-'95	S142
		Washington, D.C. '95	S153

FROMMER'S FAMILY GUIDES

(Guides to family-friendly hotels, restaurants, activities, and attractions)

California with Kids	F105	San Francisco with Kids	F104
Los Angeles with Kids	F103	Washington, D.C. with Kids	F102
New York City with Kids	F101		

FROMMER'S WALKING TOURS

(Memorable strolls through colorful and historic neighborhoods, accompanied by detailed directions and maps)

Berlin	W100	San Francisco, 2nd Ed.	W115
Chicago	W107	Spain's Favorite Cities (avail. 9/95)	W116
England's Favorite Cities	W108	Tokyo	W109
London, 2nd Ed.	W111	Venice	W110
Montréal/Québec City	W106	Washington, D.C., 2nd Ed.	W114
New York, 2nd Ed.	W113		
Paris, 2nd Ed.	W112		

FROMMER'S AMERICA ON WHEELS

(Guides for travelers who are exploring the U.S.A. by car, featuring a brand-new rating system for accommodations and full-color road maps)

Arizona/New Mexico	A100	Florida	A102
California/Nevada	A101	Mid-Atlantic	A103

FROMMER'S SPECIAL-INTEREST TITLES

Arthur Frommer's Branson!	P107
Arthur Frommer's New World of Travel (avail. 11/95)	P112
Frommer's Caribbean Hideaways (avail. 9/95)	P110
Frommer's America's 100 Best-Loved State Parks	P109
Frommer's Where to Stay U.S.A., 11th Ed.	P102
National Park Guide, 29th Ed.	P106
USA Today Golf Tournament Guide	P113
USA Today Minor League Baseball Book	P111

FROMMER'S BEST BEACH VACATIONS

(The top places to sun, stroll, shop, stay, play, party, and swim—with each beach rated for beauty, swimming, sand, and amenities)

California (avail. 10/95)	G100
Florida (avail. 10/95)	G101
Hawaii (avail. 10/95)	G102

FROMMER'S BED & BREAKFAST GUIDES

(Selective guides with four-color photos and full descriptions of the best inns in each region)

California	B100
Caribbean	B101
East Coast	B102
Eastern United States	B103
Great American Cities	B104
Hawaii	B105
Pacific Northwest	B106
Rockies	B107
Southwest	B108

FROMMER'S IRREVERENT GUIDES

(Wickedly honest guides for sophisticated travelers and those who want to be)

Chicago (avail. 11/95)	I100
London (avail. 11/95)	I101
Manhattan (avail. 11/95)	I102
New Orleans (avail. 11/95)	I103
San Francisco (avail. 11/95)	I104
Virgin Islands (avail. 11/95)	I105

FROMMER'S DRIVING TOURS

(Four-color photos and detailed maps outlining spectacular scenic driving routes)

Australia	Y100
Austria	Y101
Britain	Y102
Canada	Y103
Florida	Y104
France	Y105
Germany	Y106
Ireland	Y107
Italy	Y108
Mexico	Y109
Scandinavia	Y110
Scotland	Y111
Spain	Y112
Switzerland	Y113
U.S.A.	Y114

FROMMER'S BORN TO SHOP

(The ultimate travel guides for discriminating shoppers—from cut-rate to couture)

Hong Kong (avail. 11/95)	Z100
London (avail. 11/95)	Z101

irreverent notes